ROUTLEDGE LIBRARY EDITIONS:
ACCOUNTING

Volume 53

THE DEVELOPMENT OF DOUBLE ENTRY

THE DEVELOPMENT OF DOUBLE ENTRY

Selected Essays

Edited by
CHRISTOPHER NOBES

Routledge
Taylor & Francis Group
LONDON AND NEW YORK

First published in 1984

This edition first published in 2014
by Routledge
4 Park Square, Milton Park, Abingdon, Oxon OX14 4RN
605 Third Avenue, New York, NY 10017

Routledge is an imprint of the Taylor & Francis Group, an informa business

British Library Cataloguing in Publication Data
A catalogue record for this book is available from the British Library

ISBN: 978-0-415-53081-1 (Set)
eISBN: 978-1-315-88628-2 (Set)
ISBN: 978-0-415-71795-3 (Volume 53) (hbk)
eISBN: 978-1-315-87098-4 (Volume 53)

Publisher's Note
The publisher has gone to great lengths to ensure the quality of this book but points out that some imperfections in the original copies may be apparent.

Disclaimer
The publisher has made every effort to trace copyright holders and would welcome correspondence from those they have been unable to trace.

The Development of Double Entry
Selected Essays

Edited by Christopher Nobes

GARLAND PUBLISHING, INC.
NEW YORK & LONDON
1984

ACKNOWLEDGMENTS

The articles in this book are reprinted by permission of the authors and the following journals:

Journal of Accounting Research: "The Florentine Bank Ledger Fragments of 1211" and "The Accounts of the Corporation of Bristol." *Abacus:* "The Development of Italian Bookkeeping." *The Accounting Historians Journal* "The Coming of Age of Double Entry" and "A New Perspective on the Evolution of Double-Entry Bookkeeping." *The Accounting Review:* "The Gallerani Account Book," "The Ledger of Jachomo Badoer," and "Selections from a Pre-Revolutionary Accounting Record." *Accounting and Business Research:* "Jachomo Badoer, Renaissance Man of Commerce." *The Accountant:* "The Ledger of John Smythe" and "The Functional Development of Double-Entry Bookkeeping." *The Journal of Accountancy:* "Accounting in Colonial Virginia." Copyright © 1974 by the American Institute of Certified Public Accountants.

For a complete list of the titles in this series
see the final page of this volume.

Library of Congress Cataloging in Publication Data

Main entry under title:

The Development of double entry.

(Accounting history and the development of a profession)
Bibliography: p.
1. Bookkeeping—History—Addresses, essays, lectures.
I. Nobes, Christopher. II. Series.
HF5605.D48 1984 657'.2 83-49442
ISBN 0-8240-6309-0 (alk. paper)

The volumes in this series are printed on
acid-free, 250-year-life paper.

Printed in the United States of America.

Contents

Introduction — *ix*

A Chronological Bibliography of Selected Writings on Surviving Account Books of the 11th to the 19th Centuries — 1

"The Florentine Bank Ledger Fragments of 1211: Some New Insights," Geoffrey A. Lee (*Journal of Accounting Research*, Spring, 1973, 47-61) — 9

"The Development of Italian Bookkeeping: 1211-1300," Geoffrey A. Lee (*Abacus*, December, 1973, 137-155) — 25

"The Coming of Age of Double Entry: The Giovanni Farolfi Ledger of 1299-1300," Geoffrey A. Lee (*The Accounting Historians Journal*, Fall, 1977, 79-95) — 45

"The Gallerani Account Book of 1305-1308," Christopher W. Nobes (*The Accounting Review*, April, 1982, 303-310) — 63

"The Ledger of Jachomo Badoer: Constantinople September 2, 1436 to February 26, 1440," Edward Peragallo (*The Accounting Review*, October, 1977, 881-892) — 71

"Jachomo Badoer, Renaissance Man of Commerce, and His Ledger," Edward Peragallo (*Accounting and Business Research*, vol. 10, no. 37A, 1980, 93-101) — 83

"The Accounts of the Corporation of Bristol: 1532 to 1835," D. M. Livock (*Journal of Accounting Research*, III, 1965, 86-102) — 92

"The Ledger of John Smythe, Merchant of Bristol," Jean Vanes (*The Accountant*, September 16, 1967, 357-361) 109

"Selections from a Pre-Revolutionary Accounting Record," Robert M. Jennings (*The Accounting Review*, January, 1962, 73-75) 115

"Accounting in Colonial Virginia: A Case Study," Almand R. Coleman, William G. Shenkir and Williard E. Stone (*The Journal of Accountancy*, July, 1974, 32-43) 118

A Note on Papers Concerning the Causes and Effects of Double Entry 131

"The Functional Development of Double-Entry Bookkeeping," B. S. Yamey (*The Accountant*, November 2, 1940, 333-342) 133

"A New Perspective on the Evolution of Double-Entry Bookkeeping," John J. Williams (*The Accounting Historians Journal*, Spring, 1978, 29-39) 143

Introduction

This compilation concerns account books, not books on accounting. It is a selection of essays, most of which analyze the account book(s) of a single person or business. In each case, the account book(s) demonstrate the presence of, at least, elements of double entry.

I have also put together an approximately chronological bibliography of writings on extant account books of the 11th century to the 19th century. Much of this has been extracted from the three bibliographies by R. H. Parker reprinted in *Bibliographies for Accounting Historians* (New York: Arno Press, 1980).

The essays themselves come in pairs. They begin with Geoffrey Lee's paper on Florentine bank ledger fragments of 1211. This is a suitable place to start, for these are the earliest relics of Italian bookkeeping. The entries are in paragraph form (to save paper?); they lead to a discussion of the early examples they contain of various phrases using *dare* and *avere*, but not yet *debit* and *credit*. There is a suggestion that capital accounts exist. The second paper is also by Geoffrey Lee. It begins with the above fragments, and then traces the development of double entry through the rest of the 13th century, mainly in Tuscany. There is a discussion of the development of the style of entries, and of personal, capital and nominal accounts.

The next two papers by Geoffrey Lee and Christopher Nobes deal with account books which contain very obvious, substantial elements of double entry. Both sets of records are of expatriate Tuscan firms: Giovanni Farolfi in Provence in 1299-1300, and the Gallerani in London in 1305-1308. Both papers analyze the accounting records in detail and discuss the nature of double entry.

There follow two of Edward Peragallo's several papers on the ledger of Jachomo Badoer of Constantinople in the mid-15th century. They comment on various aspects of Badoer's commercial methods and the contents of his ledger. Double entry is much in evidence, though in a form which lacked strict precision. There are currency conversions, verification procedures and compound entries.

Next, there are two papers about accounts kept in Bristol: by D. M. Livock on those of Bristol Corporation from 1532 to 1835, and by Jean Vanes on those from 1538 to 1550 of a merchant (who, incidentally, had been Mayor of the Bristol Corporation). The Corporation's accounts are seen to change gradually over the centuries, not really achieving full double entry until 1786. The accounts of the merchant show a detailed system, with several books and the calculation of profit on ventures.

The following two papers concern accounting in colonial North America. There is a paper by R. M. Jennings on early use of double entry at the start of the 18th century in Rhode Island, and one by Coleman, Shenkir and Stone on the accounts of a store in Virginia from 1733 to 1779. They illustrate the use of balance sheets, valuation techniques and the accruals convention.

Finally, there are two papers (by B. S. Yamey and by J. Williams) which are exceptional, in the context of this compilation, in that they do not discuss particular accounting records but analyze the causes of the development of double entry, using the evidence of others.

The selection of papers here is clearly not intended to be exhaustive, but illustrative. Perhaps the most obvious writings that might have been included are those by Yamey (in the bibliography) and the renowned paper by de Roover on the development of accounting prior to Pacioli; all of these have already been reprinted recently.

A Chronological Bibliography of Selected Writings on Surviving Account Books of the 11th to the 19th Centuries

This bibliography is in approximate chronological order. It deals mainly with commercial and "local authority" account books, most of which have at least elements of double entry. In an effort to increase accessibility, it excludes most publications of before 1950, except those in widely available journals. It also excludes cost accounts. Thus, the chronology is very selective, especially of publications in a language other than English.

1 S D Goitein, "Bankers' Accounts from the Eleventh Century AD", Journal of the Economic and Social History of the Orient, IX, 1966, pp 28-68.

2 De Roover, Florence Edler, "Partnership Accounts in Twelfth Century Genoa", Bulletin of the Business Historical Society, XV, 1941, pp 87-92, and in A C Littleton and B S Yamey, Studies in the History of Accounting, London, Sweet and Maxwell, 1956.

3 R A L Smith, "The Central Financial System of Christ Church, Canterbury, 1186-1512", English Historical Review, LV, 1940, pp 353-369.

4 Searle, E and Ross, R, Accounts of the Cellarers of Battle Abbey 1275-1513, Sydney University Press, 1967, 199 pp.

5 T Antoni, "The Pisan Document of Philadelphia (La Carta Pisana di Filadelfia)", Accounting Historians Journal, IV, 1977, pp 17-24.

6 M Chiaudano, (Ed) Libro Vermiglio di Corte di Roma e di Avignone del Segnale del C, della Compagnia Fiorentina di Iacopo Girolami, Filippo Corbizzi e Tommaso Corbizzi, 1332-1337, Turin, V Bona Tipografio, 1963, 212 pp.

7 G A Lee, "The Oldest European Account Book: A Florentine Bank Ledger of 1211", Nottingham Mediaeval Studies, XVI, 1972, pp 28-60.

8 G A Lee, "The Florentine Bank Ledger Fragments of 1211: Some New Insights", Journal of Accounting Research, XI, 1973, pp 47-61.

9 G A Lee, "The Development of Italian Bookkeeping 1211-1300", Abacus, IX, 1973, pp 137-155; reprinted in B S Yamey (ed), The Historical Development of Accounting: A Selection of Papers, New York, Arno Press, 1978.

10 A Castellani, Nuovi testi fiorentini del Dugento, Florence, G C Sansoni, 1952, I vol in 2 pts, xii + 946 pp.

11 T Zerbi, Le Origini della Partita Doppia, Milan Marzorati, 1952, xiv + 520 pp (extracts throughout).

12 F Melis, Storia della Ragioneria, Bologna, Zuffi, 1950, v + 872 pp (particularly part II and bibliography).

13 R De Roover, "The Development of Accounting prior to Luca Pacioli according to the Account-Books of Medieval Merchants", pp 114-184 of A C Littleton and B S Yamey, Studies in the History of Accounting, London, Sweet and Maxwell, 1956.

14 C Pierard (Ed), *Les plus anciens comptes de la ville de Mons (1279-1356)*, Tome 1, Brussels, Palais des Academies, 1971, xivi + 785 pp; Tome 2, Brussels, Palais des Academies, 1973, 213 pp (indexes) + 5 pp of plates.

15 G A Lee, "The Coming of Age of Double Entry: The Giovanni Farolfi Ledger of 1299-1300", *Accounting Historians Journal*, IV, 1977, pp 79-96.

16 A Sapori, *I libri degli Alberti del Guidice*, Milan, Garzanti, 1952, xcii + 365 pp.

17 T Antoni, "Il 'Lou dels Pizans' del 1303", *Bollettino Storico Pisano*, XXIX, 1970, 31-40.

18 G Bigwood and A Grunzweig (eds), *Les Livres des Comptes des Gallerani*, Brussels, Academie royale de Belgique, vol 1, 1961 and vol 2, 1962, 271 pp and 354 pp.

19 C W Nobes, "The Gallerani Account Book of 1305-1308", *Accounting Review*, LVII, 1982, pp 303-310.

20 P Meyer and G Guigue, "Fragments du grand livre d'un drapier de Lyon (1320-1323)", *Romania*, XXXV, 1906, pp 428-44.

21 R S Lopez and I W Raymond, *Medieval Trade in the Mediterranean World*, New York, Columbia University Press, 1955, pp 359-377.

22 S Gibson, "The Oldest Account Book of the University of Oxford", *English Historical Review*, XXIV, 1909, pp 735-743.

23 R De Roover, *Le Livre de comptes de Guillaume Ruyelle, changeur à Bruges (1369)*, Bruges, reprinted from *Annales de la Societe d'Emulation de Bruges*, vol 57, 1934, 95 pp.

24 E B Fryde, *The Wool Accounts of William de la Pole*, York, St Anthony's Press, 1964, 29 pp.

25 T Antoni, *Il Bilancio di una Azienda Laniera del Trecento*, Pisa, Columbo Cursi, 1966, 69 pp.

26 T Antoni, *Il Libro dei Bilanci di una Azienda Mercantile del Trecento (il libro della Ragione di Biagio e Guido Delle Broche, dal 1326 al 1356)*, Pisa, Columbo Cursi, 1967, 280 pp.

27 E Forestié (Ed), *Les Livres de comptes des Freres Bonis, marchands montalbanais du XIVe siecle*, Paris, Honoré Champion, 1890 and 1893, vol 1, ccxiii + 243 pp; vol 2, vii + 654 pp.

28 T Antoni, "Sull'origine del Bilancio nelle Aziende del Sec XIV in Pisa", *Rivista Italiana di Ragioneria e di Economia Aziendale*, LXXIII, 1973, pp 425-431.

29 M Chauvin, *Les Comptes de la Chatellenie de Lamballe, 1387-1482*, Universite de Haute Bretagne, Institut Armoricain de Recherches Economiques et Humaines, 1977, 349 pp + 11 plates.

30 R Ross, "The Accounts of the Stewards of the Talbot Household at Blakemere: An Example of Medieval Accounting Practice", *Abacus*, IV, 1968, pp 51-72.

31 E M Myatt-Price, "Cromwell Household Accounts, 1417-1476", pp 99-113 of A C Littleton and B S Yamey, *Studies in the History of Accounting*, London, Sweet and Maxwell, 1956.

32 G S Pryde, "Ayr Burgh Accounts, 1428-1429", Scottish Historical Review, XXXI, 1952, pp 139-146.

33 E Peragallo, "The Ledger of Jachomo Badoer: Constantinople September 2, 1436 to February 26, 1440", Accounting Review, LII, 1977, pp 881-892.

34 E Peragallo, "Jachomo Badoer, Renaissance Man of Commerce and his Ledger", Accounting and Business Research, X, 1980, pp 93-101.

35 E Peragallo, "Closing Procedures in the 15th Century Ledger of Jachomo Badoer, a Venetian Merchant", Accounting Review, LVI, 1981, pp 587-595.

36 E Peragallo, "Merchandising of Slaves as Portrayed in the 15th Century Ledger of Jachomo Badoer, a Venetian Merchant", Accounting and Business Research, XII, 1981, pp 61-65.

37 E Peragallo, "Development of the Compound Entry in the 15th Century Ledger of Jachomo Badoer, a Venetian Merchant", The Accounting Review, LVIII, 1983, pp 98-104.

38 P Kats, "Double Entry Bookkeeping in England before Hugh Oldcastle", Accountant, LXXIV, 1926, pp 91-8.

39 E M Myatt-Price, "The Twelve at Tattershall", Accounting Review, XXXV, 1960, pp 680-5.

40 J Heers, Le Livre de Comptes de Giovanni Piccamiglio, homme d'affaires Genois 1456-1459, Paris, SEVPEN, 1959, 377 pp.

41 J Schneider, Le livre de comptes des merciers messins Jean Le Clerc et Jacquemin de Moyeuvre (1460-1461), Metz, Librairie M Mutelet 1951, 105 pp.

42 K L Wood-Legh (Ed), A Small Household of the XVth Century, Manchester, University Press, 1956, xxxvi + 90 pp.

43 M Mollat, Comptabilité du Port de Dieppe au XVe siecle, Paris, Armand Colin, 1951, 139 pp.

44 E M Myatt-Price, "Examples of Techniques in Medieval Building Accounts", Abacus, II, 1966, pp 41-8.

45 P H Wolff, "Une comptabilité commerciale du XVe siecle", Annales du Midi, LXIV, 1952, pp 131-48.

46 P Heath, Medieval Clerical Accounts, York, St Anthony's Publications No 26, 1964, 59 pp.

47 F A Ritson, "Halyburton's Ledger and his Times", Accountant's Magazine, LXX, 1966, pp 124-133.

48 E Stone, "Profit-and-Loss Accountancy at Norwich Cathedral Priory", Transactions of the Royal Historical Society, 5th ser, XII, 1962, pp 25-48.

49 T and A Constable (eds), "Accounts of Sir Duncan Forestar", in Miscellany of the Scottish History Society, vol 9, Edinburgh, 1958, pp 57-81.

50 G Parsloe (Ed), Wardens' Accounts of the Worshipful Company of Founders of the City of London 1497-1681, Athlone Press, University of London, 1964, LVIII + 491 pp.

51 K Rossman, "Bruchstucke aus Handlungsbuchern von 1508 der Welser - Vohlinschen Handelsgesellschaft in Augsburg", Scripta Mercaturae, I, 1967, pp 48-56.

52 P Pickl, Des Alteste Geschäftsbuch Osterreichs, Graz, Verlag der Historischen Landeskommission, 1966, 495 pp.

53 G E Connell-Smith, "Ledger of Thomas Howell", Economic History Review, 2nd ser, III, 1950, pp 363-70.

54 L F Tremel, Das Handelsbuch des Judenburger Kaufmannes Clemens Korbler 1526-1548, Graz, Beitrage zur Erforschung steirischer Geschichtsquellen XLVII, Heft 1960, XXXIX + 127 pp.

55 D M Livock, "The Accounts of the Corporation of Bristol: 1532 to 1835", Journal of Accounting Research, III, 1965, pp 86-102.

56 J Vanes, "The Ledger of John Smythe, Merchant of Bristol", Accountant, September 16, 1967, pp 357-361.

57 J Vanes (Ed), The Ledger of John Smythe, 1538-1550, London, Royal Commission on Historical Manuscripts, JP 19, HMSO 1974, VII + 363 pp.

58 D W Crossley (Ed), Sydney Ironworks Accounts 1541-1573, London, Royal Historical Society, Camden Fourth Series, vol 15, 1975, 269 pp.

59 A Korzendorfer and Th G Werner, "Fragment des Schuldbuches der Augsburger Welser von 1554 bis 1560", Scripta Mercaturae, I, 2, 1969, pp 109-151.

60 M Zell, "Accounts of a Sheep and Corn Farm, 1558-60", Agricultural History Review, XXVII, 1979, pp 122-128.

61 E Duverger, Jan, Jacques en Grans De Moor, Tapijtwevers en Tapigthandelaars Te Oudenaarde, Antwerpen en Gent (1560 tot ca 1680), Ghent, Centre Universitaire d'étude de l'histoire de la tapisserie flamande, 1960.

62 R Tittler (Ed), Accounts of the Roberts Family of Boarzell, Sussex c 1568-1582, Lewes, Sussex, Record Society, vol 71, 1977-79, XXVIII + 181 pp.

63 A K Longfield (Ed), Fitzwilliam Accounts 1560-65 (Annesley Collection), Dublin Stationery Office for the Irish Manuscripts Commission, 1960, XII + 139 pp.

64 B Oden, "A Netherlands Merchant in Stockholm in the Reign of Erik XIV", Scandinavian Economic History Review, X, 1962, pp 3-37.

65 G R Batho (Ed), The Household Papers of Henry Percy, Ninth Earl of Northumberland (1564-1632), Camden 3rd ser, vol 93, London, Royal Historical Society, 1962, LVII + 190 pp.

66 C T McInnes (Ed), Accounts of the Treasurer of Scotland, vol 12, 1566-1574, HMSO, Edinburgh, 1970, 529 pp (previous volumes published from 1877-1916 with different editors).

67 L B Taylor (Ed), Aberdeen Shore Works Accounts, 1596-1670, Aberdeen University Press, 1972, X + 668 pp.

68 P Ramsey, "Some Tudor Merchants' Accounts", pp 185-201 in A C Littleton and B S Yamey, Studies in the History of Accounting, London, Sweet and Maxwell, 1956.

69 J O Winjum, "The Journal of Thomas Gresham", Accounting Review, XLVI, 1971, pp 149-155.

70 C Read, "Lord Burghley's Household Accounts", Economic History Review, 2nd ser, IX, 1956, pp 343-8.

71 W Brulez, De Firma Della Faille en de-Internationale Handel van Vlaamse Firma's in de 16e Eeuw, Brussels, Paleis der Academien, 1959, 634 pp.

72 B H Slicher van Bath, "Een Fries Landbouwbedrijf in de tweede helft van de Zestiende eeuw", Agronomisch-Historische Bijdragen, IV, 1958, pp 69-208.

73 H Thierfelder (Ed), Rostock-Osloer Handelsbeziehungen im 16 - Jahrhundert Die Geschaftspapiere der Kaufleute Kron in Rostock und Bene in Oslo, Weimar, Hermann Bohlaus Nachfolger 1958, 256 pp.

74 A Simpson, "Encounters with Accounts", pp 1-21 of The Wealth of the Gentry 1540-1660, Chicago, University of Chicago Press, and London, Cambridge University Press, 1961, 226 pp.

75 S W Shelton, "The Goldsmith Banker", Three Banks Review, No 27, 1955, pp 42-52.

76 A Montgomerie, "An East Lothian Executor's Accounts, 1645-1650", Scottish Historical Review, XXX, 1971, pp 144-153.

77 B S Yamey, H C Edey and H W Thomson, Accounting in England and Scotland: 1543-1800, London, Sweet & Maxwell, 1963, 228 pp (particularly pp 180-201).

78 F W Munslow, "Executorship Accounts in 1653", Accountant, CXL, 1959, pp 218-219.

79 J Bankes and E Kerridge (Eds), The Early Records of the Bankes Family at Winstanley, Manchester University Press for Chetham Society, 1973, VIII + 113 pp.

80 G A Lee, "The Francis Willoughby Executorship Accounts, 1672-1682; An Early Double-Entry System in England", Accounting Review, LVI, 1981, pp 539-553.

81 V Baladouni, "The Accounting Records of the East India Company", Accounting Historians Journal, VIII, 1981, pp 67-70.

82 B S Yamey, "Two Seventeenth Century Accounting Statements", Accounting and Business Research, XII, 1982, pp 111-114.

83 F A Palmer, The Blacksmith's Ledgers of the Hedges Family of Bucklebury, Berks, 1736-73, University of Reading, Institute of Agricultural History Research Paper, No 2, 1970, 12 pp.

84 E Ogura, "The Nakai Family's Bookkeeping System", Accounting and Business Research, XII, 1982, pp 148-152.

85 L Kreiser, "Early American Accounting", Journal of Accountancy, CXLII, 1976, pp 77-80.

86 W E Stone, "Managerial Accounting on the US 1758 Frontier", Accounting Historians Journal, IV, 1977, pp 107-111.

87 D A R Forrester, "Early Canal Company Accounts: Financial and Accounting Aspects of the Forth and Clyde Navigation, 1768-1816", Accounting and Business Research, X, 1980, pp 109-123.

88 A J Voke, "Accounting Methods of Colonial Merchants in Virginia", Journal of Accountancy, XLII, 1926, pp 1-11.

89 A R Coleman, W G Shenkir and W E Stone, "Accounting in Colonial Virginia: A Case Study", Journal of Accountancy, CXXXVIII, 1974, pp 32-43.

90 R M Jennings, "Selections from a Pre-revolutionary Accounting Record", Accounting Review, XXXVII, 1962, pp 73-75.

91 W E Stone, "A 1794 Ledger Demonstrates an Economic Transition", Accounting and Business Research, XI, 1981, pp 243-248.

92 W E Stone, "1794 Middletown, Delaware - From Accounting Records", Accounting Historians Journal, VI, 1979, pp 39-52.

93 A T Hart, Country Counting House, London, Phoenix House, 1962, 142 pp.

94 G W Daniels, "Trading Accounts of a London Merchant in 1794", Economic Journal, XXXIII, 1923, pp 516-22.

95 "Mr Chest and Mr Box", Westminster Bank Review, August 1952, pp 14-17.

96 W T Baxter, House of Hancock, Cambridge, Mass, Harvard University Press, 1945, and New York, Russell & Russell, 1965, XXVII + 321 pp.

97 K H Burley, "Some Accounting Records of an Eighteenth-Century Clothier", Accounting Research, IX, 1958, pp 50-60; reprinted in B S Yamey (Ed), The Historical Development of Accounting: A Selection of Papers, New York, Arno Press, 1978.

98 W A Pemberton, "A Parson's Account Book", Local Historian, XIII, 1979, pp 397-405.

99 P Moureaux, Les comptes d'une société charbonniere a la fin d l'Ancien Régime, Brussels, Palais des Academies, 1969, 249 pp.

100 A K Longfield (Ed), The Shapland Carew Papers, Dublin Stationery Office, 1946, X + 228 pp.

101 L H Kistler, "The Middlesex Canal - An Analysis of the Accounting and Management", Accounting Historians Journal, VII, 1980, pp 43-58.

102 H McCredie, "An early Ledger of the Firm Messrs Cooper & Levey, 1823-5", Bulletin of the Business Archives Council of Australia, I VII, 1960, pp 19-41.

103 W E Stone, "Accounting Records reveal History: The Virginia Cobbler", Journal of Accountancy, CXLII, 1976, pp 60-66.

104 R H Parker, "Bookkeeping Barter and Current Cash Equivalents in Early New South Wales", Abacus, XVIII, 1982, pp 139-151.

105 D S Macmillan and H McCredie, "Accounting for a Scottish Venture in Colonial Development", Bulletin of the Business Archives Council of Australia, I IX, 1961, pp 66-83.

106 A C Littleton, Accounting Evolution to 1900, New York, American Institute Publishing Co, 1933, reprinted by Russell & Russell, New York, 1967, 373 pp.

ALPHABETICAL INDEX OF AUTHORS IN THE PRECEDING BIBLIOGRAPHY

Antoni, T; 17, 25, 26, 28
Baladouni, V; 81
Bankes, J; 79
Batho, G R; 65
Baxter, W T; 96
Bigwood, G; 18
Brulez, W; 71
Burley, K H; 97
Castellani, A; 10
Chauvin, M; 29
Chiaudano, M; 6
Coleman, A R; 89
Connell-Smith, G E; 53
Constable, A; 49
Constable, T; 49
Crossley, D W; 58
Daniels, G W; 94
De Roover, R; 2, 13, 23
Duverger, E; 61
Edey, H C; 77
Forestié, E; 27
Forrester, D A R; 87
Fryde, E B; 24
Gibson, S; 22
Goitein, S D; 1
Grunzweig, A; 18
Guigue, G; 20
Hart, A T; 93
Heath, P; 46
Heers, J; 40
Jennings, R M; 90
Kats, P; 38
Kerridge, E; 79
Kistler, L H; 101
Korzendorfer, A; 59
Kreiser, L; 85
Lee, G A; 7, 8, 9, 15, 80
Littleton, A C; 106
Livock, D M; 55
Longfield, A K; 63, 100
Lopez, R S; 21
McCredie, H; 102, 105
McInnes, C T; 66
Macmillan, D S; 105
Melis, F; 12
Meyer, P; 20
Mollat, M; 43
Montgomerie, A; 76
Moureaux, P; 99
"Mr Chest and Mr Box"; 95
Munslow, F W; 78
Myatt-Price, E M; 31, 39, 44
Nobes, C W; 19
Oden, B; 64
Ogura, E; 84
Palmer, F A; 83
Parker, R H; 104
Parsloe, G; 50
Pemberton, W A; 98
Peragallo, E; 33, 34, 35, 36, 37
Pickl, P; 52
Pierard, C; 14
Pryde, G S; 32
Ramsey, P; 68
Raymond, I W; 21
Read, C; 70
Ritson, F A; 47
Ross, R; 4, 30
Rossman, K; 51
Sapori, A; 16
Schneider, J; 41
Searle, E; 4
Shelton, S W; 75
Shenkir, W G; 89
Simpson, A; 74
Slicher van Bath, B H; 72
Smith, R A L; 3
Stone, E; 48

Stone, W E; 86, 89, 91, 92, 103
Taylor, L B; 67
Thierfelder, H; 73
Thomson, H W; 77
Tittler, R; 62
Tremel, L F; 54
Vanes, J; 56, 57
Voke, A J; 88
Werner, Th G; 59
Winjum, J O; 69
Wolff, P H; 45
Wood-Legh, K L; 42
Yamey, B S; 77, 82
Zell, M; 60
Zerbi, T; 11

The Florentine Bank Ledger Fragments of 1211: Some New Insights

GEOFFREY A. LEE*

Since their transcription in 1887 by Pietro Santini [11], the ledger accounts of 1211 on the flyleaves of the *Codex Aedilis* 67 in the Biblioteca Medicea-Laurenziana, Florence, have been recognized as the earliest long fragments of pure Italian, and especially Tuscan, prose. As such they were reprinted in 1889 by Monaci [7], and in 1926 by Schiaffini [12], both philologists like Santini. In 1930 the accounts were expounded by Chiaudano [4], as an important document in the economic history of Italy in the 13th century. Historians of accounting, however, have accorded them only brief and summary treatment—Besta in 1922 [2], Melis more fully in 1950 [6], and Raymond de Roover in 1956 [10].

In a previous article [5], I have given what is probably the first extended account in English of this celebrated text, including a complete translation and notes. In the present paper, I provide the main findings, suitably illustrated, for the consideration of accountants who might otherwise overlook the longer article, published as it is in a journal whose readership is mainly among the members of arts faculties.[1]

---

* Lecturer, University of Nottingham.

[1] Acknowledgment is made to the Editor of *Nottingham Mediaeval Studies*, Professor Lewis Thorpe (Head of the Department of French, University of Nottingham), for permission to reproduce the material which follows; to his wife, Dr. Barbara Reynolds (Reader in Italian Studies, Department of English), for invaluable aid in elucidating the meaning of the text, and for advice on the spelling of names; and to the Director and staff of the Biblioteca Medicea-Laurenziana, Florence for the supply of excellent photographs of the MS., which have proved most helpful in interpreting the printed transcripts.

The Manuscript

The text is written cursively on both sides of two sheets of parchment, each measuring 43 x 28 cm., and forming the flyleaves of the *Codex Aedilis* 67, a 14th century MS. of the *Digestum Novum cum glossa,* a legal work in the Biblioteca Medicea-Laurenziana. On the two *recti* the writing is generally well-preserved and legible. On *carta* 1 *verso,* however (the inside of the front flyleaf), some three-fourths of the original text has been scraped off completely and overwritten with the table of contents of the *Digestum,* leaving only the bottom one-fourth of the 1211 text still legible, and that mutilated. *C.* 2 *verso* is free from overwriting, but has been scraped all over, so that only a few words here and there are decipherable with the naked eye. Nevertheless, Santini was able to read most of it by applying chemicals to bring up the writing. But this has done further damage to the MS. Besides a few worm-holes and tears, there is one larger hole in each sheet—seemingly original, as the writing goes round them without any lacunae, and pointing to the use of cheap, inferior parchment for records intended to have but a short life.

From the character of the contents it is clear that the fragments are those of the customers' ledger of an unidentified firm of bankers, operating in Florence, Bologna and Pisa in the year 1211. All but one or two entries relate to loans made by the bank, and to repayments of the principal. Each page is ruled down the middle, and each of its two columns divided by horizontal lines into six to eight blocks of varying depth. Each block is allocated to one loan, the book-keeper leaving what he deemed to be adequate space; sometimes it was not quite filled, sometimes it proved too little and writing had to be crowded in. The entries are not in chronological order, even as regards the original advances, but must have been made as and when evidence of the loan was furnished to the book-keeper—very quickly if the transaction took place locally, a few days later if it occurred at a distance [11].

Each block of entries (except one) exhibits, in embryo, the features of a modern ledger account. First comes a statement of the borrower's name, the amount advanced, and the date, followed in many cases by the due date of repayment, the rate of interest to be charged for late payment (almost always, 4 *denari* per *libra* per month, or 20 percent per annum), sometimes the names of two or more witnesses, and sometimes, again, the name of a guarantor of the loan. Then follow repayments of the principal, generally by installments. Nothing is said about interest as a rule. The successive entries are written straight on in prose, separated only by an abbreviation of "item." All sums of money, in *libre, soldi* and *denari* (1 *libra* = 20 *soldi,* 1 *soldo* = 12 *denari*), are set out in Roman numerals, with no attempt to order them in columns. There are no totals or balances. When repayments were adjudged equal to the advance (they are not always precisely so), the account was closed by striking through it with slanting lines—as has been done in all cases in the MS. In other words, the first entry in each block was equivalent to a debit in a personal account, and the other entries to credits. Balancing was probably performed by setting up beads on the abacus for the amount of the advance, and taking them away for the amount of the repayments, the account being cancelled when there were no beads left in position—an operating sequence uncannily like that of a present-day computer.

The two leaves of the MS. are not consecutive. *C.* 2 seems to be the earlier, since it relates largely to loans made in Bologna for the fair of San Procolo (or Proculo—called "San Brocolo" in the original), which opened on 1st May [4]; most of the advances in *c.* 1 were made in June. The dates are all given according to the *consuetudo bononiensis* (custom of Bologna), by which the first 15 days of the month were counted directly, while the last 15 or 16 were reckoned backwards from the end of the month. Thus, 2nd August is *due dì intrante agosto,* while *tredici di anzi kal* [*endi*] *luglio* means 18th June; contrary to what Melis suggests [6], the Bolognese do not appear to have followed the ancient Roman practice of counting in the kalends (first day of the next month) as the first of the stated number of days. Since, however, it is clear that the main business was in Florence, it cannot be presumed that the ledger was kept at Bologna; possibly the book-keeper was a native of Bologna.

Book-Keeping Conventions in the Early 13th Century

There are 42 blocks of entries which can be read in whole or in part. A number of these appear below in full, in Italian and English, with notes and commentary. Connoisseurs of medieval Italian will note that, as might be expected, the text has no pretensions to literary grace, that its vocabulary is severely limited by the subject matter, and that it contains a large proportion of commercial terms, as well as ordinary words used in a technical sense. Nevertheless, the fragments are invaluable as evidence of the proficiency which quite ordinary Florentines had already attained in the writing of the vulgar tongue, and of its nearness, even at that period, to the language of Dante and Boccaccio. They are also remarkable as a specimen of the use of Italian in accounts having something of a public character, since they were apparently admissible as evidence in judicial proceedings for recovery of debts at a time when all official and legal records in Florence were in Latin and continued to be so for centuries. Indeed, the 1211 accounts contain many stereotyped phrases and formulas which seem to have been literally translated. Santini [11] suggests that in view of the determination of medieval legislators to preserve Latin forms in legal documents, accounts in Italian must have been in use for a long time among merchants and bankers to have broken down the prejudice of lawyers against them. The relative sophistication, too, of the accounts indicates a historical development extending well back into the 12th century; but evidence to confirm this supposition is wanting.

The writing itself is small, tolerably neat, but employs many abbreviations, particularly of words which frequently recur. The less obvious ones have been resolved in the transcripts which follow, with the adoption of some suggestions of Schiaffini [12] in preference to those of Santini. In particular, *pō*, which Santini renders as *posto*, is here given as *ponemmo* ("we added"), which is more consistent with the countervailing use of *levammo* ("we deducted"), as explained below. The spelling of proper names has been modernized throughout. Amounts of money are given in Arabic figures, using the pre-1971 British notation of £.s.d. (pounds, shillings, pence) to denote *libre, soldi* and *denari*. One or two small errors, made in the Nottingham translation [5], are here corrected.

C. 1 recto, col. 1, acc. 1

MCCXI
Aldobrandino petro e buonessegnia falkoni
No dino dare katuno in tuto lib'. lii per liure
diciotto d'imperiali mezani arrascione di trenta e cinque meno terza
ke demmo loro tredici dì anzi k. luglio e dino pagare tredici dì anzi kal. luglio.
se più stanno, a iiii d'. lib'. il mese quanto fusse nostra voluntade.
testi alberto baldovini e quitieri alberti di porte del duomo.
Item die dare buonessegnia s. xii per u massamutino.
Buonessegnia falkoni ci a dato lib'. xl: rekò
iakopo a termine. Item die auire lib'. iiii e s. ii:
leuammo di rascione buonessegnie oue douea auire
per ser kalkagnio vi dì anzi k. luglio. Item diè lib'. iii meno
d'. xii per tornaquinci, kei pagò nei panni suoi.
Item ci diè Buonincontro dappopio s. xl di ssua mano
tre dì anzi kal. luglio. Item ci diè aldobrandino lib'. iii meno d'. xii:
rekò giannozo.

1211
Aldobrandino Pietro and Buoninsegna Falconi
are due to give us, each [for himself], in total £52. 0. 0d. for £18. 0. 0d. in Imperial *mezzani* at the rate of 35 less a third [*libre* in *mezzani* in 100 *libre* Florentine] which we gave them on 18th June, and they are to pay on 18th June; if [the moneys] are outstanding longer, [interest is] at 4d. in the £ per month, for as long as we may permit. Witnesses: Alberto Baldovini and Guittieri Alberti, of the Porta del Duomo.

Item Buoninsegna is due to give 12s. 0d. for one *massamutino*.

Buoninsegna Falconi has given us £40. 0. 0d.; Jacopo brought it at the due date. *Item* he is due to receive £4. 2. 0d.; we deducted from Buoninsegna's account what he was due to receive in respect of Ser Calcagno on 25th June. *Item* he gave £2. 19. 0d. on behalf of Tornaquinci, whom he paid in cloths of his. *Item* Buonincontro da Poppio (?) gave us £2. 0. 0d. personally on 28th June. *Item* Aldobrandino gave us £2.19. 0d.; Giannozzo brought it.

This is a somewhat complex example to take, as it includes transactions in foreign exchange. *Mezzano* is defined by C. Battisti and G. Alessio [1] as a coin having half the value of a standard coin; the identity of the currency concerned is thus conjectural. The exchange is stated to be "at the rate of 35 less a third," resulting in a liability of £52. 0. 0d. Florentine for £18. 0. 0d. in *mezzani*. If the rate is interpreted as £34.13. 4d. in *mezzani* to £100. 0. 0d. Florentine, the sum works out very closely—to £51.18. 6d.; hence, this seems the most probable explanation. (Acc. 4 in this same column relates to a similar transaction, on the same day, involving the same amounts in both currencies, but with two different borrowers.) The *massamutino,* according to Battisti and Alessio [1], was a Hispano-Arabian gold coin of the 12th century; the repayments in the second part of the account do not appear to cover it, yet the account is cancelled like all the others in the MS.

Apart from all this, the account repays closer analysis, as it contains examples of most of the standard phrases used in the ledger, as follows.

(no) die/dino dare: "is/are due to give (us)"	*die/dino avire:* "is/are due to receive"

These represent the earliest, and most natural, usage of the words *dare* and *avere* in their book-keeping senses of "debit" and "credit." In 13th century book-keeping, though, they are not yet thought of as direct opposites, for with them are associated, respectively:

(ci) diè/diede/ha(nno) dato: "gave (has/have given) (us)"	*(li) demmo/avemmo dato:* "we gave (have given) him/them"

Thus the early medieval book-keeper evidently thought of two sets of fluxes and refluxes—a loan *to* someone, and its repayment, on the one hand, and a loan or deposit *from* someone, and its repayment, on the other. (Mutatis mutandis for sales and purchases, in a merchant's books.) He was also familiar with the idea that the same customer might deposit money with the bank *and* take a loan from it, and equally with the practice whereby a customer used his deposit to pay a debt of his own to another customer who had borrowed from the bank. In either case a transfer between the deposit account and the loan account, in the banker's books at the depositor's request, would settle the borrower's liability in whole or in part. Hence arose a third pair of opposed entries, of which many examples occur in the 1211 ledger, viz.—

levammo ove die/dovea avere: "we deducted what he is/was due to receive" (i.e., "we debited his account which has/had a credit balance")	*ponemmo che die/dovea avere:* "we added what he is/was due to receive" (i.e., "we credited his (loan) account with what stood to the credit of his (or another's) (deposit) account")

The author has scrupulously avoided rendering any of these six expressions, or their variants, by phrases involving the words "debit" and "credit"; to do so would have been anachronistic.

e dene/dino pagare . . . :
"and is/are due to pay (on a certain date)"

In the example, this is the actual date of the advance! More usually, it is one (occasionally two) months later. The significance of the date is clearer from the phrase which normally follows:

se più stanno, a iiii d'. lib'. il mese:
"if [the moneys] are outstanding longer, [interest is] at 4d. in the £ per month"

In other words, it appears that interest began to run, at the rate of 20 percent per annum (quite normal for those times), from the due date which, as in the first account, might be the date of the advance. In that case the borrower paid the full 20 percent for as long as the loan was outstanding. Otherwise he had (say) one month free of interest (there was normally no intention that he should pay within that time), so that his average rate was somewhat less than 20 percent. This rate is charged on 15 accounts altogether, so far as they can be read, and there is one (*c. 2 verso, col. 2, acc. 4*) in which the interest is nil for one month, 20 percent per annum for the next two months, and 30 percent thereafter; perhaps the borrower's credit was worse, or the bankers did not wish him to extend the loan unduly. Besides these, there are many accounts for small sums where no interest is mentioned; but this does not necessarily mean that it was not charged.

It is noteworthy, too, that the word "interest" is never expressed in the terms of a loan, except in the account last referred to, where it is called a "penalty" (*pena*). The reason probably lies in the Church's ban on "usury," making it desirable to disguise the charging of interest as the exaction of a penalty for late payment. For the same reason, perhaps, no charge for interest (*prode*) is entered in the personal accounts in the 1211 ledger, except in some few cases where it forms part of a balance brought forward from another page; the entry of its receipt in the cash book was presumably sufficient as a record, in the normal case.

quanto fusse nostra voluntade:
"for as long as we may permit"

This formula gave the bankers the right to call in the loan at any time after the due date. In fact, many loans run on considerably beyond it, and there is no evidence of a policy of punctually enforcing payment.

testi (abbreviated "*tt*") *A.B. e C.D.*:
"witnesses: A.B. and C.D."

The names of two or more witnesses appear in connection with 11 of the loans in the fragments. The amounts advanced range from £8.10. 0d. to £52. 0. 0d., with one mutilated account (*c. 1 verso, col. 2, acc. 1*) whose repayments indicate a larger sum. However, advances as high as £107. 7. 8d. (*c. 2 recto, col. 2, acc. 1*) are made without specifying witnesses. There would be a notarial record in all cases, except where the sums were trivial, and the first "witness" was probably the notary, as is suggested by the recurrence of names; that of Alberto Baldovini occurs six times. The witnesses' names were probably omitted to save space, once it was realized that a legal record existed anyway.

di sua mano:
"personally" (literally, "with his own hand")
reko A.B.:
"A.B. brought it"

This could refer to A.B. either as a messenger who brought money to the bank or as a partner who received it and accounted for it to the firm. The recurrence of the same Christian names suggests the latter, in the majority of cases. Eight names occur, in these and other contexts, between three and eight times each, and it would seem that they were those of the partners. They are, with the number of appearances: Arnolfino (8); Jacopo (6); Albizzo, Aldobrandino and Cambio (5); Giannozzo and Tornaquinci (4); and Tegghiaio (3).

The surnames are omitted, as being unnecessary for identification within the firm. In any case, fixed surnames were only gradually coming into use among the nonnoble classes of Florence, as may be seen from the frequent identification of a customer by his father's Christian name, or by his trade.

a termine:
"at the due date" (already written)

Further Illustrations of Accounting Methods

The first account illustrates some of the ways in which settlement was made in the books of the 1211 bankers. The £52. 0. 0d. loan was evidently in the joint names of Aldobrandino Pietro and Buoninsegna Falconi; Aldobrandino repaid £2.19. 0d. directly to the bank, and Buoninsegna £40. 0. 0d. Another £4. 2. 0d. was produced by offsetting (in modern terms, crediting) either a sum of money paid into the bank on Buoninsegna's behalf by "Ser Calcagno" (and thus credited to his deposit account, elsewhere in the ledger), or a bill of exchange or promisory note accepted or made by Calcagno, and endorsed by Buoninsegna to the bankers, with, again, a debit to another account in his name. £2.19. 0d. was credited in respect of a payment in kind: cloths to that value delivered to Tornaquinci, one of the partners; and the last £2. 0. 0d. was paid in by Buonincontro da Poppio (or Poppi), perhaps a debtor of one of the borrowers. (The author does not accept the emendation of Melis [6], *Buonincontro da proprio,* presumably meaning "B. for his own part.")

In *c. 1 recto, col. 1, acc. 5,* a new feature appears, in the shape of a guarantor of the loan, interest and principal:

MCCXI
Buonagiunta dassomaia die dare lib'. xxiii
e sol. xviii per liure uentitre ke i prestammo i die anzi kl. luglio:

ponemmo ke die aire [sic] e dene pargare in k. agosto: se piu stanno a iiii d'. lib'. il mese, quanto fosse nostra voluntade: e s'ei no pagasse si no promise di pagare buonone f [iglio] farolfi da duomo prode e kapitale quant'elli sstesero. tt. prestorso d'oltrarno ellutieri f. galgani balsimi ed ugolino f. sassolini dackapiano. Item buoriketto del greccio ci diè lib'. xxiii e sol. xviii. ponemmo.

1211

Buonagiunta da Somaia is due to give £23.18 0d. for £23. 0. 0d. which we lent him on 30th June; we added what he is due to receive, and repay, on 1st August. If [the moneys] are outstanding longer, [interest is] at 4d. in the £ per month, for as long as we may permit; and if he does not pay, then Buonone, son of Farolfo of the Duomo [parish], promised to pay us interest and principal, as much as they shall amount to. Witnesses: Prestorso of Oltrarno, Lutieri, son of Galgano Balsimi, and Ugolino, son of Sassolino da Capiano. *Item* Buorricchetto del Grecio gave us £23.18. 0d.; we added it.

Altogether, eight accounts have guarantors. Among them are the first two on *c. 2 recto,* which is headed, in *col. 1, In nomine domini. ame[n] San brocolo.* The fair of San Procolo at Bologna, as this pious headnote indicates, was a profitable time for the bank, which evidently had a branch, or resident partner, in the city. In *acc. 1* "Orlandino the leatherdresser (*galigaio*), of Santa Trinità" borrows £26. 0. 0d. in Bolognese coin at Bologna for the fair, and his guarantor is Angiolino Bolognini, leatherdresser. Orlandino duly pays, directly and otherwise. Simultaneously (as it would seem), in *acc. 2,* Angiolino borrows £40. 0. 0d., with Orlandino as guarantor; the account reads:

Angiolino galigaio no die dare lib'. xl per bulongnini ke i demmo a bolongna per lo mercato sanbrocoli, e dè pagare per metzo matgio: se più sstanno a iiii d'.; e s'elli non pagasse sinno promise di pagare orlandino galigaio prode e capitale quant'elli istessero. tt. matzinto, mainetto d'albitzoco, e bernardo bertti.

Angiolino ci a dato lib'. xl di ssua mano quatro dì anzi k. giugnio. Item ci diè benivieni galigaio per angiolino lib'. iii e sol. x: rekò albizo dafferra sic, pezzaio di lungarno a questo termine. Item ci diè orlandino lib'. x: rekò kabio da lo scotto pezzaio lib'. x: reko kabio da lo scotto pezzaio lib'. tre, e da iakopo del cāpo lib'. quatro meno soldi tre, e le tre l'. e le tre sol. diede orlandino di ssua mano a questo termine di ssopra.

Item angiolino di ssua mano sol. cx un die anzi k. giugnio. Item ci diè orlandino lib'. iiii e sol. iii: rekò kābio da bernardo lo pezaio tre di intrante giugnio. Item ci die orlandino di ssua mano sol. xl ā kon sic arnolfino i die anzi metzo giugnio. Item diede orlandino sol. iii, ed a pagato in quiderdone de la ssu parte a aldobrandino per 1—giugnio.

Angiolino the leatherdresser is due to give us £40. 0. 0d. for Bolognese coin which we gave him at Bologna for the fair of San Procolo, and is due to pay by mid-May. If [the moneys] are outstanding longer, [interest is] at 4d. [in the £ per month]; and if he does not pay, then Orlandino the leatherdresser promised to pay us interest and principal, as much as they shall amount to. Witnesses: Mazzingo, Mainetto d'Albizzocco (?), and Bernardo Berti.

Angiolino has given us £11. 0. 0d. personally on 28th May. *Item* Benevieni the leatherdresser gave us on behalf of Angiolino £3.10. 0d.: Albizzo da Ferrara (?), leatherseller of Lungarno, brought it at the date aforesaid. *Item* Orlandino gave us £10. 0. 0d.; Cambio brought £3. 0. 0d. from Scotto the leatherseller, and £3.17 0d. from Jacopo del Campo, and Orlandino gave £3. 3. 0d. personally, at the date given above.

Item Angiolino [gave us] personally £5.10. 0d. on 31st May and has paid the interest. *Item* Orlandino gave us £3.16. 0d. on behalf of Jacopo on 31st May. *Item* Orlandino gave us £4. 3. 0d.; Cambio brought it from Bernardo the leatherseller on 3rd June. *Item* Orlandino gave us personally £2. 0. 0d. on account of (?) Arnolfino on 14th June. *Item* Orlandino gave [us] 3s. 0d., and has paid in settlement of his liability to Aldobrandino by mid-June.

Thus it was that, in the end, the guarantor Orlandino had to pay £20. 2. 0d. of the principal, as against £20. 0. 0d., and the interest, paid by the borrower Angiolino, or on his behalf by his own debtors—a net overpayment of 2s. 0d., unless this included Orlandino's share of interest. Both were Florentines, as shown by their addresses, and the amounts are all stated in terms of Pisan *denari*, the common silver currency of Tuscany at that period; Florence did not begin to coin silver *fiorini grossi* (= 12d.) until 1237, or gold *fiorini d'oro* (= 29s. 0d.) until 1252 [3, 9]. Bologna had her own coinage already, and the silver *buolognini* are known, from other accounts in the 1211 ledger, to have been reckoned generally at 22s. 0d. Bolognese to 20s. 0d. Florentine. Thus in *c. 2 recto, col. 2, acc. 2:*

Serr ackorri f. pankonsole no die dare lib'. vi di bonlongnini ke li li prestoa arnolfino a bolongnia per san brokolo.

Item ci diè ser ackorri sol. cviiii di pisãni: rascionamo i bolognini sol. due l'.

Ser Accorri, son of Panconsole, is due to give us £6. 0. 0d in Bolognese coin which Arnolfino lent him at Bologna for San Procolo.

Item Ser Accorri gave us £5. 9. 0d. in Pisan coin; we made an allowance on (?) the Bolognese coin of 2s. 0d. in the £.

This evidently means that the £6. 0. 0d. Bolognese was multiplied by the factor 20s./22s. to reduce it to Florentine; to the nearest *denaro* it would be £5. 9. 1d., and the calculation in the text is therefore very close.

Again, despite the nominal equality at that time of the silver *denari* of Pisa, Lucca, Florence and Sienna [3, 4], it appears from the fragments that *new* Pisan coin stood at a premium, ranging from 1s. 3d. to 1s. 7d. in the £, over ordinary Florentine coin. Thus in *c. 2 verso, col. 1, acc. 4:*

MCCXI (Item die dare per prode sol. xlviiii)*

Lutieri kalkagni no die dare lib'. xliiii e sol. xi per liure quaranta due meno d'. diciotto di nuovi k'ebbe in pisa a quindici d'. l'. undici dì intranto giugnio, e dene pagare xi die intrante luglio: se più stanno a iiii d'. lib'.: disse kessono trallui e kardinale. Item die dare kardinale lib'. xxiiii e d'. xxx per la rescione rinucini f.

* Inserted afterwards

macene (ke sodāmo xiii dì intrante nouēbre)*

Lutieri ci a dato dissua mano lib'. ii e sol. x e l—tredici dì intrante luglio. Item ci diede kardinale lib. ii (?) sol. xv e d'. v. ponemmo.

Item lib'. cinquanta di nuoui ke diede per noi e quarneri f. gaiazzi di porre san pie [tro], ke li fecie dare a bernardo bankiere di pisa xiii dì intrante nouebre. Item ci diè luttieri e kardinale lib'. xv e sol. xvi e d'. viii innanzi viiii pergamene.

1211 (*Item* he is due to give for interest £2. 9. 0d.)*

Lutieri Calcagni is due to give us £44.11. 0d. for £41.18. 6d. of new coin which he received in Pisa at [a charge of] 1s. 3d. in the £ on 11th June, and is due to pay it on 11th July; if [the moneys] are outstanding longer, [interest is] at 4d. in the £ [per month]. He said that [the moneys] are between him and Cardinale. *Item* Cardinale is due to give £24. 2. 6d. in respect of the account of Rinuccino, son of Macigno (?) (which we settled on 13th November).*

Lutieri has given us personally £2.10. 6d. on 13th July. *Item* Cardinale gave us £2.15. 5d. (?); we added it.

Item £50. 0. 0d. of new coin which he gave on our behalf to Guarnieri, son of Gaiazzo of the Porta San Pietro, which [money] he caused to be given to Bernardo, the banker of Pisa, on 13th November. *Item* Lutieri and Cardinale gave us £15.16 6d., nine parchments further on.

Here the total debits (including the interpolated sum for interest) amount to £71. 2. 6d., and the total credits to £71. 2. 5d. This is arrived at after emending Cardinale's first payment from *lib'. li sol. xv e d'. v* (£51.15. 5d.), as read by Santini, to *lib'. ii*, etc.; perhaps the odd 1d. might be similarly found. (This part of the MS is now virtually illegible, and I am unable to check the transcript directly.) Oddly, there is no extra allowance for the £50. 0. 0d. of new Pisan coin given to the banker in Pisa. Final settlement seems to have been effected by transferring a credit balance, or part of one, in the names of Lutieri and Cardinale on a later page, after inserting an amount on the "debit side" for accrued interest.

The Rudiments of Double Entry

It is now necessary to form an opinion as to how far the unknown bankers of 1211, and their clerks, had progressed on the road to double entry book-keeping, which, as is generally known, was attained in Genoa by 1340 [6]. The ledger fragments are particularly valuable, since they are not only the earliest existing relics of Italian book-keeping, but antedate by more than forty years the oldest of the several specimens of the art which survive from the second half of the 13th century—viz., the Sienese mercantile accounts of 1255–62 [6].

The bankers of 1211 operated in the period just before Florence rose to the commercial, and political, hegemony of Tuscany. Siena had already taken the place of Pisa as the leading mercantile and financial center of the region, thanks largely to the expertise of its bankers, who were employed by the Papacy to collect and manage the revenues of the Church. It was only in the latter part of the 13th century that the great

Florentine houses of Bardi and Peruzzi were to surpass them. Yet Florence was already autonomous (despite the suzerainty of the Holy Roman Emperor), with a population of some 50,000, an extensive dependent territory, or *contado,* and preeminence in the manufacture and exportation of fine cloths, assisted by easy communications with the other cities of central and northern Italy [9]. In the 1211 accounts, the sums dealt in are small—mostly under £50, and seldom over £100. But the firm had a flourishing branch in Bologna, a city which served the merchants of Florence as a base for opening up the rich markets of the North Italian plain, and beyond that, of France [11]; while the ledger reveals relatively complex modes of settling debts, by setoff between the accounts of different customers, and (perhaps) by the use of negotiable instruments between customers and third parties. (In *c. 2 recto, col. 1, acc. 4,* a sum of **£9.13. 4d.** lent to one Diede Bilicozzi is paid by Mainetto Tornaquinci—a regular customer, as it would seem—to a creditor of the bank, to whom it was owed on behalf of a fourth person, and he was owed it on behalf of a fifth!)

The degree of financial sophistication thus indicated, and the fact that banking partnerships were maintained for about five years at a time, and often renewed with some or all of the same partners [4], would call for more complex accounting records than the generality of businesses at the time. A cash book and personal ledger would be indispensable, and the latter would include both loan and deposit accounts. None of the latter is extant, but their presence is indicated by numerous setting-off entries in the loan accounts. Possibly they were in a separate volume, as there is a reference, in *c. 1 verso, col. 2, acc. 1,* to a payment *iera iskritta in quaderno nu*[*ouo*]—"written yesterday in the new register" (or "ledger"—though *quaderno* is not used in this sense in later accounting texts from Florence [10]). Transactions relating to the principal, if not the interest, of loans would, of course, appear in both ledger and cash book; but the 1211 ledger shows no cross-references. This, however, is not conclusive proof that there were none; the same feature is seen, for instance, in the Farolfi ledger of 1299–1300 [3, 6], where transfers to other accounts in the ledger are cross-referenced. To refer with any ease from the cash book to the ledger, one would need folio numbers at the least; but in working from the ledger back to the cash book the dates would give a sufficient clue, as the cash book entries would be in chronological order, probably with the receipts in the front half of the book and the payments in the rear half, as in the Sienese mercantile cash book of 1277–82 [6], and the cash book of Ruggiero da Firenze, treasurer to Pope Nicholas III in the Marches, 1279–80 [3, 6].

No-one has ever suggested that the unknown Florentines of 1211 had achieved double entry. There is no evidence of nominal accounts, even for interest received and paid, and for purposes of profit determination—normally on the winding-up of the firm only, and by single-entry methods—an analysis of the cash book would have sufficed. Yet there would still have been need for some record of capital contributed, and perhaps of drawings made, by each partner; and in this regard the author believes that he has found evidence overlooked, or not properly understood, by his predecessors. This is the enigmatic sequence of entries in *c. 2 verso, col. 1, acc. 6,* as follows:

In nomine domini, amen.
Arnolfino porta seco a la badia lib'. ciii e sol. xv di veronesi ke i tolemmo da qualterotto. Item porta lib'. xxxi di veronesi . . . di cambio (?) Item porta sol. xx di bo[lon]gnini perrispese. Montano i veronesi lib'. lxxviii. Item die dare lib'. viiii meno sol. iii ke le demmo per lui a quaskone f. rineri ubertini per lo storamento dei veronesi. ponemmo ke die auire. Item per paganello del garbo lib'. lxxxx e d'. xxv. Item per lo bene prestasini lib'. xlvii e sol. xvii e d'. iii. Item buonessengnia de l'anquillaia lib'. xlv e sol. iiii e d'. i (?). Item per ser (?) arrigo rinieri mediki lib' lxxxxiiii e sol. v l—. Item per rugieri figliastro buonfantini lib'. lxviiii e sol. xiii e d'. iiii. [Item] per arrigo f. rinieri mediki lib'. liii e sol. ii. Item die dare per lo prode lib'. xiiii e sol. iii Item per benciuenni kōpagnio querieri sol. xlvi, d'. . . . Monta in tutto lib'. Diiii e sol. viiii e d'. ii. Item rauemmo trappagatori per quelli di laska lib'. Diiii e sol. xii.

In nomine Domini, amen.
Arnolfino is carrying with him to the Badia £103.15. 0d. in Veronese coin which we took for him from Gualterotto. *Item* he is carrying £31. 0. 0d. in Veronese coin . . . [illegible] *di cambio* (?). *Item* he is carrying £1. 0. 0d. in Bolognese coin for expenses. The Veronese coin amounts to £78. 0. 0d. *Item* he is due to give £8.17. 0d. which we gave on his behalf to Guascone, son of Rinieri Ubertini, for the exchange (?) of the Veronese coin. We added what he is due to receive: *item* from Paganello del Garbo, £90. 2. 1d.; *item* from Bene Prestasini, £47.17. 3d.; *item* [from] Buoninsegna dell'Anguillaia, £45. 4. 1d. (?); *item* from Ser (?) Arrigo, [son of] Rinieri Medici (?), £94. 5. 6d.; *item* from Ruggiero, stepson of Buonfantino, £69.13. 4d.; [*item*] from Arrigo, son of Rinieri Medici (?), £53. 2. 0d.; *item* he is due to give for the interest £14.3. 0d.; *item* from Bencivenni, partner (?) of Guarniero, £2. 6. ?d. . . . [illegible] It amounts in total to £504.9. 2d. *Item* we recovered (?), including payments by those whose debts had been remitted (?), £504.12. 0d.

This is certainly not an ordinary loan account, and the Latin headnote suggests a rather important set of entries. Interpretation is not helped by two lacunae, though from inspection of the photocopy neither seems very long. The section concerns Arnolfino, a partner in the bank, who begins by carrying to the "Badia" two sums in Veronese coin, totalling £134.15. 0d., as well as £1. 0. 0d. in Bolognese coin for expenses. The illegibility of a few words makes the nature of the transaction uncertain; then it is stated that the Veronese coin amounts to £78. 0. 0d.—presumably, its exchange value in Florentine currency, at the rate of approximately 20s. 0d. Veronese to 11s. 7d. Florentine. What "Badia" means in this context is hard to say; it is unlikely to have been the Benedictine abbey in Florence. More probably it was the meeting-place of the *Arte di Cambio,* the guild of moneychangers and bankers, or, still more probably, its equivalent in Bologna; the ready availability of Veronese coin on that side of the Apennines, and the use of *bolognini* for expenses, suggest that city as the venue. (The corresponding building in Milan was called *la badia de' mercanti cambiatori* [8].) Indeed, the words *di cambio* are doubtfully read by Santini after the lacuna, and the author has not attempted to translate them out of context.

There follows a statement that Arnolfino owes the bank £8.17. 0d. for a payment on his behalf for *storamento* of the Veronese coin. This seems to refer to the charge for changing it; Battisti and Alessio [1] give *contraccambiare* (exchange?) as an old meaning of *ristorare,* and this appears to be the only interpretation which fits here. It is then stated that the bank has "added" what Arnolfino is owed *per* ("from") six named persons (one of them mentioned twice), of whom one is also said to owe interest; the total due from them is £416.13. 3d., plus between 1d. and 11d. from the last-named Santini was unable to read the number of *denari.* After another lacuna come the words "It amounts in total to £504. 9. 2d." Lastly it is stated that "we recovered (?), including payments from those whose debts had been remitted (?), £504.12. 0d." This rendering assumes *laska* to be a mistake for, or misreading of, *lascia* ("remission of payment") [1], presumably accounting for the difference of 2s.10d. in the two amounts, which are much the largest in the fragments.

The only sense I can make of all this is as a record of cash introduced into the firm, and loan debtors assigned to it, by the partner Arnolfino as original, or additional, capital contributed, less expenses paid by the firm on his behalf. He appears to have brought in £78. 0. 0d. in cash and £504. 9. 2d. in debtors, and refunded expenses of £8.17. 0d., a net sum of £573.12. 2d., on the assumption that the second gap in the text contained at least one further debtor of the order of £88. 0. 0d. to make up the sum of £504. 9. 2d. (The £1. 0. 0d. in Bolognese currency was presumably the firm's money.) Correspondingly, £78. 0. 0d. would appear as a receipt in the cash book, and £8.17. 0d. as a payment; eight loan accounts would be opened for a total of £504. 9. 2d., plus an account for Arnolfino, "credited" with £78. 0. 0d. and "debited" with £8.17. 0d. Subsequently, when a total of £504.12. 0d. had been recovered from the debtors, some of whose balances appear to have been written down, this sum would be transferred to Arnolfino's account, whose credit balance would then be £573.15. 0d.

If this interpretation is sound, then the entries just described constitute the earliest evidence yet discovered of the keeping of capital accounts in a business firm—44 years earlier than those of the unidentified Sienese merchant-bankers of 1255–62, analyzed by Melis [6]—as well as the earliest reference to the writing down of bad or doubtful debts. Had all the partners' capital consisted merely of cash introduced and undrawn profits, there would have been no need of regular capital accounts. The total profits, over the whole (rather short) life of the firm, could have been ascertained on liquidation, by single-entry methods, and divided among the partners as agreed; after which each partner's contributed capital would be added to his share, and his total drawings deducted from it, to give the amount finally due to him. In Arnolfino's case, however, a large part of his contribution was in kind, in the form of book debts, perhaps carried over from an earlier firm in which he was a partner or sole proprietor. If these were recorded only in the middle of the personal ledger there would be danger of overlooking them later, and there must, almost certainly, have been some sort of capital account, in the same or another book, presumably for each partner or, at any rate, notes of these matters, whether in proper account form or not. Even so, it is not very likely that there was any accounting for shares of profit or loss (except on liquidation), and thus the Florentines of 1211 were still considerably short of the achievement of true double entry book-keeping.

To trace the evolution of double entry over the following century or so is beyond the scope of this article. What may be said, finally, is that the concept of debit and credit, though not yet clearly formulated, underlies the 1211 accounts, despite the absence of the two-sided presentation. Indeed, as Melis makes plain [6], the paragraph form continued to dominate Tuscan accounting beyond 1300, partly from conservatism, but more practically because of the relative dearness of parchment, and even of paper. Paragraph accounts wasted little of the space on each page, whereas a two-sided account with many debits and few credits (or vice versa) would leave much of the page blank. Paper would seem to have become appreciably cheaper in the 14th century since from about 1340 when it is first observed) the modern layout completely displaced the older one in Italy. For all that, paragraph accounts were no bar to the development of double entry, which rests not upon a particular visual presentation but upon the dichotomy between the assets and liabilities of an entity, with equity as their net difference. In the view of Melis [6] and Castellani [3] this was recognized, however dimly, by 1300, and full double entry may have emerged in the books of Rinieri Fini & Brothers (1296–1305) and of the Farolfi Company (1299–1300), both Florentine firms trading in France, and both using the paragraph layout in their ledgers. Such were the ramifications of the modest system whose traces survive through the random choice by a 14th-century scribe of two old pieces of parchment for his flyleaves.

REFERENCES

1. Battisti, C., and G. Alessio. *Dizionario Etimologico Italiano*. Florence, 1950.
2. Besta, Fabio. *La Ragioneria*. 2d ed. Milan, 1922.
3. Castellani, Arrigo. *Nuovi Testi Fiorentini del Dugento*. Florence, 1952.
4. Chiaudano, Mario. *Studi e Documenti per la Storia del Diritto Commerciale Italiano nel sec. XIII*. Turin, 1930.

5. LEE, GEOFFREY A. "The Oldest European Account Book: A Florentine Bank Ledger of 1211," *Nottingham Mediaeval Studies*, Vol. XVI, 1972.
6. MELIS, FEDERIGO. *Storia della Ragioneria*. Bologna, 1950.
7. MONACI, ERNESTO. *Crestomazia Italiana dei Primi Secoli*. Città di Castello, 1889.
8. PETROCCHI, P. *Novo Dizionario Universale della Lingua Italiana*. Milan, 1908.
9. RENOUARD, YVES. *Les villes d'Italie de la fin du Xè siècle au début du XIVè siècle*. Paris, 1961–62.
10. ROOVER, RAYMOND DE. "The development of accounting prior to Luca Pacioli according to the account-books of mediaeval merchants," in A. C. Littleton, and B. S. Yamey, *Studies in the History of Accounting*. London, 1956.
11. SANTINI, PIETRO. "Frammenti di un libro di banchieri fiorentini scritto in volgare nel 1211," *Giornale Storico della Letteratura Italiana*, Vol. X (1887).
12. SCHIAFFINI, ALFREDO. *Testi Fiorentini del Dugento e dei Primi del Trecento*. Florence, 1926.

GEOFFREY ALAN LEE

The Development of Italian Bookkeeping 1211-1300

The Florentine bank ledger fragments of 1211, the earliest surviving commercial accounts in Europe, have received considerable attention from historians of accounting. Transcribed by Pietro Santini (1887)[1] and Alfredo Schiaffini (1926),[2] discussed at some length by Mario Chiaudano (1930)[3] and Federigo Melis (1950),[4] and briefly by Raymond de Roover (1956),[6] they were translated into English, and commented on, by the present author (1972, 1973).[7, 8] This article takes a more comprehensive view of Italian (especially Tuscan) bookkeeping in the thirteenth century, and endeavours to trace the lines of evolution from the surprisingly sophisticated ledger of 1211 to the emergence of double entry, or approximations to it, about 1300.

The task is easiest in relation to Florence, thanks to Arrigo Castellani (1952)[5] who, in the interests of philology, transcribed virtually all extant Florentine prose texts up to 1300—most of them account-books or extracts therefrom. Other Tuscan accounts, besides being scarcer, are much less accessible, and the author has been compelled to depend upon extracts, mainly in Melis. Beyond Tuscany, and Tuscan firms abroad, there is practically nothing before the famous Genoese municipal accounts of 1340; but books have survived, from the first half of the fourteenth century, of several Florentine banking, commercial and industrial firms, at home and in Flanders, France and England.[4, 6]

EVOLUTION OF THE PERSONAL LEDGER ACCOUNT

The 1211 fragments are confined, with one exception noted later, to debtors' accounts. In general they combine the functions of borrowers' ledger and loans register; the account for each loan (of any size) is headed with details of the borrower's name, amount advanced, rate of interest, witnesses, and sometimes guarantor(s), followed by particulars, in narrative form, of repayment of the principal. This was effected, sometimes in cash, sometimes by set-off against a deposit account, for the same customer or for some other person—probably by means of a bill of exchange or promissory note, frequently accepted or made by a third party. When an account was settled the paragraph was cancelled with oblique lines. There are no totals or balances, and calculations must have been done on the abacus or with counters. Many loans are complicated by transactions in non-

---

GEOFFREY ALAN LEE is Lecturer in Accounting in the Department of Industrial Economics, University of Nottingham.

Florentine currency—principally that of Bologna, where the bank had a branch or resident partner—but all amounts are converted to the standard silver *denari* of Pisa, the money of account. On the other hand, interest (normally at 20 per cent per annum, often with one month's grace before it began to run) is not entered in the accounts, except as part of a balance transferred from another page. Such transfers are common, but the only cross-references are in the form '*x* parchments further on (*or* back)'; there are no references at all to the cash book, which must have been indispensable.

After 1211 there is in Florence a gap of 48 years before one reaches the extract (1259-67) from the books of Castra Gualfredi and the Borghesi Company, and of 51 years to the next actual account-book, the first ledger of Bene Bencivenni (1262-75). Apart from public accounts in charge and discharge form, the only other Italian specimens are fragments of the accounts of Cambio and Giovanni di Detacommando (1241-72) at Poppi; of a creditors' journal at Imola (1260-2); and of a memorandum book of the Ugolini Company of Siena, trading to the fairs of Champagne (1255-62).[3, 4, 6] The language of all these accounts was the Tuscan dialect, already developing into the literary tongue by the efforts of Dante's precursors; public and ecclesiastical accounts were still kept in Latin.

The Detacommando accounts have survived in similar circumstances to those of 1211, as guard-leaves to a thirteenth-century MS. in the Biblioteca Communale at Poppi. Only one leaf is in good condition, and of this Melis[4] offers an excerpt from 1261, in which a contract is made by Don Detesalvi, Rector of San Zeno, and other clerics to supply 105 *staie* of wheat and barley, in four annual instalments from 26 February 1261, at 10 *libre* per *staia;* followed by sundry deliveries, stated in quantities only, over an uncertain period, and amounting in total to 53½ *staie* of barley and 52½ *staie* (less one *bacino*) of wheat. This scarcely represents an advance in technique over 50 years; nor does the Imola journal of 1260-2, in which notes of indebtedness incurred are merely struck through, presumably as the creditors were paid. The Ugolini book is considered also, by those who have inspected it,[3, 4, 6] to be a series of memoranda, rather than accounts in proper form; but it may have constituted a basis for entries in regular ledgers, and is interesting for another reason, as explained later.

The main stream of development thus flows through Florentine channels. Extant ledgers from about 1260 onwards present many common features, and it is instructive to compare representative accounts with those of 1211. All are still in 'paragraph' form, with entries arranged consecutively down the page and amounts of opposite sign (indebtedness incurred and discharged) differentiated by the form of words employed. Sums of money are still expressed in Roman numerals (allegedly more difficult to falsify than Arabic ones), though the setting-out is generally neater than in 1211, with each entry started on a fresh line. It is still exceptional, though, for any totals to be provided, and settlement of an account, or the carrying forward of a balance to another page, is still denoted by striking through the paragraph with slanting lines. The lesson that a set of accounts should be in a single currency has, however, been well learnt; most use the reformed silver coinage (*fiorini grossi*) introduced in Florence from 1237, converting gold florins (*fiorini d'oro*), minted from 1252, at a rate of exchange stabilized, by 1277, at 29 silver *soldi* to the gold florin.

Three main advances in technique are noticeable. Firstly, the functions of register and ledger account have become separated. The elaborate headnotes of 1211 have largely disappeared, though it is still stated, on occasion, that the proprietor holds a bond (*carta*) for the sum lent—sometimes for a larger amount than was actually advanced—and the name of a guarantor (*mallevadore*) may also be given. Secondly, the accounting itself has become more comprehensive, by the inclusion of interest in the body of the account—under the euphemisms of *guadagno, prode* or *dono* (gain, profit, gift), to evade the (seldom enforced) ecclesiastical prohibition of usury. (The rates are also lower—generally 8 to 12 per cent per annum.) Thirdly, there is more systematic cross-referencing of items between two accounts (e.g. set-offs, or transfer of a balance to another page) —the leaves being generally numbered. However, there is still no cross-referencing to the cash book (which has in no case survived with the ledger)*, perhaps because the date was sufficient in a book where all the entries were (more or less) in chronological order.

SURVEY OF PERSONAL LEDGERS, 1211-96

1. *Unknown Florentine banking firm, 1211:*

Two leaves of parchment, used as front and rear flyleaves to a fourteenth-century MS. of *Digestum Novum cum Glossa,* in Biblioteca Medicea-Laurenziana, Florence; transcribed by P. Santini (1887)[1] and A. Schiaffini (1926),[2] and translated, with a commentary, by G. A. Lee (1972).[3,4] Debtors' accounts only, except for one section of uncertain import (see later). The following extracts (translated) illustrate most of the points made earlier.

Carta 1 *recto, columna* 1

1211

Jacopo, son of the Barone degli Acquarelli, and Simone his brother are due to give us, each [for himself], £52. 0. 0d. for £18. 0. 0d. in Imperial *mezzani* which we gave them on 18 June at [the rate of] 35 less a third†; and they are due to repay us on 18 June. If [the moneys] are outstanding longer (*se più stanno*), [interest is] at 4d. in the £ per month, for as long as we may permit (*quanto fosse nostra voluntade*). Witnesses: Alberto Baldovini, Gagliette da Pecora, Buontalento Macchetti, and Ruggiero, stepson of Buonfantino of Borgo San Lorenzo.

Item Buonincontro, son of the Barone degli Acquarelli, gave us £14. 11. 0d.: Cambio and Tornaquinci [partners?] brought it on 27 July. *Item* Arrighetto Arrigoni gave us

* The earliest extant cash book is that of an unknown Sienese firm (1277-82); this, and the cash book of Ruggiero da Firenze (1279-80), Treasurer to Pope Nicholas III in the Marches, have receipts in the front half and payments in the rear half, with periodic netting-off of the smaller total against the larger.

† I.e. £34.13.4d. in *mezzani* ('halves' of an unspecified monetary unit) for £100 Tuscan.

£5. 0. 0d.: [signed] Buonincontro; Tegghiaio [partner?] brought it at the above date. *Item* Jacopo has given us £15. 0. 0d., of which Ricovero, partner of Piero Rossi of San Firenze, received £6. 0. 0d., Buonafede Varliani £5. 0. 0d., and Testa di Codarimessa £4. 0. 0d., on 2 August on our behalf (*per noi*). He also gave on our behalf to Cambio Morandi (?) £10. 3. 0d. on 19 September. *Item* Jacopo gave us £5. 6. 0d.; Jacopo brought it on 26 September. *Item* we were due to receive £2. 0. 0d. in respect of (*per*) Dato Guidotti (?) on 8 October. *Item* Jacopo gave us £1. 10. 0d.; Aldobrandino [partner?] brought it.

C. 1 r., *col.* 2
1211

Donato, son of Ciaffero, and Guido della Spada are due to give us, each [for himself], in total £107. 7. 8d. for Bolognese coin which we gave them in Bologna for the fair of San Procolo, and are due to pay on 1 June; if [the moneys] are outstanding longer, [interest is] at 4d. in the £ per month.

Buonaccolto Salintorri has given us £17. 17. 10d.; Messer Aldobrandino, son of Rinieri Foresi, received £14. 0. 0d. of it on behalf of Simone Gianrolandi, and Albizzo [partner?] brought the remainder on 13 June, when Rinieri, son of Martinello the bin-maker*(?), brought us the £14. 0. 0d. *Item* Rinieri (?) Rinucci gave us £17. 17. 11d.; we received £5. 10. 0d. of it from Corbizzo della Pressa; Jacopo [partner?] brought it, and Giannozzo [partner?] brought the remainder at the date aforesaid. *Item* he [Donato] gave on our behalf to Torsello Giugni £18. 0. 0d.; we paid it on behalf of Capo the dyer on 8 June. *Item* Donato gave us £9. 10. 0d.; Albizzo brought it at the date aforesaid. *Item* Ciaffero gave us personally (*di sua mano*) £18. 12. 0d. on 11 June. *Item* he is due to receive £17. 17. 10d. which Arrigo dell'Erro gave us; we deducted from his account what he was due to receive at the due date. *Item* he is due to receive £2. 0. 0d. in respect of Caro the goldsmith; we deducted it from the account of Guarnelletto, son of Gregorio, on 5 July. *Item* he gave on our behalf to Accolto, son of Ughetto of San Firenze, £4. 0. 0d.; Donato, son of Ciaffero, paid it on 9 July. *Item* Donato gave us £1. 12. 0d.; and his share of the interest he accounted for to (?) Tornaquinci on 9 July.

Each page of the ledger is ruled down the middle, and each of the two columns is divided into six or eight blocks. Each represents an account, with the writing fitted in as the bookkeeper could best contrive; hence, the various repayments are separated only by the word '*item*'. In the translation the spelling of proper names has been modernized, and the presentation of figures regularized.† Totals and balances are absent, but it is fairly obvious that the first set of entries in each account are effectively debits, and the second set credits, and that when the two were equal or deemed to be so, the account was cancelled with oblique lines,

* *Arciolaio*—a word otherwise unknown, and given (it seems) in no dictionary. It seems to be derivel from *arcile,* a Lucchese word for a flour-bin (per Parodi, in a commentary on Santini's original article (1887)).

† In the original, the days of the month are counted forwards in the first half, and backwards (from the end) in the second; e.g. 18 June is *tredici dì anzi kal* [*endi*] *luglio* (13 days before the kalends (1) of July), and 2 August is *due dì intrante agosto* (two days into August). Sums of money, in *libre, soldi* and *denari,* have been rendered for convenience as pounds, shillings and pence, in Arabic instead of Roman numerals; in the original the enumeration is not always straightforward—e.g. £17.17.10d. stands as *lib' xviii meno den. xxvi* (£18 less 26d.).

as stated above. (In fact, the first account has total debits £52.0.0d. and credits £51.10.0d., while in the second the two totals are £107.7.8d. and £107.7.7d.) There are no entries for interest, though the headnotes prescribe a rate of (in effect) 20 per cent per annum from the date of each advance; in other cases one or two months' grace is often allowed, so that the true rate is less.

The 1211 accounts are equally interesting as witnesses to the existence in thirteenth-century Italian of a specialized vocabulary of bookkeeping, perhaps originating in literal translations from Latin. The most significant terms are those relating to positive and negative movements in the balance of the account, of which two pairs may be distinguished, viz.:

	(a)		(b)
1	(a) (*no*) *die/dino dare*	and	(b) *die/dino avere*
	is/are due to give (us)		is/are due to receive;
2	(a) (*ci*) *diè/diede/ha* (*nno*) *dato*	and	(b) (*li*) *demmo/avemmo dato*
	gave (has/have given) (us)		we gave/have given him/them;

From the first pair is derived the modern Italian usage of *dare* and *avere* as the equivalents of 'debit' and 'credit'—a locution familiar to Pacioli. The thirteenth-century bookkeeper, however, did not think of them as direct opposites, but regarded 2 (a) as opposed to 1 (a), and 2 (b) to 1 (b)—that is, he thought on the one hand of a loan *to* someone, and its repayment, and on the other hand, of a loan *from* someone, and its repayment (or, in a mercantile business, of sale of goods and receipt of cash, and of purchase and payment therefore). The mediaeval ledger-keeper also became familiar with the procedures of offsetting the balance of a customer's loan account against that of his deposit account, and of using a transfer from a debtor's deposit account to his creditor's deposit account, or against his creditor's loan account (with the agreement of both customers), as a means of settling their reciprocal indebtedness. Examples of both types occur in the 1211 ledger, and thence arose two more pairs of opposed entries, viz.:

	(a)		(b)
3	(a) *ponemmo che die/dovea avere*	and	(b) *ponemmo che die/dovea dare*
	we added what he is/was due to receive		we added what he is/was due to give;
4	(a) *levammo ove die/dovea avere*	and	(b) *levammo ove die/dovea dare*
	we deducted what* he is/was due to receive		we deducted what* he is/ was due to give.

Thus, *ponemmo* meant 'we added (to the balance of the opposite account)', and *levammo* 'we subtracted (from the balance of the opposite account)'. If a

* Or, 'we deducted (it) where', etc., according to context.

customer's deposit account balance was offset against his (or another's) loan account balance, there would be an entry of type 4 (a) in the debtors' ledger, and of type 4 (b) in the creditors' ledger; if he made a transfer from his deposit account to that of his creditor, there would be a 3 (a) entry in the debtor's account and a 4 (a) entry in the creditor's—both in the creditors' ledger of the bank. Hence *ponemmo* in a debtor's account (with a debit balance) came to mean 'we credited the (creditor's) account affected', and in a creditor's account, 'we debited the (debtor's) account affected'; while *levammo* had the meaning, in a debtor's account, 'we debited the (creditor's) account affected', and in a creditor's account, 'we credited the (debtor's) account affected'. Not all of these types of entry are found in the 1211 fragments.

2. *Castra Gualfredi and the Borghesi Company, 1259-67:*

Part of the notarial extract (1287) of deposit account of Gualtieri dal Borgo, guardian of the sons of Rinieri Ugelletti; like all the following extracts, it is translated from A. Castellani's transcripts (1952)[5] of MSS mainly in Archivio di Stato, Florence. Taken from 'old book' (1259-60) and 'new book' (1260-7).

Old Book

[QQ] 1259

Gualtieri dal Borgo and Tuccio Saverigi, guardians of the sons of Rinieri Ugelletti, are due to receive (*deo* [*no*] *avere*) £133. 13. 4d. on 1 August on behalf of Messer Maccio dalla Badia; we added [it] in his account where he is due to receive, back in MM.

And they are due to receive for interest (*merito*) £16. 11. 8d. to 1 August [12] 60.

We have given (*hanno dato*) Gualtieri and Tuccio £150. 5. 0d. on 1 August [12] 60; we gave it to Gualtieri himself; we added what he is due to receive, further on in TT.

TT. 1260

Gualtieri dal Borgo, guardian of the sons of Rinieri Ugelletti, is due to receive £150. 5. 0d. on 1 August on behalf of Gualtieri himself and Tuccio Saverigi; we deducted [it] where they were due to receive, back in QQ.

And he is due to receive £236. 12. 0d. this day on behalf of Ser Arrigo Buonaccorsi and his partners; we added [it] where they are due to give, back in BB.

This account we have cancelled (*dannato*) and entered here above in one sum, and this day what he is due to receive here above we have added where he is due to receive in the new book at folio 23; and all these entries (*partite*) which he had here below, collected at one date in total, are added at the foot of the above account aforesaid in the new book, at 24 November [12] 61.

We have given Gualtieri £12. 0. 0d. on 14 August; Ugo Monaldi counted (*annoverò*) into his hand 20s. in florins for corn.

[There follow 18 such 'debit' entries, totalling £117. 7. 4d., mainly for corn, bread, wine, oil and clothes.]

New Book

1260

Gualtieri dal Borgo, guardian of the heirs of Rinieri Ugelletti dei Macci, is due to receive £386. 17. 0d. at 1 August [12] 60; they were written in the old book at TT.

We have given Gualtieri £129. 8. 0d. [sic] at 24 November [12] 61; they were written in the old book at the foot of the above account, where he was due to receive; they were written in several entries; we have brought them all to this day, making the dates the same.

We have given £17. 7. 0d. at 15 July [12] 63; we deducted [it] from his account in the old book, where he was due to give at GG.

[There follow four similar 'debits', totalling £28. 4. 0d.: then—]

We have given [amount left blank], which Gualtieri gave to Guiduccio, son of Rinieri Ugelletti, in Spain during the 28 months which he spent with him, and for all his expenses; when the total sum which he gave is known, it is desired to reimburse Gualtieri.

As compared with the 1211 fragments, the Borghesi extracts show many of the tendencies enumerated earlier—neater setting-out, simplification by removal of 'register' details, inclusion of interest in the body of the account, and proper cross-referencing to other ledger folios (here denoted by letters). The extracts are also important, as containing the earliest surviving account for a creditor or depositor. There are still no proper totals, but there is some attempt at balancing. It will be noted that the balance 'carried forward' (in modern terminology) is described as 'given' to the depositor, and that it is stated to have been 'added' on the new page; while on that page the balance 'brought forward' is conversely stated to have been 'deducted' on the old page. Likewise, in the 'new book', the debit of £17.7.0d. is stated to have been 'deducted' from Gualtieri's loan account at GG in the 'old book'; this must mean that it was credited to an account with a debit balance, thus reducing that balance. The summarization of the credits and debits in the old book, when carrying them forward to the new one, also shows some advance in technique, despite the arithmetical error of 8d. in respect of the debits. The blank in the last entry is partly explained by the narration; perhaps the amount was itself the subject of the litigation for which the notary (Lotte Formaggi) made the extracts. The money of account is the new Florentine silver currency, based on the *fiorino da dodici* of 12 *denari;* the excerpt gives an example of the contemporary idiom '20 *soldi* in florins', meaning 240 silver florins counted as one *denaro* each—though in reality they amounted to £12.0.0d. of standard money, as the rest of the entry makes clear.

3. *Bene Bencivenni (first ledger), 1262-75:*

Domestic ledger of a wealthy Florentine who died between 1296 and 1298;[5] comprises mainly debtors' accounts, but includes one for a large investment in a firm (see later). Extracts consist of the religious formula at the beginning, and one page of accounts.

C. 1 verso

In Dei nomine, amen*, and of profit and good fortune, of increase of persons and goods, and of every good thing which God may give us, amen.

---

* In the original, *In Dei domine*.

C. 2 recto

1263

Currado and Lutieri, brothers, sons of Benevieni da Petriuolo, are due to give us £12. 0. 0d. which we lent them on 15 May of the above indiction. They had from us 20s. in *fiorini da dodici;* Bene Bencivenni counted it into their hands. We have a bond in respect thereof by the hand of Ser Ruggieri who lodges with Ser Parisci in Borgo Sant'Apostoli, and I have the bond by me.

Currado and Lutieri have given us £6. 13. 0d. in florins at 15 May [12] 64; we received £7. 3. 0d. in *piccioli*. We added it (*ponemmo*) to their account where they are due to receive, in the large book, in respect of a piece of land which we bought from them in Le Sciabbie, five *staiora* and five *panora*.

Currado has paid us for the third part.

Ferrante has paid us for his part.

1263

Ser Martinello di Balla is due to give us £6. 0. 0d. which we lent him on 1 November, in three instalments (*tra tre volte*) personally; he said that someone else would repay us, for his hose and shoes and his other expenses.

He is due to give 10s. 0d. at 15 December, which we lent him personally at Cisti's shop in Porta Santa Maria.

He is due also to give 10s. 0d. on 10 June, which we lent him personally in the Mercato Vecchio at [blank]'s bank (*tavola*).

Ser Martinello has given us, himself, £7. 0. 0d. on 1 November [12] 64, in that we received from him two *cogni* of new wine, at £3. 10. 0d. per *cogno*.

Arriguccio, son of Bellondani da Petriuolo, is due to give us £1. 10. 0d. for one mantle and some skins which we sold him, [the mantle?] of Arras cloth, on 15 October.

Guccio has given us £1. 10. 0d. at the due date (*al termine*); we added [it] where he was due to give, two parchments further on.

These accounts, being private ones, are less sophisticated than those in the previous extract, and show somewhat less evolution from the standards of 1211. There is still, for example, mention of the security for a loan, and interest is not entered; nor are there proper cross-references. There also appears some inconsistency in the use of *ponemmo*, in the first account. It will be noted, too, that some debts are settled in kind, and that there is now a divergence between the purchasing power of the silver florin and of the old Pisan currency (*piccioli*), since £6.13.0d. of the first are taken as equal to £7.3.0d. of the second. The pious formula at the beginning of the ledger (and repeated annually) was common form by 1262; a similar sentence occurs in the Borghesi transcript, dated 1253. More significant, though, is the practice (not illustrated above) of balancing, at each 1 January, those debtors' accounts which were still open; earlier books of account are too fragmentary to prove or disprove any hypothesis as to its prevalence before 1262.

4. *Estate of Baldovino, son of Jacopo Riccomanni, 1272-8:*

Accounts (in Biblioteca Nazionale, Florence) of the administrators of a citizen of Florence who died on 14 September 1272. They begin with lists of legacies, creditors' claims and expenses paid out of the estate, and continue with collection of debtors' balances, investments in banking firms on behalf of the heirs, and purchases of land on their account. Extract shows the latter part of the account for the principal investment, in the family firm.

C. 8 *recto*

1276, 1 January

Simone Baldovini, Riccomanno Jacopi, Nero Cambi del Tedesco & Co. are due to give in florins, on 1 January, £1,978. 1. 0d.; we deducted [it] from their account where they were due to give, one and a half sheets back, and these moneys belong to the brothers Giovanni and Donato, sons of the late Baldovino Jacopi.

Simone, Riccomanno & Co. have given in florins, on 1 January [12] 76, £725. 13. 7d., which moneys they have withdrawn for their [Giovanni's and Donato's] petty expenses; for the dowry of their sister Tora, which she had when she married Lapo, son of Messer Uberto di Rovinoso; for the dowry of their sister Bice, which she had when she married Ciaino, son of Inghilberto Acciai; and for other expenses which they have incurred up to this day, just as they are written in their book of the bank by the hand of Nero Cambi. And these are all the expenses incurred by them with the Commune of Florence; and also they had of us moneys which were paid to Canci dei Visdomini for rent of the land which we bought from him, since two years' rent were taken by him, amounting to £45. 0. 0d. in florins.

Simone, Riccomanno & Co. have given in florins, on 1 January [12] 76, £1,252. 7. 5d.; we added [it] where they are due to give on this same page.

1276, 1 January

Simone Baldovino, Riccomanno Jacopi, Nero Cambi del Tedesco & Co. are due to give in florins, on 1 January [12] 76, £1,252. 7. 5d.; we deducted [it] from their account where they were due to give on this same page, above.

Simone, Riccomanno & Co. are due to give in florins, on 10 February [12] 75, £573. 10. 0d. Lamberto dell'Antella & Co. gave them to them on our behalf; we deducted [it] from their account where they were due to give, two sheets back.

Simone, Riccomanno, Nero Cambi & Co. have given us, at the [above] date, £1,825 17. 5d., the which moneys they paid to Giovanni and Donato for their share in the bank of the said firm, as is contained in the articles (?) and in a book entry (*sì come si contiene per ordine e per partita di libro*) of the said firm. Everything which has passed, before and since, will be found written in that book.

The accounts for the lesser debtors (some of them inherited from the deceased) are fairly similar to those in the Bene Bencivenni ledger; interest is charged at 10 per cent per annum, and there is the additional complication, in some cases, of conversion from gold florins to silver, taking the *fiorino d'oro* as 27s. 0½d. The proceeds of these debts were distributed to the heirs, or invested on their behalf, and the accounts closed. The need to charge interest on a compound basis with yearly rests appears to be the main reason for the systematic balancing of the debtors' accounts at every 1 April. Cross-referencing is less sophisticated than elsewhere, perhaps because of the small number of leaves, nine in all.

The account for the main investment extends over two full sides of parchment, of which the second is translated above. Into it (as from 2 January 1274) have been fed the balances from six other accounts receivable (all appearing elsewhere in the ledger), as well as sundry amounts in cash and, as at 1 January 1276, interest allowed by the firm at 8 per cent per annum. Just over a month later the account is closed, its balance having been used to purchase a share in the bank for the deceased's two sons.

5. *Gentile de' Sassetti and Sons, 1274-1310:*

Mainly domestic accounts, but include a large investment in the family business. Consist of 27 leaves of debtors' accounts from front of ledger, and 5 of creditors' accounts from back of it. Extracts are from the debtors' section, and include an account for rent receivable. (N.B. There is evidence that Gentile regarded 25 March as the official New Year's Day—as in England up to 1752—and the years have, where necessary, been renumbered accordingly).

C. 9 verso

In nomine Domini, amen. 1280 [-81], 1 January. May God give us good, this [year] and all others, and grant them for increase of persons and of property and for joy and good fortune which God give us, amen! and grant them to be for great profit of soul and body.

Borgo Corbaccioni and Cione da Campi, his son, of the San Martino quarter, are due to give, on 9 January 1281 [-82], 67 gold florins for 60 gold florins which I gave him on 9 January 1280 [-81]; guarantors Nazzo his brother, Puccio Romei, Tuccio Albaggi, and Pietro Monti da Campi, of the San Martino quarter; bond by the hand of Ser Jacopo Orlandi da Campi, of the San Lorenzo quarter. Borgo fetched [the money] himself; Gentile counted it into his hand: we have the bond executed, and Borgo paid for it.

Borgo himself gave us, on 9 March 1283 [-84], 4 gold florins: Borgo brought them himself, and gave them to my lady (*madonna*) personally.

Borgo himself gave us, on 21 August 1284, 70 gold florins: Nardo Gunte the dyer in orchil* (*oricellaio*) gave them to us on his behalf, and Lapo and Pino, sons of Lo Strozza, gave them to us on behalf of Nardo Gunte; we added [it] where Lapo and Pino themselves are due to give, at [folio] 19.

Borgo himself gave us, on 1 September, 3 gold florins; we added [it] where Borgo is due to give, further on at [folio] 19.

C. 11 recto

1281 [-82]

Caino the blacksmith is due to give, on 1 January of the above indiction, £5 0. 0d. for the fourth part of the rent of the shop where he lodges, for one year.

Caino gave us, on 20 July, £2. 7. 6d.; he counted them to Gentile.

Caino gave us, on 1 January, £2. 7. 6d.; he counted them to Gentile.

* Orchil (*oricello*) is a lichen extract, used in dyeing. The word *oricellaio* does not seem to be otherwise known, and is found in no dictionary; but Petrocchi[9] gives *oricellare* as an obsolete word, 'to dye'. Castellani defines *oricellaio* as 'merchant of orchil'; but he adduces no proof, and his interpretation seems to me less likely than my own.

These accounts show rather less system than some earlier ones. In particular, there is no real attempt to reduce all entries to a single currency. They are in a mixture of gold florins, silver florins, and *piccioli,* with a general propensity to express the first in terms of the third, at rates varying from 33s. 0d. to 36s. 10d. to the gold florin. The second of the two accounts illustrated shows a debt of £5.0.0d. discharged by two payments totalling £4.15.0d. The first sum must have been in *piccioli,* the other two sums in *fiorini da dodici;* at a rate of 33s. 0d. *piccioli* to 29s. 0d. *fiorini,* the £4.15.0d. would become £5.8.1d. in *piccioli*—the extra being perhaps regarded as interest.

The loan account, also, is not balanced in any obvious way, except that a residual sum is carried forward to another page. A debt of 67 gold florins is payable in one year's time against an actual advance of 60 at 9 January 1280-1; in effect, interest is charged at 11.67 per cent per annum. The total receipts, plus the balance at 1 September 1284, are 77 florins. The extra 10 must represent further interest charged; but compound interest at 11.67 per cent per annum, with annual rests, would come to more than 10 florins, and one can only suppose that the charge fluctuated. All in all, the Sassetti accounts are inferior in technique to some of their contemporaries; yet they are important evidence, as will be seen, for the development of equity accounting, as well as being the first proven example of a ledger with debtors at the front and creditors at the back.

6. *Bene Bencivenni (second ledger), 1277-96:*

A continuation, after a short interval, of (2) above. Similar to the 1262-75 volume, but contains some novel features, as shown below.

C. 4 verso

1277

Guadagnino Soldi, of Porta San Pancrazio, is due to give us £2. 0. 0d. in *piccioli;* we deducted them in the other ledger (*quaderno*). I lent him them in Pisa, personally, when he was there with Count Guido Novello, on 8 May, when King Charles went to Rome; there is no bond (thus would I have it done!) which remains in my favour.

I do not think that I shall ever get any money.

Secca of Peretola is due to give us 10s. 0d. in *piccioli,* which I lent him in Florence when he paid a fine of his, £5. 0. 0d., to the Commune, in the time of the Ghibellines in [12] 65.

This man is dead; I do not think that I shall ever get any money at all.

Donna Albanese, widow of the late Melliorello della Riccia, of Petriuolo, is due to give us £1. 0. 0d. in *piccioli,* which I lent her husband on 15 June, personally at Petriuolo.

The husband is dead; I do not think that I shall ever get any money at all.

I do not think I shall ever get any money.

These are the earliest unmistakable instances of the writing off of debts as bad; several more occur, in 1277 and later. This ledger, like the preceding one, is important also in the history of equity accounting.

Of several other domestic ledgers transcribed by Castellani,[5] the most remarkable is that of Lapo Riccomanni, brother-in-law of Dante Alighieri; there is regrettably no mention of the poet. Extending from 1281 to 1297, it is if anything even less systematic than the Sassetti ledger, with accounts in a mixture of currencies, unconverted. Like the Baldovino Riccomanni accounts, it includes a loan to the family firm.

DEVELOPMENT OF CAPITAL AND NOMINAL ACCOUNTS TO 1296

It will have been observed that most surviving thirteenth-century Florentine ledgers related to domestic, rather than business, concerns. They are essentially memoranda of financial matters which it would have been imprudent to commit to memory alone—principally debtors' and creditors' balances, and changes therein, with cash movements recorded in separate cash books, of which very few have survived. Some account books include notes of real property purchased, but without the prices. In no case are there materials for ascertaining the proprietor's wealth at any date, let alone any form of capital or equity account; neither are there any 'nominal' accounts—the entries in the cash book, plus interest charged/allowed in debtors'/creditors' accounts, would be sufficient for the bookkeeper's purposes.

Nothing like a complete set of business accounts has come down to us from before 1296. The art of bookkeeping was most highly developed among the bankers, merchants and clothworking firms of Florence. Their businesses showed a high degree of continuity from year to year (unlike the mercantile enterprises of Venice or Genoa, with their concentration on separate trading ventures), and they were carried on by stable partnerships, who needed to ascertain and divide profits from time to time, as well as to record the drawings of each partner for deduction from his share. Unfortunately such partnerships tended to be shortlived, being wound up and re-formed (sometimes with the same partners) every four or five years as a rule. Once the old firm had been 'liquidated' and the partners' claims agreed and the new set of books had been opened (often with assets and liabilities transferred from the old firm), no-one was very interested in preserving the old books; on the contrary, since parchment was expensive the pages were often washed or scraped, and reused. Thus it is that most thirteenth-century business accounts have reached posterity only by fortunate accidents, or in brief extracts prepared for legal purposes.*

For this reason it is difficult to find any direct evidence as to how proprietors'

* Castellani has, however, transcribed some accounts of a Florentine cloth-merchants' firm for 1278-9, relating to goods and money sent to branches in Pisa and Lucca, and debts collected there. The inventories of stocks of cloth, in quantities and values, occupy many pages; the extended values are neatly ranged in columns, with a total at the foot of each page.

shares of equity and profit/loss were accounted for, or how the books were balanced. The earliest clue, albeit equivocal and hard to interpret, is found in the 1211 ledger, in a section inserted abruptly among the debtors' accounts, but plainly not of the same nature with them. It may be translated thus:

C. 2 *verso, col.* 1

In nomine Domini, amen.

Arnolfino is carrying with him to the Badia £103. 15. 0d. in Veronese coin which we took for him from Gualterotto. *Item* he is carrying £31. 0. 0d. in Veronese coin . . . [illegible] *di cambio* (?). *Item* he is carrying £1. 0. 0d. in Bolognese coin for expenses. The Veronese coin amounts to £78. 0. 0d. *Item* he is due to give £8. 17. 0d. which we gave on his behalf to Guascone, son of Rinieri Ubertini, for the exchange (*storamento*) of the Veronese coin. We added what he is due to receive: *item* from (*per*) Paganello del Garbo, £90. 2. 1d.; *item* from Bene Prestasini. £47. 17. 3d.; *item* [from] Buoninsegna dell' Anguillaia, £45. 4. 1d. (?); *item* from Ser (?) Arrigo, [son of] Rinieri Medici (?), £94. 5. 6d.; *item* from Ruggiero, stepson of Buonfantino, £69. 13. 4d.; *item* from Arrigo, son of Rinieri Medici (?), £53. 2. 0d.; *item* he is due to give for the interest £14. 3. 0d.; *item* from Bencivenni, partner (?) of Guarniero, £2. 6. ?d. . . . [illegible] It amounts in total to £504. 9. 2d. *Item* we recovered, including payments by those whose debts had been remitted (?) (*ravemmo trappagatori per quelli di laska*), £504. 12. 0d.

As is explained at greater length in the author's two previous articles,[7, 8] his opinion is that this obscure sequence of entries (whose Latin headnote suggests something of special importance) relates to the introduction of capital, in cash and in the form of debtors of his own, by a partner named Arnolfino. He carries to the 'Badia' (probably the meeting-place of the bankers' gild in Bologna) two sums in Veronese coin totalling £134.15.0d., plus £1.0.0d. in Bolognese coin for expenses. The Veronese coin is apparently exchanged for £78.0.0d. Florentine; then it is stated that Arnolfino owes the bank £8.17.0d. for a payment on his behalf for exchange of the money. The bank then states that it has 'added' what Arnolfino is owed *per* ('on behalf of', or in this context, perhaps 'by') six persons (one of them named twice); the total due from them is £416.13.3d., plus an uncertain number of *denari* from the last-named. Another name and amount appear to have become illegible; after which the text reads, 'It amounts in total to £504.9.2d.' Lastly comes the statement tentatively rendered as 'We recovered, including payments from those whose debts had been remitted, £504.12.0d.'—the recovered write-offs presumably accounting for the excess of 2s. 10d.

Arnolfino's contribution appears to have been £78.0.0d. in cash and £504.9.2d. (or £504.12.0d.) in debtors (assuming one more account of about £88.0.0d. in the second lacuna), less refunded expenses of £8.17.0d. (if the £1.0.0d. was the firm's money)—a net sum of £573.12.2d. (or £573.15.0d.). The inconspicuous position of these entries in the middle of the debtors' ledger, and the fact that they are struck through as settled, are strong arguments for the existence elsewhere of capital accounts for Arnolfino and the other partners, at least in note form; otherwise it is hard to see how a proper settlement could have been made on winding up the firm. The last 'item', too, seems to be the earliest extant reference to the writing down of debts as bad—66 years before the first *undoubted* entries of this nature, in the second ledger of Bene Bencivenni (1277).

No authentic, fully-balanced capital accounts have come down to us from the thirteenth century; the oldest are in the *libro segreto,* or private ledger, of the Alberto del Giudice bank of Florence (1302-29). The oldest apparent reference, after 1211, to equity accounts occurs in the memorandum book kept by a partner in the Ugolini Co. of Siena (1255-62): the relevant entries, as transcribed by Melis,[4] may be rendered thus:

C. 60 *recto*

Our old firm is due to receive £6. 2. 6d. in coin of Provins, at the Tresetto fair [12] 61, for our share of £20. 0. 0d. which we collected from the Abbot of Flavigny.

Item it is due to receive £35. 5. 3d. in coin of Provins, at the fair of Bar [-sur-Aube], [12] 62, for our share of £150. 0. 0d. which we collected from the Abbot of Flavigny.

Item [it is due to receive] £9. 10. 0d. in coin of Provins, at the said fair, for our share of £38. 0. 0d. which the Bishop of Toul paid us.

If these sums represent interest received on loans made at the fairs of Champagne, then 'our old firm' may indicate the existence, in the ledger proper, of an account similar to those found in many fourteenth-century Florentine books of account. In these the ledger was opened, on the setting up of a new firm, by making the 'old firm', now liquidated, a creditor for assets, and a debtor for liabilities, taken over from it; individual accounts being opened, with debit balances for assets and credit balances for liabilities. The 'old firm' account then functioned, in effect, as a single equity account for all partners, being annually (or more frequently) credited with income and capital introduced, and debited with expenses, partners' salaries, and drawings. The individual partners' shares were analysed separately, so that a proper settlement could take place when the firm was wound up—often by transferring its assets and liabilities to yet another 'new firm'. The 1261-2 fragment is evidence of the antiquity of this practice; but it is hazardous to argue, as Melis does,[4] that it indicates the presence of double entry bookkeeping, or any close approach to it, at so early a date

Apart from the Ugolini memoranda, the best evidence for early capital accounting is found in domestic ledgers. These include several accounts for investments in business firms, usually as lenders, but in two cases as partners. These records, which may well be 'mirror images' of accounts in the firm's books, are described below.

1. *Gentile de' Sassetti & Sons, 1274-1310:*

Contains the only fully-developed account for a partnerhip share which survives from this period. It relates to the share of (presumably) Gentile himself in the firm of Sassetto Azzi & Co., from 1 January 1278-9 to 1 January 1289-90—thus 'leapfrogging' from page to page through the ledger. It is summarized below in modern form, the original being in the old 'paragraph' layout. One or two arithmetical errors are noted in their places.

Sassetto Azzi & Co.

1279			£	s	d	1280			£	s	d
Jan.	1	Balance b/d	2,583	12	0	Jan.	1	Drawings	63	13	0
1280						,,	1	Balance c/d	3,446	13	0
Jan.	1	Interest	206	13	0						
,,	1	Profit	720	0	0						
,,	1	[Error]		1	0						
			£3,510	6	0				£3.510	6	0
1280						1281					
Jan.	1	Balance b/d	3.446	13	0	Jan.	1	Drawings	408	16	0
1281						,,	1	Balance c/d	3.805	9	0
Jan.	1	Interest	275	14	0						
,,	1	Profit	400	0	0						
,,	1	'Other account'	91	18	0						
			£4,214	5	0				£4,214	5	0
1281						1283					
Jan.	1	Balance b/d	3,805	9	0	Jan.	1	Drawings	1,380	17	0
1283						,,	1	Balance c/d	4,537	18	0
Jan.	1	Interest (2 years)	639	6	0						
,,	1	Profit (2 years)	1.400	0	0						
,,	1	'Two other accounts'	74	0	0						
			£5.918	15	0				£5,918	15	0
1283						1284					
Jan.	1	Balance b/d	4,537	18	0	Jan.	1	Drawings (per			
1284								detailed account)	99	0	0
Jan.	1	Interest	364	10	0	,,	1	Balance c/d	4,802	8	0
						,,	1	[Error]	1	0	0
			£4.902	8	0				£4,902	8	0
1284						1284					
Jan.	1	Balance b/d	4.802	8	0	May	6	Cash	4.926	14	0
1284											
May	6	Interest									
		(4 months)	124	6	0						
			£4.926	14	0				£4,926	14	0
1284						1285					
May	8	Cash	4.000	0	0	Jan.	1	Balance c/d	4,206	0	0
1285											
Jan.	1	Interest (8 months)	206	0	0						
			£4,206	0	0				£4.206	0	0

1285					1287					
Jan.	1 Balance b/d	4,206	0	0	Jan.	1 Drawings	749	1	0
1287					„	1 Balance c/d	4,156	16	0
Jan.	1 Interest (2 years)	696	17	0					
„	1 [Error]	3	0	0					
		£4,905	17	0			£4,905	17	0
1287					1288				
Jan.	1 Balance b/d	4,156	16	0	Jan.	1 Drawings	1,048	13	0
1290					1290				
Jan.	1 Interest (3 years)	904	14	0	Jan.	1 Cash	3,327	17	0
					„	1 Cash	685	0	0
		£5,061	10	0			£5,061	10	0

All amounts are in silver florins. The interest (*prode*) works out, very closely in most cases, at 8 per cent per annum, compound with annual rests at 1 January. In the first four years there are also shares of profit (*guadagno*)—evidently estimated, in view of the round amounts allowed, with the mysterious 'other accounts' (*altre ragione*) perhaps representing later adjustments. On the other side are drawings (*danari per ispese*), which continue even after 'profit' dries up. At 6 May 1284 the 'old' firm was apparently liquidated, with a final balance to Gentile of £4,926.14.0d.; two days later a new firm was set up, and a round £4,000.0.0d. invested in it, until the second liquidation on 1 January 1289-90. The drawings for the year ended 1 January 1283-4 are shown in detail in a separate account, whose balance is transferred to the investment account; otherwise the annual drawings are given in one sum, probably derived from statements rendered by Sassetto Azzi & Co., and/or from a memorandum book (or cash book analysis) kept by Gentile. The 'errors' noted in the summary are net discrepancies in the figures as transcribed; it is not clear whether they are scribal, editorial or typographical in origin.

2. *Bene Bencivenni* (*second ledger*), *1277-96:*

This contains a lengthy account (1285-96) of the proprietor's drawings (*tratta*) from the family business, more detailed, but less sophisticated, than the 'capital' account in the Sassetti books. Most sums are stated to be taken 'from the warehouse' (*dal fondaco*), and are expressed in gold florins, converted to silver at 29s. 0d. each. A few small amounts in *piccioli,* unconverted, are said not to be from the warehouse, and are excluded from the page totals. The latter are carried forward and summarized, up to 1292, at each 1 July—evidently the balancing date for the firm's books; after 1292 there seems to be no regular balancing date for the drawings account. In no case, though, is the grand total for the year transferred to any other account, nor is there any specific reference to a share of partnership; probably the firm's books were also under Bene Bencivenni's control, he saw no reason to duplicate the capital account therein, and he debited it annually with his total drawings as summarized in his private books. In other words the private ledger was merely one part of a larger system, imperfectly articulated. The first page of the drawings account is translated below; the total is 4s. 0d. too much (as the figures stand in Castellani [5]) and for the first balancing period (23 October 1285 to 1 July 1286) the total is given as £120.2.0d., though the recorded drawings add up to £170.14.0d. (Did the book keeper, or the editor, write *lb. cxx s. ij* instead of *lb. clxx s. ij?*) In the rest of the account, though, the arithmetic is generally accurate.

C. 17 *verso*

1285

Bene Bencivenni is due to give for his drawings £26. 2. 0d. in florins at 23 October, which he had of us from the warehouse, 18 gold florins for new wine and other household expenses.

And he is due to give £52. 4. 0d. in florins, at the above date, which he had of us from the warehouse, 36 gold florins, which they gave on my behalf to Galluzzo Orlandi, who received them on behalf of Messer Bernardino and Cecco de' Caponsacchi, brothers, in respect of half of the 13 *staiora* of land which I bought from them, jointly with Guccio Bellondani, and for which I have a deed by the hand of Ser Pepo, notary, of [blank].

And he is due to give £8. 14. 0d. at 17 November, which he had of us from the warehouse, 6 gold florins, of which he gave 2 gold florins to Messer Giovanni Angiolini, and the others were for his expenses.

And he is due to give £5. 16. 0d. at 24 November, which he had of us from the warehouse, 4 gold florins for expenses.

And he is due to give £5. 16. 0d. at 28 November, which he had of us from the warehouse, 4 gold florins, from which he paid the levy (*libbra*) of 25s. 0d. per cent for the term [of office] of Messer Giliuolo da Padova*; collectors Ser Berlinghieri, notary, and the late Arrighetto Doni of Porta Rossa, both of them.

This page (*faccia*). £98. 16. 0d. [*sic*]

Tuscan accounts up to 1296 afford little evidence of the keeping of nominal accounts; there are none in the domestic ledgers, and few traces in business books. The Ugolini fragment suggests that items of income and expenditure were carried direct to a quasi-equity account; but more than this would be needed if annual profit, and the sharing thereof, were to be regularly ascertained. At a minimum, interest receivable and gains on the sale of goods would be credited to an account for 'profit' (*avanzo*), and interest payable, losses on sales and expenses debited to 'loss' (*disavanzo*)—the totals of each for the year being transferred to 'capital' under whatever name. The earliest direct testimony to such practices is found in a notarial transcript of 1298 (in Archivio di Stato, Florence), of a loan account of 1292-3 in the ledger of Filippo Peruzzi & Co., the great Florentine banking house;[6] it may be translated thus:

* Evidently the *podestà* for the year.

Fo. 49

1292

Giovanni Gianfigliazzi is due to give us, at 29 July [12] 92, in florins, £76. 6. 3d.; he had from us 52 gold florins, and 18s. 4d. in [silver] florins; he said that he was giving them to Messer Ispinello Gianfigliazzi, who said that Rosso left them to him.

[14 more debits of the same nature, then—]

Total £837. 19. 1d. in florins, with this page below, 29 September [12] 92.

And he is due to give for interest (*guadagno*) up to 25 February 92 [i.e. 1293], in florins, £27. 10. 0d.; we added [it] to profit (*avanzo*) in the small ledger (*quadernetto*) at [folio] 3.

Giovanni has given us, at 25 February 92 [i.e. 1293], in florins, £865. 9. 1d.; we deducted [it] where he was due to receive at [folio] 451.

From other references in the extract, it would seem that Rosso had died, and that the account was that of his administrator. Mention of a ledger folio 451 indicates the scale of operations of the Peruzzi bank; but Melis's assertion[4] that the firm probably kept its books by double entry goes far beyond the evidence.[6]

DID THE FLORENTINES INVENT DOUBLE ENTRY?

All the trends so far described are brought together in what Melis[4] and Castellani,[5] but not de Roover,[6] regard as the first sets of books kept by double entry—those of Rinieri Fini & Brothers (1296-1305), and of Giovanni Farolfi & Co. (1299-1300), both in Archivio di Stato, Florence.[5] Consideration of these celebrated accounts raises questions too complex to be disposed of at the end of an article: the author intends to make them the subject of a further paper, and only his general observations can be given here.

Both sets of books relate to Florentine mercantile firms operating in France—the Fini Brothers at the fairs of Champagne, and the Farolfi Co. at Nîmes and other towns in Provence; both kept their accounts in *livres tournois*. Both still use the paragraph layout, and both ledgers have accounts with debit balances at the front, and with credit balances at the back. Most are for debtors or creditors, with interest included; but in addition there are accounts for sales, with the balance of profit or loss transferred (along with interest) to *avanzo, disavanzo* and related accounts, which also survive. In the Farolfi ledger there are even allocations of prepaid expenditure to successive years—surely an advanced concept for the late thirteenth century.

The two ledgers are indeed in double entry, in the sense that, so far as can be observed, there is (supposed to be) a debit for every credit, with full cross-references—except that in Farolfi there are no specific references to the cash book, now lost. Both ledgers contain accounts of an 'equity' nature—a capital account in Fini, and a head office account in Farolfi, whose books relate to the Salon branch only. The Fini books, however, do not appear to be regularly balanced, but run on from year to year, without any closing-off of the nominal accounts. Those of Farolfi, on the other hand, are closed by means of a 'balance account' (unfortunately incomplete), as is the common practice today on the Continent. Examination of the accounts has nevertheless revealed to the author several errors, of principle and of arithmetic, which would have made proper balancing impossible; and his tentative opinion is, that the profit or loss for the year was found by a refinement of 'single entry' methods, involving a comparison of total assets with total liabilities plus capital, as at the year-end—a type of 'quasi-double entry' commonly used in fourteenth-century Florence. It therefore seems premature to claim that the Tuscans had discovered double entry before 1340; but they had certainly worked out all the underlying principles by trial and error, and it needed only a more rigorous application of them, and the use of two-sided accounts, to achieve complete success. It may even be that the *massari* of Genoa, or their bookkeepers, built on the foundations laid in Tuscany, and that it is no exaggeration after all, to designate Florence as the original home of the key technique of modern accounting.

BIBLIOGRAPHY

1. Pietro Santini, 'Frammenti di un libro di banchieri fiorentini scritto in volgare nel 1211', *Giornale storico della letteratura italiana,* vol. X (1887), pp. 161-77.
2. Alfredo Schiaffini, *Testi Fiorentini del Dugento e dei Primi del Trecento,* Firenze, 1926.
3. Mario Chiaudano, *Studi e Documenti per la Storia del Diritto Commerciale Italiano del sec. XIII,* Torino, 1930.
4. Federigo Melis, *Storia della Ragioneria,* Bologna, 1950.
5. Arrigo Castellani, *Nuovi Testi Fiorentini del Dugento,* 2 tomi, Firenze, 1952.
6. Raymond de Roover, 'The development of accounting prior to Luca Pacioli according to the account-books of mediaeval merchants', in A. C. Littleton and B. S. Yamey (eds), *Studies in the History of Accounting,* Sweet & Maxwell, London, 1956.
7. Geoffrey Alan Lee, 'The oldest European account book: a Florentine bank ledger of 1211', *Nottingham Mediaeval Studies,* vol. XVI, 1972, pp. 28-60.
8. Geoffrey Alan Lee, 'The Florentine bank ledger fragments of 1211: some new insights', *Journal of Accounting Research,* Spring 1973.
9. Policarpo Petrocchi, *Nova Dizionario Universale della Lingua Italiano,* Milano, 1908.

Geoffrey A. Lee
SENIOR LECTURER
UNIVERSITY OF NOTTINGHAM

THE COMING OF AGE OF DOUBLE ENTRY: THE GIOVANNI FAROLFI LEDGER OF 1299-1300

Abstract: This article examines the branch ledger of a Florentine firm in 13th century Provence, and its relationship to contemporaneous Tuscan account books. It is concluded that the ledger was part of a sophisticated accounting system, with a debit and credit for every item and a serious attempt at annual balancing, thus constituting the earliest known example of commercial double entry.

In previous published papers the author dealt with the earliest evidence of business bookkeeping in Florence—the bank ledger fragments of 1211, transcribed in 1887 by Pietro Santini—and with the development of accounting in Tuscany during the 13th century, as evidenced in the account-books, or extracts therefrom, which constitute the bulk of Arrigo Castellani's *Nuovi testi fiorentini del Dugento e dei primi del Trecento* (1952). There were traced the gradual standardization of techniques, and incorporation of elements of double entry, within the framework of the "narrative" or "paragraph" type of accounting record *(a sezioni sovrapposte)*, perhaps derived from the "charge and discharge" format used in public accounts. The survey ended with the emergence of double entry itself, in the ledgers of Renieri (or Rinieri) Fini & Brothers (1296-1305) and Giovanni Farolfi & Company (1299-1300). The latter's records are better preserved and more completely transcribed than the other's, and display somewhat more advanced techniques; hence they constitute the main subject of this paper.

The Ledger of Giovanni Farolfi & Company

This document is preserved in Archivio di Stato, Florence, and filed under *Carte Strozziane, 2ª serie, n. 84 bis.* It consists of 56 leaves of paper, about 33 x 24 cm., consequently numbered. The first 47 leaves are lost; the extant ones run from 48 to 110, with numbers 66, 74, 87, 93, 105, 106 and 109 missing. Leaves 92, 94 and 103 are damaged in their lower halves, and 92 and 110 are out of sequence—92 bound after 96, and 110 at the beginning. In this article reference is made to the leaves, recto (r.) and verso (v.), as in Castellani. The bookkeeper, however, numbered only the recto of each pair of facing pages, and counted them as one folio; thus, a cross-reference to an entry *nel lxiii carte* meant that the counterpart appeared on either 62v. or 63r. Some references extend beyond the extant pages, mentioning folio numbers as high as 129, and it therefore seems that less than half the book has survived.

The ledger is entirely in one hand, that of Amatino (or Matino) Manucci, one of the partners who acted as bookkeeper. The writing is neat, legible and well-preserved for the most part; but occasionally two pages have stuck together and some of the surface of one has adhered to the other, forcing Castellani to use a mirror to read the text, or to leave a lacuna where the facing page is lost. The entries are set out in lines, going close to the left-hand edge but leaving a wide right-hand margin, into which are extended the sums of money, in Roman numerals and neatly ranged in a column. In the first section of the ledger, up to page 92v., the upper half of each account contains the debits, and the lower half the credits; in the second section, from 94n., the sequence is reversed. The debits and credits are each totaled in the middle of the page, and (normally) demonstrated to be equal. As in other old Italian ledgers, all accounts are struck through with slanting lines, denoting settlement. The arithmetic, performed on the abacus or with counters, is in general very accurate. The money of account is the *livre tournois* of France, divided into 20 *sols*, and each *sol* into 12 *deniers*. The language is the Tuscan vernacular of Dante's time, recognizably like modern Italian and spelt much as today, with some abbreviation of common words. A few Provençal expressions are also found, mainly weights and measures.

The Business of Giovanni Farolfi & Company

Giovanno Farolfi & Company, as appears from their ledger, were a firm of Florentine merchants whose head office was at Nîmes in Languedoc, in the kingdom of France. The ledger, however, relates exclusively to the branch at Salon, a town in the independent county of Provence, about 45 miles from Nimes and 25 east of Arles, with a population in 1300 of some 2,000 to 3,000. It was dominated by the Archbishop of Arles, Rostang de Capre, who held the see from 1286-1303,[1] and was one of the Count of Provence's principal vassals. He resided often at his Château de l'Empéri, crowning the hill on which Salon stands, and appears in the Farolfi accounts as their most important customer, and largest supplier of agricultural produce. His patronage must also have shielded the Florentines from any trouble over the Church's official ban on "usury", which in any case was not seriously enforced, provided the rate of interest was not extortionate; the Archbishop himself borrowed from the Farolfi at 15 per cent per annum. Rostang de Capre was also friendly with another powerful magnate, Bertrand des Baux, Count of Avellino, who held the limestone hills of the Alpilles to the north of Arles. He is mentioned more than once, in accounts with the Archbishop, and his goodwill, if not his custom, was doubtless important to the Farolfi.

Salon's economic significance lay in its position as the chief market town between Arles and Aix, the capital of Provence. Situated in the plain north of the Etang de Berre, with its salt-pans (a monopoly of the Count's), close to the arid, pebbly wastes of La Crau with its flocks of sheep, the town was, and is, a centre of the olive oil industry, and formed an ideal collecting-point for the other bulk commodities in which the Farolfi dealt — wheat, barley, oats, wine, and wool. It was also well situated for the company's other main trade, in cloth, yarn, and dyeing materials; most of the goods were locally produced, but the finer cloths mentioned must have been imported through Marseilles. The company additionally engaged in moneylending and moneychanging, as a sideline and mainly for the accommodation of their trade customers. On one occasion the Salon branch consigned 220 quintals of merchandise (evidently bulk grain and/or oil) to Florence in the care of the partner Ughetto Buonaguida, and paid freight of 68*l.* 8*s.* 0*d.*, presumably from Marseilles.

The senior partner was Giovanni Farolfi, otherwise Giovanni Filippi or (in one place) Giovanni, son of Ubaldino; next to him ranked (it seems) Compagno (or Pagno) Franchi. Amatino (Matino) Manucci kept the books. Bacchera Baldovini was apparently in charge of the Salon branch, and was its chief buyer. Other partners were Borrino (Burrino) Marsoppi, Vitale Marsoppi, Ughetto Buonaguida, and Francesco Cavalcante. Tommasino Farolfi and Giometto Verdiglione may also have been partners, but the evidence is equivocal.[2] Such partnerships in medieval Italy were normally constituted for only a few years at a time, and it is not known how long the Farolfi firm lasted. The ledger shows balances brought forward from a previous one, and ending balances in 1300 closed off to the firm's account; but this may have been because the ledger was full, or because the firm kept a separate volume for each year.

Besides the Archbishop of Arles, major customers included Guillaume de Lambesc, perhaps a merchant in a little town 8 miles to the east; Gilles Vacquier, a draper in Salon; three Italian merchants,

Ghiberto Doni, Tano (Gaetano) da Figliano, and Ischiatta della Fiorentina[3] from L'Isle-sur-la-Sorgue in the Comtat Venaissin (the Papal territory north of Provence); and Giovanni Giuserani or Jean Jusserand — he may have been either Italian or Provençal. The main suppliers were, again, the Archbishop, Tano da Figliano and Giuserani/Jusserand, together with Tommasino Farolfi of Mondragon (north of the Comtat) and Astruc Durand Loncantaire, a Jew of Salon. Other Jews are mentioned, some as Astruc's partners; Provence and the Comtat were more tolerant of their race than was France, and they formed communities, with synagogues, in several towns. Nothing appears to be known otherwise of any of these persons.[4]

Structure of the Farolfi Accounting System

From the surviving ledger it is evident that it was only one account-book among several. The first half contained the debtors' and expenditure accounts, and the debit side of the head office account, which on closure of the ledger became the balance account. In the second half were the creditors' and profit accounts, and the credit side of the balance account. The total of the latter was carried to page 92v. and compared with the total of the debit half; theoretically they should have been equal, but were not, for reasons given later.

In both halves of the General Ledger (as it may conveniently be called) the earlier accounts show balances transferred from a "White Ledger" *(quaderno bianco)*, with cross-references to numbered folios therein, ranging from 23 to 99. The folios up to 69 refer to debit balances, those from 70 upwards to credit ones. This White Ledger must therefore have been an earlier volume of the General Ledger, divided similarly into two halves, rather than (as Castellani thought) "a waste-book of prime entry" *(uno scartafaccio di prima nota)*. Since the balances were transferred directly from the old personal accounts to the new, it seems clear that the old ledger had no closing balance account; nor was there an opening one in the new volume, such as is found in the Peruzzi ledger of 1335-43.

From numerous references it is apparent that the main merchandise accounts — for wheat, barley, oats, olive oil, wine, wool, and yarn — were contained in a separate "Red Book" *(libro rosso)*; folio numbers from 14 to 141 are mentioned. These accounts were debited with purchases (in the front of the ledger) and credited with sales (in the rear half), and closing inventory balances were transferred to the debit of the balance account in the General Ledger. The Profits Account *(avanzi)* was in the last pages (127-129) of the

General Ledger, which are lost; it would seem that any excess of credits over debits in the Red Book accounts was transferred at intervals to the credit of Profits, and any contrary excess to the debit of Current Expenses *(spese corse).* Indeed, the latter account is debited on 20 June 1300 with 95*l.* 4*s.* 5*d.* "which we lost on wheat that we purchased", cross-referenced to Red Book, folio 22. In many General Ledger accounts, though, a debit for goods sold to a customer is followed by a statement that "we have a bill made by the hand of Maître Bertrand Arnaud *(maestro Bertrano Arnaldi),* notary of Salon". There is usually no cross-reference to any other account or book. The account is balanced, then follows the statement: "It shows that for us there is a profit of (so much): we added to Profits, further on at folio 129". This sum appears to stand outside the debtor's account, which balances without it, and thus to constitute a mere memorandum in that place. The credit to Profits cannot now be followed through, and the question arises: where was the corresponding debit? The most likely hypothesis, on the whole, is that it was made in (say) the Wheat Account in the Red Book, as representing the gross margin on the sale; the bill of exchange was used as the posting medium — hence the lack of a reference to the credit for the sale in the Red Book. This belief is strengthened by consideration of the order of amounts involved, and by a curious piece of evidence on page 77r. Beside an account showing a sale of 15*l.* 0*s.* 0*d.*, with a profit noted as 3*l.* 5*s.* 0*d.*, there appear in the left margin the *Arabic* figures 11 and 15, vertically. These look like a note of the cost price, 11*l.* 15*s.* 0*d.*, taken from the Red Book on the debit side.

A third book is referred to once — the Cloth Ledger *(quaderno dei panni).* This obviously contained merchandise accounts (as in the Red Book) for various kinds of cloth. The references (to folio 4 and 16) occur in an account for Druggets *(sargie)* at page 63v., the beginning of which is mutilated; the debit and credit totals from the Cloth Ledger have been transferred here, and further sales entered, with a profit figure (credited to Profits) which appears arithmetically wrong. The balance account in the General Ledger shows no debits for ending inventories of cloth; presumably there were none left. Apart from the Druggets Account, moreover, there are several debits to customers for cloth sales, without cross-references; bills have been drawn up by Maître Arnaud, as described above.

A fourth book was the Expenses Ledger *(quaderno delle spese);* there are references to folios from 6 to 37. It seems to have contained accounts relative to fixtures *(masserizie)* and current expenses *(spese corse),* and possibly other items. Corresponding entries appear in the General Ledger; then the closing totals of the Expenses Ledger accounts have been transferred to Fixtures, and Current Expenses, Accounts, and further entries made therein, as with the Cloth Ledger.

Last among the main books of account was the Cash Book *(libro dell'entrata e dell'escita).* This is never mentioned in the text, and no folio references to it are given for the numerous debits and credits relating to cash paid and received, or for the sum of 1*l.* 10*s.* 0*d.* transferred at 16 August 1300 to the debit of the balance account. This item is described as moneys, "which we gave them in cash in Nîmes: Matino counted it out." It must be the final cash balance, as it follows a series of debits for ending inventories of various goods, from the Red Book. The Cash Book was probably in the form then standard in Italy, with receipts in the front half, payments in the rear half, and periodical balancing of the two totals. The absence of folio references in the General Ledger is explained by the relative ease of referring back to the Cash Book by dates alone; there would, for obvious reasons, have been ledger references in the Cash Book.

These five books — general ledger, two merchandise ledgers, expenses ledger, and cash book (with the White Ledger as a sixth) — constituted what looks very like a true double entry system, though for the Salon branch only. In addition there were at least two subsidiary books, occasionally referred to in the General Ledger. The first was the *libro piloso,* a term which, curiously, occurs also in the contemporary Fini ledger, in what seems to be the same sense. The best translation, in the author's judgment, is "Plush Book", taking *pelo (pilo)* to mean (as in Edler) the nap or "pile" on cloth. It was kept by the partner Borrino Marsoppi, evidently as a memorandum book of business expenses out of pocket; folio numbers from 5 to 55 are mentioned. It was periodically summarized, and the total debited to Expenses and credited to Borrino's account. The second subsidiary book was the "Memorandum Ledger" *(quaderno memoriale),* for which no folio references are given. There are only three entries from it in the General Ledger; they concern out-of-pocket expenses of partners other than Borrino Marsoppi, and the Memorandum was presumably a generalized form of his Plush Book.

All these records add up to a bookkeeping system of uncommon sophistication, even by contemporary Italian standards. Wonder grows when one remembers that these were the books of one branch only of a sizeable mercantile enterprise, and they arouse in the inquirer a strong, but fruitless, desire to know what elaborate arrangements must have been in force at the Nîmes head office of the company.

The Farolfi Ledger and the Evolution of Double Entry Bookkeeping

It has long been recognized by accounting historians that double entry bookkeeping did not suddenly appear in Genoa in 1340, and is most unlikely to have had any single inventor. Examination of Tuscan account-books, business and private, of the 13th century by Federigo Melis and Raymond de Roover, as well as by Arrigo Castellani, has revealed considerable sophistication and increasing systematization in the "paragraph" format, and done much to correct the view of earlier historians, such as Edward Peragallo, that there was little systematic business accounting before the rise of the great Florentine banking houses and cloth manufacturers of the 14th century. The present author has entered into his great predecessors' labours, and in a previous study traced the emergence, between 1211 and 1296, of the main components of double entry.

These may be identified, in descending order of obviousness, as:

(1) the concept of the individual proprietor or (more clearly) the business partnership as an *accounting entity,* whose books record its financial relationships with other economic agents;
(2) the concept of *algebraic opposition,* firstly between increases and decreases in a physical holding of cash or goods, secondly between increases and decreases in the level of indebtedness by or to another economic agent or entity, thirdly between indebtedness by, and to, other entities in general, and fourthly, and least obviously, between assets and liabilities of the entity accounted for;
(3) the concept of a *single monetary unit,* to which amounts in other currencies are converted, thus making the entries additive overall;
(4) the concept of *proprietors' equity,* as the algebraic sum of assets and liabilities;
(5) the concept of *profit or loss,* as the net increment or decrement to equity resulting from one or more acts of exchange between the entity and its economic environment (excluding the proprietors); and
(6) the concept of an *accounting period,* over which profit or loss may be measured.

It would be flying in the face of the evidence to suggest that these ideas were all considered of equal importance, or that there was any steady and consistent progress in adopting them, among the businessmen of 13th century Florence. No-one had any theory as to what an accounting system ought to be, or if he had it was never put into writing, as far as anyone knows. Each man of substance kept whatever records he needed for his own purposes, with little regard for overall coherence or consistency. He was concerned mainly to keep track of his current position with respect to cash, debtors and creditors, and sometimes his investment in the family firm. There are no nominal or equity accounts in early private ledgers, and no means of ascertaining either the wealth of the owner at any time, or his income or expenditure over any period. The only basic concepts followed with any consistency are those of the accounting entity (the proprietor himself), and of algebraic opposition between increments and decrements to the balances of individual debtors' and creditors' accounts (including interest receivable and payable), and presumably to cash balances, though no private cash books have survived. Not all account-books adhere closely to the concept of a single monetary unit. Some use the silver florin as the unit, and convert gold florins at the rate (from 1277) of 1 gold florin = 29 silver *soldi;* but others, such as that of Gentile de' Sassetti and his sons (1274-1310), use a mixture of currencies — gold florins, silver florins, and Pisan silver *piccioli* — with little attempt to unify them, though the same unit is normally used for all entries in a given account. Some loan accounts are balanced at the same date each year (as in the first ledger of Bene Bencivenni, 1262-75), but only, it seems, in order to compute interest.

Remains of 13th century Italian business accounts are very fragmentary, and have survived only by various accidents. Banking and mercantile partnerships were formed for only a few years at a time, and when the firm was wound up and partners' shares paid out to them, no-one was concerned to preserve the books. Indeed there was an incentive, owing to the dearness of parchment, to scrape or wash the pages and reuse them — as in the case of the 1211 bank ledger pages, utilized as flyleaves to a 14th century legal MS. About the only other first-hand documents of the period are fragments of the Detacommando ledger at Poppi (1241-72), of a creditors' journal at Imola (1260-62) (both very crude), and a memorandum book of the Ugolini Company of Siena (1255-62), together with two cash books — of an unknown Sienese firm of 1277-82, and of Pope Nicholas III's treasurer in the Marches, 1279-80 — and inventories of stock, cash and book debts of the Lucca and Pisa branches of a Florentine cloth-merchants' firm, 1278-79. (The two last have been transcribed by Castellani). At second hand, we have 13th century transcripts of two bankers' ledger extracts, for use in lawsuits — a deposit account from the ledger of the Borghesi Company (1259-67), and a loan account from that of the Peruzzi Company (1292-93). At one further remove, there are "mirror images" in private ledgers, of a partner's drawings account, 1285-96 (Bene Bencivenni's second ledger, 1277-96), and of his capital account (Gentile de' Sassetti and his sons, 1274-1310).

From this scanty testimony it would be hazardous to form any dogmatic conclusions as to the evolution of accounting at this period. Yet evidence emerges of the gradual acceptance and application by entrepreneurs and their bookkeepers — often one and the same person — whether consciously or not, of the six concepts formulated above, and of their progressive convergence to form a coherent system, approximating to double entry. The first three are already present in the 1211 ledger: (1) the firm is clearly distinguished from outsiders; (2) there is offsetting, not only of increments and decrements to the same account balance but as between loan and deposit account balances, and there are even quite complex transfers between different customers' accounts in settlement of liabilities to third parties; and (3) all entries are in Pisan currency, with many intricate conversions of sums in Bolognese, Veronese, German Imperial, French, English and Arabian coin. The tightly-knit *Arte di Cambio* of Florence was unlikely to have let such knowledge remain the preserve of any one firm, nor yet to have allowed it to perish. What little we know of later 13th century business accounts shows building on these foundations, and the addition of the other three basic ideas.

All are exemplified in the private ledger counterpart of Gentile de' Sassetti's capital account with Sassetti Azzi & Company. It started at 1 January 1278-79 (the year then began officially on 25 March) with a balance, in silver florins, of 2,583 *libbre,* 12 *soldi,* 0 *denari,* which grew to 4,926*l.* 14*s.* 0*d.* at 6 May 1284, when it was paid out in cash. On 8 May 1284 Gentile invested 4,000*l.* 0*s.* 0*d.* in a new partnership with the same firm, and on 1 January 1289-90 this, too, was liquidated, with a payment to him of 4,012*l.* 17*s.* 0*d.* The account is consistently balanced at 1 January in each year (except 1281-82), when it is debited (credited, in the firm's books) with interest at 8 per cent per annum on the opening balance. To this is added, up to 1 January 1282-83, a share of profit, in a round sum plus a supplementary broken amount after the first year; after 1283 there is only interest. Drawings for the year are credited at 1 January (debited in the firm's books). The total gain to Gentile from the first partnership was 4,295*l.* 8*s.* 0*d.*, and from the second 1,810*l.* 11*s.* 0*d.* (subject to three small arithmetical errors) — altogether, 6,105*l.* 19*s.* 0*d.* From this record one may deduce that Sassetti Azzi & Company's accounting system not only incorporated concepts (1) to (3) above, but also included: (4) a capital account for each partner; (5) regular ascertainment and division of profit and loss; and (6) annual balancing of the partners' accounts, if not of the books as a whole. What cannot be proved is that the firm used double entry. More probably, the partners at the year-end totaled the assets and liabilities, deducted the latter from the former, then subtracted the opening balances on the capital accounts, and added back the partners' drawings, less any capital contributed during the year. The result was a sufficient approximation to the annual profit or loss, which was then divided, and credited or debited to the capital accounts (which were debited with drawings). Such was the common practice in Florence in the first half of the 14th century, as shown in the *libro segreto* of the Alberto del Guidice Company, 1302-29.

None of this, however, precludes the use in such books of nominal accounts, debited with expenditure and losses *(disavanzo)* and credited with revenue and profits *(avanzo).* Theoretically, the excess of the latter over the former should have been equal to the excess of closing net assets over opening capital, plus contributions, minus drawings, for the year; but this happy result could seldom, if ever, have been achieved in medieval Italy, owing to the bookkeeper's propensity for making one-sided adjustments, and to human error. Hence there was almost always a difference between total debits and total credits; if it was not too large the bookkeeper was satisfied, and adjusted the profit total to fit. In the Sassetti Azzi ledger there may have been a preliminary computation of profits as *avanzo* less *disavanzo,* with round-number "dividends" transferred to capital accounts, followed by a more precise calculation, and adjusting entries; but without the books there is no way of settling the question.

Of nominal accounts there is no direct evidence before the Peruzzi ledger extract of 1292-93. This includes a debit to Giovanni Gianfigliazzi's loan account in respect of interest, 27*l.* 10*s.* 0*d.*, stated to be added "to profit *(avanzo)* in the small ledger *(quadernetto)* at (folio) 3". The first extant ledger to include such accounts comes, though, not from Italy but from France; it is nevertheless in Italian, and preserved in Archivio di Stato, Florence, under *Capitani d' Orsammichele, n. 220.* It has been partly transcribed by Arrigo Castellani.

The ledger is that of Renieri (Rinieri) Fini de' Benzi & Brothers, and extends from 1296 to 1305. The three brothers, Baldo, Renieri (who wrote most of the ledger) and Schiattino, were the sons of Fino de' Benzi, from Figline in Val d'Arno. The two elder sons had been factors to Biccio and Musciatto Franzesi, financiers to Philip IV of France (1285-1314), and all three brothers were merchants and moneylenders at the Fairs of Champagne. Unfortunately the MS., of some 91 leaves of paper, is in poor condition; also, Castellani transcribed only the entries up to 1300 — about one-fifth of the whole.

Accounts with debit balances appear in the first half, those with credit balances in the second. In both halves are accounts for Renieri Fini, who was cashier as well as bookkeeper; they seem to be the two sides of the Cash Account. The debtors' accounts relate mainly to loans at the Fairs of Champagne, but include a loan of 16,000 *livres tournois* to the King of France in 1299. The second half of the ledger has an account for "Baldo Fini and his brothers"; credits include five years' "salary" at 200 *livres* per annum, paid to Renieri by "Biccio Franzesi and his Franzesi partners". More significantly, nominal accounts are found for the first time — in the first half, for Interest (payable) and for Expenses of Clothing and Footwear, and in the second half for Profit *(avanzo)*, mainly interest receivable. All the entries, so far as can be traced, have counterparts in personal accounts, or in Renieri Fini's cash account. The ledger thus exhibits a combination of accounting *a sezioni sovrapposte* with double entry, in the sense that every debit has its credit and vice versa, at least in intention, and that impersonal, as well as personal, aspects of transactions are dealt with. What is missing is any evidence that the ledger was ever balanced. The accounts, as far as they have been transcribed, appear to run on from year to year, with no general closing off, no striking of annual or other balances of profit or loss, and no transfers of nominal account balances to capital; nor does there seem to be any partitioning of equity between the partners. Perhaps these matters were settled when the ledger was full or the firm was wound up, and judgment must be suspended until a complete transcript of the surviving entries is to hand.

With the doubtful exception of the Fini ledger, then, evidence for full double entry before 1299 is tenuous to say the least. The lack of accounting periods of fixed length is not, however, a fundamental objection to the classification of an accounting system as double entry; the Florentines made use of them from the 14th century, but the Venetians, for example, did not, and Luca Pacioli (1494) did not prescribe them. What matters is that *at some stage* all balances on a ledger shall be brought together in one view, debits against credits, and some genuine attempt be made to prove the two totals equal. If that is done, even without complete success in the last point, then the system complies with concept (6) above, and shows an accounting period over which profit or loss can be measured — even if that period is merely the time from opening, to closing, of a volume of the ledger. This process one cannot find in the Fini accounts and, pending further research, must refuse to certify them as true double entry. It will now be demonstrated that the Farolfi ledger exhibits all six of the basic concepts, including final balancing, and that the system therefore qualifies as the earliest proven example now extant of commercial double entry bookkeeping.

The Giovanni Farolfi Accounts As a Double Entry System

Like the Fini ledger, the Farolfi one includes "real" and "nominal", as well as "personal", accounts. The goods accounts now accessible comprise the Druggets Account (for purchases and sales of coarse woollen cloth), and several accounts for purchase and resale of individual packhorses. Both are stated, rather quaintly, to be "due to give" their purchase prices, and to "have given" their sale proceeds — a sign that the conventional bookkeeping formulae were losing their literal meanings and becoming purely indicators of the difference between debit and credit. The nominal accounts are more interesting than in the Fini ledger. There are separate ones for Fixtures (debited with purchases and credited with proceeds of sale — both items brought forward from the Expenses Ledger), Expenses of Eating and Drinking, and Current Expenses, the two latter being more conventional.

Most extraordinary for so early a date is the presence of four accounts for prepaid rent on various premises. In the case of a warehouse rented from Pierre Guillaume, for example, 16 *livres* were paid on 17 May 1299, for four years in advance; this sum was transferred from the old White Ledger to the debit of the rent account. At 17 May 1300 one year's rent, 4 *livres,* was credited to the account and debited to Current Expenses. At the closing of the ledger the remaining 12 *livres* were transferred, as an open balance, to the debit of the balance account. Similar treatment was accorded to advance rent of a shop (12 *livres* for four years — 3 *livres* written off); of a second warehouse, 1*l*. 10*s*. 0*d*. for one year (all written off);

and, more subtly still, to the balance of 4 *livres* (out of 12 *livres* paid in advance for three years on 6 October 1297) for a second shop. Such a grasp of the principles of revenue/cost matching in relation to time-based expenditure would have been creditable four or five centuries later; in 1300 it seems to border on the miraculous.

Posterity has been less fortunate as regards the total loss of the Profits Account, which was credited separately on folios 127 to 129. The author has listed all the extant debits cross-referenced to it, totalling 127*l*. 8*s*. 8*d*.; but there must also have been gross profit figures transferred from the now-lost Red Book and Cloth Ledger.

Finally comes the acid test of any alleged double entry system — the balancing process. Amatino Manucci does not disappoint. On page 88r. begins an account headed *Giovanni Farolfi e' compangni n(ost)ri di Nimmisi.* To its debit side are transferred almost all the debit balances open on the General Ledger to that point, including some on missing folios (2 to 7) at the beginning, after which there is an abrupt jump to the extant part of the ledger, from folio 48 onwards. The account continues to the bottom of page 90v., with each page separately totalled; on page 91r. comes a summary of open debit balances on the Red Book — ending inventories of produce — followed by what is clearly the ending balance of cash in hand, from the Cash Book. (Balances on the Cloth Ledger and Expenses Ledger have already been taken up into the General Ledger.) Page 91v. sweeps up a few debit balances previously overlooked, or added after the balancing began, then summarizes the totals of pages 88r. to 91r., making a grand total of 2,745*l*. 6*s*. 1*d*. *tournois.*

The credit side of this balance account is, exasperatingly, lost; it occupied folios 111 to 114, tantalisingly just beyond where the MS. ends. It is clear that it summarized all the open credit balances in the second half of the General Ledger, for there are many cross-references to it. The extant ones total to 2,846*l*. 9*s*. 5*d*., and there must have been others, yet the credit balance brought forward to page 92v. (the grand summary) is only 2,762*l*. 19*s*. 0*d*. There is no obvious explanation for the discrepancy of 83*l*. 10*s*. 5*d*.; inclusion of the missing Profits Account credit balance would increase, not diminish, it. If the total is right, then folios 115 to 129 must have contained debits, and there is at first sight nowhere whence they could legitimately have come. On the other hand there are no references to any folios from 115 through 126, and there may have been adjustments here — perhaps partners' drawings in cash, debited to personal accounts and transferred to the debit of the balance account on folios 111 to 114, either directly or via the Profits Account.

The grand summary on page 92v., then, begins with a credit total of 2,762*l.* 19*s.* 0*d.*, dated 4 August 1300. Against it is set the debit total from page 91v., 2,745*l.* 6*s.* 1*d.*, dated 27 June 1300. To this is added an unreferenced debit of 42*l.* 6*s.* 0*d.*, described as interest on the preceding sum at 15 per cent per annum up to 4 August; it does, in fact, work out very closely as 15 per cent per annum on 2,745*l.* 6*s.* 1*d.* from 27 June to 4 August. This interest was evidently designed to bring both totals to a common basis as at 4 August, and to offset interest at the same rate already debited to Current Expenses and credited to Giovanni Farolfi & Company, up to 1 September 1300; 15 per cent was presumably an estimate of a fair rate of return on the capital invested in the branch, and one which had to be earned before a net profit was recognized. The somewhat muddled adjustment of 42*l.* 6*s.* 0*d.* ranks in double-entry terms as a one-sided entry; it should also have been credited to Profits, and seemingly has not been. Hence, if it is ignored, the apparent difference on the books is 17*l.* 12*s.* 11*d.* excess of credit over debit.

Close scrutiny of the General Ledger, with translation into modern two-sided accounts and careful checking of casts and postings, has revealed to the author several errors, of arithmetic and of principle, which would in any case have vitiated the balance. There are also a large number of entries on both sides that seem at first sight to have no counterparts. From these one can at once eliminate the cash items — they must have gone through the Cash Book. There are likewise many unreferenced purchases and sales of goods, especially where a bill of exchange was accepted in payment; again, there must have been corresponding entries in the Red Book or Cloth Ledger, otherwise the inventory balances would not have agreed with the physical stocks.

If the obvious bookkeeping errors are first adjusted, the apparent difference on the General Ledger is reduced as follows:

Page 92v. Credit total brought forward, 4/8/1300		2,762*l.* 19*s.* 0*d.*
Less Page 62r. Credit entered twice, only one debit	40*l.* 2*s.* 10*d.*	
Pages 75v., 96r., 96v. and 102v. Four small arithmetical errors	2*l.* 11*s.* 2*d.*	
		42*l.* 14*s.* 0*d.*

Revised credit total				2,720*l.*	5*s.*	0*d.*
Page 92v. Debit total brought forward, 27/6/1300				2,745*l.*	6*s.*	1*d.*
Less Page 84r. Debit entered twice, only one credit	40*l.*	0*s.*	0*d.*			
Pages 63r. and 88v. Two small arithmetical errors		1*s.*	1*d.*			
				40*l.*	1*s.*	1*d.*
Revised debit total				2,705*l.*	5*s.*	0*d.*
Revised apparent difference (credit exceeds debit)				15*l.*	0*s.*	0*d.*

Now, as it happens, there is one credit of exactly 15*l.* 0*s.* 0*d.* with no cross-reference to a corresponding debit. It occurs on the very first extant page, 48r., in the account of the Archbishop of Arles, and is described as an allowance to him "for harvesting the wheat at Miramas and Saint-Chamas", as at 10 June 1299. If this credit is indeed one-sided, *and there are no further errors,* then after debiting Current Expenses 15*l.* 0*s.* 0*d.* one can balance the books of Giovanni Farolfi & Company to the exact *denier* as at 4 August 1300!

It is only fair to point out that there are several small items which may or may not be errors vitiating the balance. In the account of Tommasino Farolfi on page 63r., the debits as given add up to 10*l.* 0*s.* 0*d.* more than the given total; the latter agrees with the (correct) credit total. Among the debits, though, are two largeish cash payments, and either may have been transcribed or printed with one *x* too many in the *livres* — only a sight of the MS. would confirm or deny this. Similar errors, of 10*s.* 0*d.* and of 1*s.* 0*d.*, occur in the Druggets Account (page 65v.); again, without seeing the Ms. one does not know whose errors they are.[5] Also there are two entries which seem to be one-sided, but may not be — a credit to Gilles Vacquier (page 65r.) of 10*s.* 0*d.* for an allowance on a horse, referenced to Current Expenses and probably debited in the Expenses Ledger; and a credit to Expenses of Eating and Drinking (page 83r.) of 1*l.* 12*s.* 0*d.* for flour and salt meat on hand at the balancing date and not, it seems, transferred elsewhere. With these doubtful exceptions, then, the ledger as we have it can be balanced precisely; even if they are errors, there must have been others exactly offsetting them in total, which cannot now be investigated.

Conclusion

On any showing, the bookkeeping system of Giovanni Farolfi & Company for the Salon branch in 1299-1300 is a most remarkable achievement for its time. Within the conventions of the traditional Tuscan paragraph format of accounts, long favoured as being more economical of writing material than the Venetian-Genoese two-sided presentation *(a sezioni contrapposte),* Amatino Manucci has managed to construct a comprehensive and fully-articulated set of double-entry records, with a regular balancing procedure on closure of the General Ledger, marred only by a few human errors. Nor was the aspect of financial control neglected. The books were logically subdivided, with segregation of cash and goods accounts from the main ledger, a perpetual inventory of each line of agricultural produce and each grade of cloth or yarn dealt in, and full records of debtors and creditors, expenses, profits, interest and partners' drawings, as well as the state of account with the head office at Nîmes, and an estimate (15 per cent per annum) of the expected rate of return on capital employed. Perhaps it was these aspects that most concerned the partners, and the balance of the ledger was of secondary importance; if it agreed within a reasonable tolerance, it was accepted.

To the author's mind, the doubts expressed by Melis, Castellani, Raymond de Roover, and Vlaemminck have been cleared up, and double entry bookkeeping stands revealed as a product of 1300 at latest, rather than 1340. The mystery remains as to how, and on what models, Amatino evolved his system, and as to why it was not adopted in full rigour by other Florentine firms before the second half of the 14th century. Yet it is clear, on the evidence, that the Farolfi ledger stands in the line of succession that leads on from the untidy, but surprisingly sophisticated, bank ledger of 1211, and that the basic ideas of rational accounting, painfully worked out in the 13th century, came together and were fully integrated into that matrix of information which we know as double entry. In short, the books of Giovanni Farolfi & Company are established as one of the major monuments of early accounting history, and Amatino Manucci as surely a strong candidate for any future International Accounting Hall of Fame.

FOOTNOTES

[1]*Dictionnaire d'histoire et de géographie ecclésiastiques: Tome 4,* art. *Arles* (Paris, 1930). No particulars are given beyond the name and dates.

[2]Only Pagno and Bacchera are otherwise known, from the books of the Gianfigliazzi Company in Dauphiné and Provence, 1320-25 (see bibliography, items 1 and 5).

[3]"Son of the Florentine woman"—perhaps illegitimate.

[4]Letters to the author from Mm. G. Giordanengo, editor of *Provence historique*, and R. H. Bautier, author (with J. Sornay) of *Les sources de l'histoire économique et sociale du moyen âge* (Paris, from 1968). Tome 1: *Provence, etc.* refers to the Farolfi ledger, but gives no additional information. The archives of Salon do not go back to 1300.

[5]The author has discovered a similar error (*libbre ii* printed as *libbre li*) in P. Santini's transcript of the 1211 bank ledger fragments (see refs. 2, 8 and 9). It had been unnoticed by two later editors of the Italian text.

BIBLIOGRAPHY

1. Arrigo Castellani, *Nuovi testi fiorentini del Dugento e dei primi del Trecento* (*2 tomi*, Firenze, 1952). The ledger of Giovanni Farolfi & Company, 1299-1300, is transcribed, almost entire, at *Tome 2*, pp. 708-803; that of Renieri Fini de' Benzi & Brothers, 1296-1305 (as far as 1300 only) at *Tome 2*, pp. 674-696.
2. Pietro Santini, "Frammenti di un libro di banchieri fiorentini scritto in volgare nel 1211", *Giornale storico della litteratura italiana*, Vol. X (1887), pp. 161-177.
3. Federigo Melis, *Storia della ragioneria* (Bologna, 1950).
4. Federigo Melis, *Documenti per la storia economica dei secoli XIII-XVI* (Firenze, 1972).
5. Raymond de Roover, "The Development of Accounting Prior to Luca Pacioli According to the Account-Books of Medieval Merchants", in A. C. Littleton and B. S. Yamey (editors), *Studies in the History of Accounting* (London, 1956).
6. Joseph-H. Vlaemminck, *Histoire et doctrines de la comptabilité* (Bruxelles, 1956).
7. Edward Peragallo, *Origin and Evolution of Double Entry Bookkeeping* (New York, 1938).
8. Geoffrey Alan Lee, "The Oldest European Account Book: A Florentine Bank Ledger of 1211", *Nottingham Medieval Studies*, Vol. XVI, 1972.
9. Geoffrey Alan Lee, "The Florentine Bank Ledger Fragments of 1211: Some New Insights", *Journal of Accounting Research*, Vol. 11, No. 1, Spring 1973.
10. Geoffrey Alan Lee, "The Development of Italian Bookkeeping 1211-1300", *Abacus*, Vol. 9, No. 2, December 1973.
11. Edouard Baratier (directeur), *Histoire de la Provence* (Toulouse, 1969) (Chs. V-VII on medieval Provence, by E. Baratier).
12. Michelin (series editors), *Provence* (22e edition, Paris, 1971) (supplemented by personal observation in 1975).
13. Florence Edler (de Roover), *Glossary of Medieval Terms of Business, Italian Series, 1200-1600* (Cambridge, Mass., 1934).
14. C. Battisti and G. Alessio, *Dizionario etimologico italiano (5 tomi*, Firenze, 1950).
15. A. J. Greimas, *Dictionnaire de l'ancien français* (Paris, 1968).
16. Emil Lévy, *Petit dictionnaire provençal-français* (Heidelberg, 1909).

THE ACCOUNTING REVIEW
Vol LVII, No 2
April 1982

The Gallerani Account Book of 1305–1308

Christopher W. Nobes

ABSTRACT: This paper examines the account book of an Italian firm operating in London in the early 14th century. The existence of the book is well known to accounting historians, but it has not previously been carefully studied by them. The history of the firm and of the book are discussed, followed by an examination of the treatment of cash and non-cash entries and of opening and closing procedures. The presence of accounts for joint-ventures, petty cash, expenses, profit, and capital; the use of a single monetary unit; the consistent method of recording; and the achievement of balance at the end of an accounting period are features that may justify a claim that this account book was part of a double-entry system.

THIS paper discusses the *Libro dell'Entrata e dell'Escita* of the London branch of the Gallerani company between the years 1305 and 1308. It appears that it has not been considered in detail before by an accountant. The question of whether it represents double entry is considered. The Farolfi ledger, which may be the earliest extant example of double entry, is only six years older [Lee, 1977]. This research should be of interest to those who are not accounting historians because it deals with the period when bookkeeping was developing into the Italian fifteen century double-entry system which is still the basis of accounting throughout most of the world. Further, because it is not immediately clear whether this account book uses double entry, it raises interesting questions about the exact nature of the characteristics of double entry.

History of the "Libro"

This surviving book of "entry and exit," which is written in medieval Tuscan Italian, is akin to a journal. It is at present in Belgium where it arrived with Tommaso Fini, who was a member of the Gallerani company and also a Flanders agent of Robert of Béthune. It is not clear exactly when and why the Gallerani left London, but it *is* clear that foreign merchants and bankers were in danger from the King, Edward II. De Roover [1956, p. 126] refers to the records of the flight of the Frescobaldi partners from England to escape arrest in 1311–1312. But difficulties were not confined to England, and Fini had to leave "Belgium" hurriedly in 1309, whereupon the documents were confiscated by the Count of Flanders and thereby preserved. They may now be found in the State Archives

I am very grateful to R. H. Parker for prompting the work leading to this paper; to him, G. A. Lee, B. S. Yamey, and anonymous reviewers for their many helpful comments on earlier drafts; and to R. Bruni for help with translation.

Christopher W. Nobes is a Lecturer in Accountancy, University of Exeter.

Manuscript received June 1980.
Revision received July 1981.
Accepted July 1981

at Ghent.[1] There they were noticed in passing by P. de Decker[2] in 1844 and subsequently transcribed by Georges Bigwood, whose work was carried on after his death in 1930 by Armand Grunzweig. The latter completed the study and published a two-volume work [Bigwood, 1961 and 1962].

The Bigwood books contain much history of the Gallerani company and its international operations, and also deal with other early fourteenth century records which relate to their Paris branch. Bigwood's transcription work is obviously of great value. However, his readers should note that it is possible to detect some errors. There are a number of simple transcription errors where the Italian date in the entry is different from that in the margin.[3] In addition, it should be mentioned that the marginal dates are sometimes the dates of the entry and, at other times, the dates of the transaction. In the present writer's opinion, there is also misinterpretation of some entries.[4]

Bigwood [1962, p. 257] suggests that the *Libro* represents "*comptabilité en partie double.*" Martinelli [1974, p. 480] quotes Bigwood in translation and does not disagree with him. However, Bigwood was not an accountant, and there is no specific backing for the claim. He was relying on a discussion with and reading of Melis [1950, p. 474], who refers to the Gallerani papers as "*partita doppia senese in piena maturita.*"[5] However, de Roover [1956, p. 123], who was consistently more skeptical about such claims, comments[6] that "... a cursory examination led Professor Melis to the conclusion that the Gallerani unquestionably kept their books in double entry. This is possible, but by no means established without more careful study." It appears that no accountant has given the question "more careful study" in published form since the publication of the transcription. It is intended to do this here, after a brief digression on the London branch of the Gallerani.

THE GALLERANI IN EARLY 14TH CENTURY LONDON

The Gallerani, we are told [Bigwood, 1962, p. 5], was a Sienese merchant company of medium size. Its London branch was closely linked with that in Paris.[7] It borrowed and lent money; bought and sold horses, lead, gems, and other merchandise; and settled and collected debts relating to other branches. Most of the bookkeeping was carried out by a London partner called Biagio Aldobrandini, as the *Libro* records. It is not clear exactly where they did business, but they paid for premises at what they called "Valbrocco" (Walbrook, in the City of London) [Bigwood, 1952, p. 120].

At the beginning of the period of the *Libro*, England was ruled by Edward I (reigned 1272–1307). The Prince of Wales was the future Edward II (reigned 1307–1327) of considerable notoriety and unusually unpleasant demise, as historians and playwrights have recorded (e.g., Keen [1973]; Marlowe [1598]). Biagio went to the coronation of Edward II, as

[1] When Melis [1950, p. 475] wrote, the *Libro* was in Brussels. However, it has now returned to the Rijksarchief at Ghent, where I worked on it in May 1981.

[2] Cited in Bigwood [1962] as de Decker [1844].

[3] For example, entries 318–323, 377, 378, 394, and 395.

[4] See entry 402 quoted in text (*Dr.* fo.128 in *GL; Cr.* fo.57 in *LDC*). Bigwood thinks fo.57 in the *LDC* is a clothes account. However, why should this be *credited*? There must have been a credit to either "cash" or "Frescobaldi." I believe fo.57 contained the Frescobaldi account.

[5] "Fully developed Sienese double entry."

[6] De Roover's writing was published five years *before* the publication of the Bigwood transcription.

[7] For more details on the activities of the company and its organization, see Melis [1950, pp. 472–476] and Bigwood [1962].

entry 402[8] records:

402. (*escita*) £7.8.0d to expenses, to be given to the Frescobaldi for gold cloth and robes they bought for us for the King's coronation.

It is clear that the Gallerani dealt with the mighty: there are many entries concerning lords, knights, and cardinals. One of the characters who looms large in the history and drama relating to this period is Piers Gaveston, the favorite of Edward II. In the Gallerani records, there are two interesting entries dealing with "Piero di Ghavestona." Entry 400 notes that on August 4, 1306, Biagio spent 28 shillings and 6 pence sterling[9] on merchandise, including some for the said Piers Gaveston. More fascinating is entry 190:

190. (*entrata*) £8.13.4d charged to the Treasurer of the Prince (*LDC* fo.37) for a horse ("*sardo leardo*") received by Piers Gaveston [see 179 and 351 below].

The Nature of the "Libro"

The *Libro dell' Entrata e dell'Escita* (*LDE*) is a form of journal organized in two parts, as was Sienese custom [de Roover, 1956, pp. 122, 123, 127]. Each page has five or six entries which consist of narratives, amounts of money in sterling, and references to other books. Although the *Libro* is clearly related to a cash book and probably evolved from it, it would be misleading to call it by such a name, for many entries have no direct cash involvement. Folios 1–26 (including the *verso* in each case up to folio 25) contain entries concerning sterling receipts or the creation of sterling debits in some other way. At the end of each piece of narrative there is a folio reference to another book of account, the *Grande Libro*. This book is missing, as are all others apart from the *LDE* itself. However, in all cases, the reference for the credit entry is to this *Grande Libro*. Where cash is received there is no reference to an account to be debited (clearly this implies a debit to cash); where another account is to be debited because cash has not been received, there is a folio reference to a third type of book, the *Libro dei Conti*.

Then there are blank pages from 26 v^0 to 36 v^0. The second part of the *LDE* runs between folios 37 and 54. It contains sterling payments or the creation of other sterling credits. In each case there is a narrative, a reference to an account to be debited in the *Grande Libro*, and, where the transaction is other than a cash payment, a reference to an account in the *Libro dei Conti* to be credited.

The first half of the *Libro* (*entrata*, inflow) contains entries involving either *da* (i.e., received from) or *che dieno* (or *debeno*) *avere* (i.e., who should have or should be credited). The second half (*escita* or *uscita*, outflow) contains entries involving either *a* (i.e., payment to) or *che dieno dare* (i.e., who should give or should be debited).[10] In the case of non-cash entries, it is often unclear why the debit, rather than the credit, goes to the *Grande Libro*, that is, why the transaction is an *escita* rather than an *entrata*. Most accounts seem to have existed in both the *Grande Libro* and the *Libro dei Conti*.

[8] Entry numbers are those allocated by Bigwood [1961]. Narratives are the author's abbreviated translations.

[9] All of the entries are in sterling, and in the pounds (£), shillings (s), and pence (d) system adopted from the Romans, and only abandoned in England in 1971. In this case, there are 12 pence to one shilling, and 20 shillings to one pound.

[10] Similar expressions were noted by Lee [1973, p. 141] in a Florentine bank ledger of 1211.

Possibly, an attempt was made to put frequent transactions through the latter in order not to clutter the former. Alternatively, perhaps stricter security and secrecy were attached to the former.

The dates of the entries are a slight problem because, as mentioned above, some are the dates of transactions, and others are the dates of recording. Many dates are missing. The *LDE* does not follow strict chronological order, which is not unusual for "early" accounting. However, within any folio the order is mostly chronological, and the two halves of the *LDE* generally move forwards, starting from May 1305 and ending in October 1308, but with several exceptions.

As has been mentioned, the *Grande Libro* and the *Libro dei Conti* are missing. However, the accounts that they contained can be inferred from the many references to them in the *LDE*. Bigwood [1962, pp. 246–254] lists the accounts that must have been on the various folios in these two books. However, he omits a cash account which, judging by closing entries in the *LDE*, would have been on folio 30 of the *Grande Libro* (entry 427, see below). The accounts in the *Libro dei Conti* are transferred to the *Grande Libro* at the end of the period (entry 423, see below).

The first two entries in the *LDE* are balances brought forward at May 1, 1305 from the previous period. Entry 1 is the cash balance of £15.0s.10d; entry 2 is the excess of all other debit balances over all credit balances remaining in the previous period's *Libro dei Conti*, £109.4s.11d (detailed as the entries necessary to close the previous *Libro dei Conti*):

		Dr.	*Cr.*
1. (*entrata*) May 1, 1305	£15.0.10d. cash left on April 30, 1305.	(Cash)	From previous *LDC* via the *GL*.
2. (*entrata*) May 1, 1305	£109.4.11d. balance of the *Libro de' Conti* i.e. 224.17.6d to be collected and 115.12.7d to be given to others. [Thus, some entries would be the opposite of those shown on the right].	Various accounts in *LDC*.	From previous *LDC* via the *GL*.

Judging by the procedure of October 1308 (discussed below), the entries to close the previous *Libro dei Conti* had their counterparts in the *Grande Libro*. The entries are here reversed to open up the new *Libro dei Conti*. The *Grande Libro* had not been closed down. Its balance could have been used to determine profit and to draw up a balance sheet. Sadly, any evidence of either of these activities has not come to light.

Turning to the end of the period on October 31, 1308 and the end of the *LDE* (*escita* half), we have a closing cash balance of £34.1s.8d as entry 427, and a closing list of debit balances (mostly personal debtors) of £153.7s.1d as entry 423:

		Dr. in *GL*	*Cr.* in *LDC*
423 (*escita*) October 31, 1308	£153.7.1d, which amount remained in *LDC* on the last day of October 1308; written to the debit of accounts in the *GL* fos. 26 to 29.	fos.26–29	Various accounts in *LDC*.
427 (*escita*) October 31, 1308.	£34.1.8d. The closing cash balance held by Nicoluccio.	fo.30, Cash	Nicoluccio fo.59 in *LDC*.

Entry 423 is supported by a detailed schedule of 26 constituent balances which are to be transferred to accounts in the *Grande Libro*, which remains open.

Thus it might be hoped that, if the *Grande Libro* is to balance, then the total of the *entrata* half of the *LDE* (which creates credits in the *Grande Libro*) would be equal to the *escita* half (which creates debits). This is almost exactly the case, as will now be shown.

There is a memorandum at the end of the *LDE* written to Nicoluccio di Cante, a Paris partner, which gives totals: *Avere* (credits) £9481.8s.9d, *Resta* ("the other" or "the rest"?) £9477.16s.1d. Bigwood has noted some errors in the folio totals which help to account for the small difference above. The present writer, taking these and another I have found[11] into account, has totaled all the *entrata* entries (£9484.12s.8d) and all the *escita* entries (£9482.19s.1d.). A degree of error of this size seems more than acceptable over a three-and-a-half-year period, particularly as many of the entries were in cumbersome Roman numerals.

Some Special Cases

There are a few exceptions to the otherwise consistent use of the rules for the use of the *LDE* explained above. There are some non-cash *entrata* entries which create only a credit, but these are matched by *escita* entries of the same date which create only a debit.[12] This practice is especially common for the purchase of horses (a purchase: 179 and 351; the subsequent sale: 190):

		Dr.	Cr.
179. (*entrata*) June 5, 1306	£7.0.6d to be credited to Paris branch for 94.16.3d. *tournois* paid for a horse ("*sardo leardo*") bought by Biagio in Paris. Written to the horse account.		fo.102 in *GL*, Paris branch.
351. (*escita*)	£7.0.6d. debit a horse ("*sardo leardo*"), for 94.16.3d. *tournois* which Paris paid and Biagio bought from a Genoese. Credit to Paris.	fo. 24 in *GL*, Horse account.	
190. (*entrata*)	(see above)	fo.37 in *LDC*	fo.24 in *GL*.

Further, for the period June 1, 1306 to November 1, 1308, a joint venture for the trading of horses was run with the Frescobaldi company. The joint venture is set up by entry 377 and closed by entry 216:

		Dr.	Cr.
377. (*escita*)	£133.6.8d debited to the Horse Joint Venture with the Frescobaldi.	fo.25 in *GL*, Horse J-V.	J-V account, fo.39 in *LDC*.
216. (*entrata*) Nov. 1, 1308	£156.14.10d to our capital in the Horse Joint Venture, including £23.8.2d. of profit.	Capital account in *Libro dei Cavalli*, i.e. fo.2	fo.25 in *GL*, Horse J-V.

[11] There seems to be a mistake in entry 281 of October 8, 1305:

£0.18.0d to equipment; given to Bindo di Pari of Florence; and £0.2.0d more for other small things.

The 2s. was missed when the folio was totaled, and not noticed by Bigwood.

[12] Entries 20 and 249, for example.

The difference between purchase and sale prices is noted as profit.[13] It is fairly clear that the bookkeeper was initially uncertain about how to deal with the joint venture. There is a canceled entry on June 1, 1306 which mistakenly credited the Frescobaldi account in the *Grande Libro* with their contribution to the capital of the joint venture. Also, the opening entry credits an account in the *Libro dei Conti* rather than the capital account in the *Libro dei Cavalli*. This seems to have been altered by the date of the closing entry, 216.

Lastly, the penultimate and pre-penultimate entries of the *escita* half of the *LDE* are to debit the expense account in the *Grande Libro* for two petty cash accounts which have been running throughout the three-and-a-half-year period. These are the *dentro* (inside the office) and *fuore* (outside) petty cash accounts. These entries are necessary because transfers from cash to petty cash are not recorded in the *LDE* as they occur (as *Dr* Petty Cash; *Cr* Cash). Thus, at the end of the period, the closing entries are not (*Dr* Expenses; *Cr* Petty Cash) but (*Dr* Expenses; *Cr* Cash).

The Essentials of Double Entry

Before asking whether the London branch of the Gallerani was using double-entry bookkeeping in 1305, it is necessary to recognize some criteria for double entry against which to judge the Gallerani system as evidenced by the *LDE*. Here we are assisted by useful precedents set by Lee, de Roover, and Martinelli. Lee [1973, p. 154] notes that double entry requires that "there is (supposed to be) a debit for every credit, with full cross-references." In a later work, Lee [1977, pp. 85 and 90] suggests more detailed criteria, including the presence of concepts of accounting entity and proprietor's equity, the use of accounting periods and a single monetary unit, the calculation of profit and loss, and the periodic collection of balances to prove equality of debits and credits.

How well does the Gallerani accounting system measure up to these criteria? It is very clear that the Gallerani company was accounted for as an entity and that there was even a strict separation of the branches within the company.[14] For instance, there are many entries of debit or credit to the account of the Paris branch.[15] Lee's criterion of monetary homogeneity is also strictly respected. Although the narratives for many entries *refer* to other currencies, the actual entries are always recorded in sterling. For example, entry 116:

		Dr.	*Cr.*
116. (*entrata*)	£0.19.0d. to the credit of the Paris branch for 12.7.6d. *livres tournois* received by Nicoluccio and charged to his account in *LDC*.	Nicoluccio's account, fo.6 in *LDC*.	fo.100 *in GL*, Paris Branch.

It is apparent from the entries in the *LDE* that the London partners, including Aldobrandini, had capital accounts. Sadly, it is not possible to tell what they contained or how the profits were split up. Nevertheless, there were accounts for profits, interest, and other expenses. For example, entries 87 and 166;

[13] Profits of about 23 per percent for the single horse, and 18 percent for the joint venture.

[14] Melis [1950, p. 475] says: "Hence, such branches had an autonomous bookkeeping system, which must have included some accounts linking up with the central office bookkeeping."

[15] Entries 116 and 179, for example.

		Dr.	*Cr.* in *GL*
87. (*entrata*) Nov. 9, 1305	£3.18.6d to the "bay horse" account. The amount has been written to the lead expenses in the *LDC* (fo.8) because the horse has become lame.[16] It has been given to God [charity?]	Expenses of lead account, fo.8 in *LDC*.	fo.10, horse account.
166. (*entrata*) August 29, 1306	£0.12.0d to profit, gained on the purchase and sale of gold doubloons.	(Cash)	fo.120, profit.

There also appears to be a regard for accounting periods: the *LDE* runs for exactly three-and-a-half years. It could be argued that this period was merely the term set for the partnership or the stint of the bookkeeper. However, even if periodicity cannot be read into this one account book, the importance of periodicity as a prerequisite for double entry might well be questioned. Surely it is more telling that, at a point in time, there are closing entries, and the balances are collected together to prove equality of debits and credits.

De Roover [1956, p. 125] would require each transaction to be recorded twice, and the existence of accounts for expenses and operating results. It has been shown that the *LDE* creates two entries for each transaction: one for the *Grande Libro* and usually one for the *Libro dei Conti*. For cash amounts, it is presumably the physical existence of the cash which acts as the record of the other entry. An actual counterpart entry is created at the end of periods when the cash is counted to establish a closing entry to the *Grande Libro*. At the same time, the *Libro dei Conti* is closed down and a total balance in the *Grande Libro* is achieved at the end of the period. It is possible that there was a separate cash book, but this seems unlikely as the *LDE* itself looks so much like a cash book which has just been adapted to include non-cash entries. As for de Roover's other point, it has been shown that there were accounts for expenses and profit.

Martinelli [1977, p. 11] would look for "the presence of two complete sets of antithetical accounts,[17] constant reference for each entry to its cross-entry, and constant application of the same monetary unit." These requirements seem to be satisfied, except for the criterion about cross-references (also mentioned by Lee, above). It is not possible to be sure on this point because of the absence of the *Grande Libro* and the *Libro dei Conti*. However, there are full references in the *LDE*.

Conclusion

The *Libro dell'Entrata e dell'Escita* (*LDE*) of the London branch of the Gallerani from 1305 to 1308 was written in Italian, using typically Tuscan expressions and with a characteristically Sienese format. Beacuse of the clear evidence for the creation of double entries, and because the two halves of the *LDE* are in almost exact balance, it seems that this bookkeeping contained, at the least, substantial elements of double entry. Incidentally, if this view is accepted, then these records represent the earliest extant accounting records using a form of double entry in the British Isles. However, as the Gallerani in London was a (short-lived) branch of a foreign firm, there is no suggestion that indigenous English records were kept in this advanced way either during or following its presence.

[16] Presumably, the lead expense account is debited because the horse became lame as a result of carrying too much of this heavy metal.

[17] It is supposed that Martinelli means "two complete sets of antithetical entries."

REFERENCES

Bigwood, G. (ed. A. Grunzweig) (1961), *Les Livres des Comptes des Gallerani, Book I* (the transcription) (Commission Royale d'Histoire, Brussels, 1961).

———, (ed. A. Grunzweig) (1962), *Les Livres des Comptes des Gallerani, Book II* (the commentary) (Commission Royale d'Histoire, Brussels, 1962).

de Decker, P. (1844), *Etudes historiques et critiques sur les Monts de Piété* (The Author, Brussels, 1844).

de Roover, R. (1956), "The Development of Accounting Prior to Luca Pacioli According to The Account-books of Medieval Merchants," in A. C. Littleton and B. S. Yamey, eds., *Studies in the History of Accounting* (Irwin, 1956; reprinted in 1978 by Arno Press), pp. 114–174.

Keen, M. H. (1973), *England in the Later Middle Ages* (Methuen, 1973).

Lee, G. A. (1973), "The Development of Italian Bookkeeping, 1211–1300," *Abacus* (December 1973), pp. 137–155.

——— (1977), "The Coming of Age of Double Entry: The Giovanni Farolfi Ledger of 1299–1300," *The Accounting Historians Journal* (Fall 1977), pp. 79–95.

Marlowe, C. (1598), *The Troublesome Raigne and Lamentable Death of Edward the Second* (London, 1598).

Martinelli, A. (1974), "The Origination and Evolution of Double Entry Bookkeeping to 1440" (unpublished doctoral thesis. University Microfilms, Ann Arbor, Mich., 1974).

——— (1977), "Notes on the Origin of Double Entry Bookkeeping," *Abacus* (June 1977), pp. 3–27.

Melis, F. (1950), *Storia della Ragioneria* (Zuffi, Bologna, 1950).

THE ACCOUNTING REVIEW
Vol. LII, No 4
October 1977

The Ledger of Jachomo Badoer: Constantinople September 2, 1436 to February 26, 1440

Edward Peragallo

ABSTRACT: The ledger of Jachomo Badoer is the only commercial document written entirely in Constantinople that has survived, in its entirety, the Turkish conquest of that city. It is a precious source of data relevant to the intense economic activities and Byzantine commerce of that era. It furnishes us with varied information on wares exchanged, their prices and marketing practices, the monetary currencies circulating in the Levant, their purchasing power and the rates of exchange, which were continuously fluctuating. It also vividly portrays the stage of development of the art of bookkeeping, which was in a fluid state. Badoer, himself, was an experimenter and innovator of new ideas in bookkeeping. The first evidence of a compound entry that has so far surfaced is found in his ledger.

THE ledger of Jachomo Badoer is a rare document, for in the holocaust that followed the fall of Constantinople to Turkish forces in 1453 few records of the Byzantine commerce survived, none in their entirety. Badoer's ledger is the only record written entirely in Constantinople that has reached us, and it throws a narrow but vivid light on the intense activities of the economic life of the Levant. It is for this reason that the Badoer ledger is of inestimable value to the history, both economic and accounting, of the Levant during the first half of the 15th century [Dorini and Bertelè, 1956].

Little is known about Badoer. He is described as a typical merchant of the Venetian nobility, not of the first rank, but nevertheless important and representative of the Venetian maritime mercantile scene at the beginning of the 15th century [Astuti, 1968–69]. His ledger reveals that he is married and has children, that he is a man of considerable wealth and that, in partnership with his brother Jeronimo, he invested a considerable portion of his capital in a commercial venture in Constantinople where he will spend more than 3 years trading for his own account and for the account of others, and that he is a man accustomed to a comfortable standard of living. His personal expense account on L.F.41 shows that he brought an apprentice with him from Venice. Merchants of Badoer's calibre and stature usually were assisted by apprentices from patrician families, who sought such positions to learn about foreign trade and to engage in mercantile practices under the guidance of their employer [Astuti, 1968–69, p. 84]. Badoer also brought a horse with the necessary feed and straw and he acquired a second horse within 2 months of his arrival in Constantinople. Curi-

Edward Peragallo is Professor of Accounting and Economics at College of the Holy Cross, Worcester, Massachusetts.

ously, he also brought 210 cantars[1] [Edler, 1934, p. 59] of wood from Venice. The account also indicates that he rented a villa in the suburbs of Pera, an important Genoese colony on the coast of the gulf of the Golden Horn not far from Constantinople, where he would vacation and rest to recuperate from the grind of trading on the Byzantine market. The account further shows that he furnished and appointed the house in a very comfortable fashion and that he acquired a young slave girl to manage the household. Occasionally Badoer, would entertain friends at his villa and, in one instance, he lists separately the expenses of a particularly sumptuous banquet he had given during the carnival of 1437 with musical entertainment for his guests. One of the more unusual expenses he incurred towards the end of his stay in Constantinople was for a gold toothpick.

Jachomo Badoer landed in Constantinople at noon on September 2, 1436, with a valuable cargo of merchandise on a fleet of four galleys captained by Piero Contarini. The cargo was partly for his own account and partly for the account of resident merchants of the Venetian nobility for whom Badoer acted as agent. Among his consignors were important people such as Piero Soranzo of the Soranzo Brothers, the Contarini family, of whom Piero was the fleet captain, and Dardi Moro, each of whom financed a galley bearing the family name.

The voyage began on July 24, 1436, with stops at Pola, one of the ports mentioned in the ledger and at ports of call along the Dalmation coast and in the Aegean Sea, and certainly at Modon or Coron, which were considered to be the "two eyes of the Republic [Lane, 1973, p. 242] where all ships were required to stop to supply and receive information pertinent to their trip. The fleet belonged to the group known as the Galleys of Romania which traded at Constantinople and at the Venetian colonies at Tana, Sinope and Trebizond on the Black Sea.

Venetian trade encompassed all of the Mediterrean basin, the Black Sea, England and the Netherlands. The trade was controlled closely by the Venetian government, which assigned galley fleets to the various trade routes covering the area. The galleys were armed and often accompanied by warships. The Levant trade was important to Venice for its spices, raw silk and silk fabrics from Constantinople, dyes, incense, sugar, raisins, furs and slaves from the Black Sea area, cotton and many other products [Lane, 1973, pp. 69, 78].

Venice at this juncture in her history enjoyed a lively prosperity. She still benefited from the defeat she had inflicted on her chief commercial rival, Genoa, in a naval battle at Chioggia. She had re-established her rule over Dalmatia, and her colonial empire appeared secured and intact. She was the active center of trade between the East and the West, and her profits were great. Venice, nevertheless, was approaching the end of an era. With the imminent fall of Constantinople a mere decade away and with the trade routes shifting to the Atlantic, her commerce and her sources of income would decline and her end would be inevitable.

All this, naturally, was still in the future when Badoer undertook his voyage. Upon reaching Constantinople Badoer lost no time in attending to his affairs. The first week was devoted to the delivery of bills of exchange (*lettere di cambio*) which he had brought from Venice and to the unloading of his wares from the galleys.

Two such bills, a total of 400 ducats,

[1] Cantar, a unit of weight, usually 100 *ruotoli*, but varying from 100 to 750 lbs. in different Mediterranean countries. (In Badoer's ledger, the cantar is 150 lbs.)

were drawn by Piero Soranzo in favor of Jachomo Marzelo, payment to be made by Badoer. To follow this transaction through Badoer's ledger, a brief explanation of his accounting system seems appropriate.

The Accounting System

Badoer used only one ledger with no formal journal, though memorandum journals for a variety of expenditures were used. Each ledger entry comprised only one debit and one credit. Transactions involving more than two elements would require a number of entries until fully recorded. The ledger format did not lend itself readily to compound entries. Each entry was in paragraph form with a rough money column in the right-hand margin. Debits were recorded on the left-hand page and credits on the facing page. The first few words or sentence of the first entry of each account, both on the debit side and on the credit side, identified the account; this would be repeated, regardless of length, when posting the second part of a transaction, debit or credit, to the other account. This was necessary for identification purposes, because ledger entries were cross-indexed, not by accounts, but by ledger folios.

Badoer's ledger was chiefly of the receivable and payable type. This served Badoer's purposes very well. His affairs dealt with the interests of resident Venetian merchants, and the debtor and creditor relationships that evolved were of paramount importance to him. The more complete double-entry system with journal and ledger, then in current use in Venice as evidenced by the Soranzos' and the Barbarigo's records (Archivio di stato di Venezia), was not needed. The tracing of Soranzo's two bills of exchange in Badoer's ledger should clarify this point further.

Bills of Exchange and Currency

The two bills, one of 250 ducats and the other of 150 ducats convertible at 3 perperi 8½ carati and at 3 perperi 9 carati, respectively, per ducat totaling 1344 perperi 19 carati, are posted to Piero Soranzo's account as a Badoer receivable. The credit is posted to Jachomo Marzelo's account on L.F.2 (Figure 1) as a Badoer payable. Jachomo Marzelo, it develops, owes Felipo Marzelo, who is not related and who resides in Venice, 900 perperi. Badoer, therefore, transfers the liability of 900 perperi to Felipo Marzelo's account on L.F.2. The balance owing Jachomo Marzelo of 444 perperi 19 carati is then settled by Badoer authorizing a transfer of bank funds to Jachomo's account on the books of the banker Chaloiani Suffiano. Badoer's liability of 900 perperi to Felipo Marzelo is settled by drawing a bill of exchange on Piero Soranzo for 300 gold ducats payable in Venice to Felipo Marzelo at the conversion rate of 3 perperi per gold ducat, and it is to be delivered by the galleys captained by Piero Contarini. Badoer, therefore, closes Felipo Marzelo's account and credits Piero Soranzo for 900 perperi.[2]

Piero Soranzo, obviously, did not provide Badoer with immediate funds to honor the two bills. His liability to Badoer was partially offset by the bill of 900 perperi drawn on him and payable in Venice to Jachomo Marzelo's creditor, Felipo Marzelo. Soranzo eventually paid the balance of his debt to Badoer with funds from the sale of goods which he had consigned to him.

[2] Byzantine currency, composed of perperi, carati and occasionally duchatelli, is used throughout the ledger There are 24 carati to a perpero and 1½ duchatelli to a carato. There is, however, the constant problem of money conversion with Venetian ducats and with Turkish asperi. Badoer was kept informed about market rates of exchange, as determined at the Rialto in Vinice, by frequent correspondence from Venice, as the account "Bill drafted for Venice" on *L.F.27* clearly shows.

FIGURE 1

SORANZO AND RELATED LEDGER ACCOUNTS

L. F 1 1436

Mr Piero Soranzo son of Mr Antonio debit 3rd day September for 2 bills of exchange payable to Mr Jachomo Marzelo son of Christofalo, one of duc 250 at perp 3 car 8½ per ducat, the other of duc 150 at perp 3 car 9 per ducat,
total.... ....L.2 perp 1344 car 19

On ditto date for Mr Nicholó Justignan son of Mr Andrea for a bill of exchange of 200 ducats payable to him at perp. 3 car. 9 per ducat,
total.......... ... .L 2 perp 675 car 0

On ditto date commission for myself Jachomo Badoer of one percent on the payment of the above bills, no commission on the money conversion was charged
...........................L.4 perp 20 car 5

10th day October for expenses incurred at the unloading and warehousing of 80 steel vessels for Soranzo's account, the ownership of which was contested in the court of the *bailo*, Mr. Christofal Marzelo, who ordered that they be consigned to Mr Marin Zen son of Mr. Jachomo,
total........................L.8 perp. 9 car. 14

14 day November for silk *zagora* from Soranzo's account for the cost of 8 pieces of silk cloth including expenses and loaded on the captain's galley of Mr Piero Chontarini,
total........................L.34 perp 424 car 3

Total perp. 2473 car. 14[a]

(a) Should be car. 17

Mr. Piero Soranzo son of Mr. Antonio debit 13th day of December for the balance forwarded from above and as shown in a statement sent via Modon by the ship of Todaro Vatazi,
total.......................L.1 perp. 286 car. 18

1436 L F 1

Mr Piero Soranzo credit 5th day September for a bill of exchange of 300 gold ducats payment to be made in Venice to Mr Felipo Marzelo son of Mr Fantin, bill to be sent by the galleys captained by Mr Piero Chontarini at perp 3 per gold ducat according to his order
L 2 perp 900 car 0

16th day October debit 12 tin vessels for his account for the net balance of that account, the funds to be drawn
L 8 perp 794 car 0

18th day ditto crisp netting for his account, net balance forwarded
L 8 perp 492 car 20

13th day December balance of this account forwarded to the account below, the balance agrees with the statement received this day via Modon by ship of Todaro Vatazi . . . . ..L 1 perp 286 car 18

Total perp. 2473 car 14

L.F.2 1436

Mr. Jachomo Marzelo son of Mr. Christofalo debit 4th day September for part of the exchange per contra which he promised to pay Mr. Felip Marzelo son of Mr. Fantin in my name.
L.2 perp. 900 car. 0

5th day ditto for Chaloiani Sufiano banker, for a bank transfer I authorized to his account in Chaloiani's bank for the balance.
L.3 perp. 444 car 19

Total...

Mr. Felipo Marzelo son of Mr. Fantin debit 5th day September for Mr. Piero Soranzo son of Mr. Antonio, for a bill of exchange of 300 ducats payment to be made in Venice to the above Felipo by Piero at perp. 3 per ducat...................L.1 perp. 900 car. 0

Total...

1436 L.F.2

Mr. Jachomo Marzelo credit 3rd day of September for 2 bills of exchange from Piero Soranzo of 400 ducats amounting to perp. 1344 car. 19, which I agreed to pay
...........................L.1 perp. 1344 car. 19

Total...

Mr. Felipo Marzelo credit 4th day of September for what Mr Jachomo Marzelo promised him in my name
L.2 perp. 900 car. 0

Total

L.F.3 1436

Chaloiani Sufiano banker debit 5th day September for funds collected from Mr. Felipo Chontarini, which were deposited in my name in Chaloiani's bank in accordance with Mr. Dardi Moro's instructions.
L. 2 perp. 1000 car 0

Etc.

1436 L F 3

Chaloiani per contra credit 5th day of September for Mr Jachomo Marzelo son of Mr. Christofalo for the balance of the bill of exchange
L d perp 444 car 19

Etc.

These transactions attest to the widespread use of the bill of exchange in Renaissance finance. Its primary purpose was to facilitate the transfer of funds between resident merchants and their agents without the risks of shipping bullion or other assets. It also served as a borrowing medium [Lane, 1973, p. 141], as Piero Soranzo's two bills indicate. There is no evidence in the Soranzo's account on L.F.1 (Figure 1) of an interest payment, though Badoer does charge a commission of one percent for honoring these bills. No charge was made for the money conversion. It should be noted that interest was not a hidden factor in the exchange rates, a practice common in Renaissance finance to avoid Church strictures for violating Church doctrine on usury. The Venetians openly differed with this doctrine. They saw nothing wrong in borrowing money at interest and it was considered nonusurious if it was determined by market conditions. The ". . . Venetian courts enforced collection (of contracts) so long as the rate of interest was moderate, 5 to 8 percent" [Lane, 1973, p. 146].

To honor Soranzo's bills of exchange, Badoer needed an account with a local banker. Dardi Moro supplied 1000 perperi by means of a bill of exchange drawn on Felipo Contarini, who in turn authorized a transfer to an account in Badoer's name on the books of the banker Chaloiani Suffiano. This was in accordance with Dardi Moro's instructions as shown in the account on L.F.3 (Figure 1).

Byzantine banking certainly was organized along the same lines as Venetian banking. Its primary function was not a bank loan, but a bank transfer (*scritta di banco*) [Edler, 1934, p. 265] made on behalf of depositors, who personally presented themselves to authorize transfer to creditor accounts. Checks were not used. In Venice, bankers, of whom there were four or five, maintained booths on the campo at the Rialto with their journals recording bank transfers as instructed by their clients [Lane, 1973, 147]. In Constantinople, Badoer had accounts with at least four bankers, who undoubtedly maintained their stalls in the market place in the Venetian quarters. Badoer appears to allude to the market as the *Bursa*.

The two credit instruments, the bill of exchange (*lettera di cambio*) and the bank transfer (*scritta di banco*), served the interests of the Renaissance merchant very well. The one took care of fund transfers between merchants residing in different localities and the other of fund transfers within a local market.

Unloading of Wares at Constantinople

Badoer's financial investment in the wares unloaded from the four galleys was substantial. Fully half of the merchandise was either for his own account or in partnership with another merchant. One of his first tasks was to defray initial merchandising expenditures (*spexe de merchadantia*), which included a customs duty of one percent payable to the '*bailo*' (*chomerchio del nostro bailo una per c.*). The bailo was an appointed government representative of considerable importance. He was considered to be the governor of the Venetian colony, its commercial consul and ambassador to the reigning emperor [Lane, 1973, p. 100]. He was also the presiding judge in his court for settling disputes between merchants. Such a dispute did, in fact, arise between Piero Soranzo and Marin Zen, which was resolved in the bailo's court in favor of the latter (Figure 1). The levying of the customs duty required a valuation of the merchandise. Badoer reached an agreement with the bailo's representative and recorded it as a memorandum notation on the debit side of the bailo's customs payable account on L.F.19 (Figure 2). The memorandum notation, it should be observed, was also an inventory of the merchandise that was unloaded and was valued at the prevailing market prices. The total valuation was 17816 perperi, and the account shows that a duty of 177 perperi was paid. The allocation of this expenditure to the various consignment accounts is recorded on the credit side of the account. Customs duties at Venice and at overseas destinations were controlled closely by the state [Lane, 1973, p. 340].

Consignments

The merchandise is recorded in consignments accounts. The accounting does not differ basically from modern practice, but there are differences which, perhaps, should be explained. The following consignment of "woolen cloth *bresani* for the account of Antonio Chontarini and Badoer" (Figure 3) should suffice.

A detailed description of twenty-five pieces of regulation size woolen cloth is first given, followed by the listing of merchandising expenditures, which include all expenditures to the point of sale. The expenditures for unloading and for delivery to warehouse are therefore recorded as of September 4, but the expenditures related to sales, which include delivery from warehouse to master Piero's shop, pic measuring and taring, warehousing and brokerage, are not recorded until the cloth is finally sold or disposed of in some other fashion, which, in this case, involved a period of 13 months. At this time, the total of 29 perperi 21 carati finally is credited to the merchandising expense account. These expenditures are all cash payments and Badoer records them in a memorandum journal as they occur and periodically posts them in total as a debit to the merchandising account and as a credit to cash. Therefore the merchandising expense account does not reflect liabilities.

FIGURE 2

CUSTOMS PAYABLE ACCOUNT (debit)

L.F.19 (debit) 1436

Customs at one percent payable to the *bailo* debit October 17 for cash payment to Mr. Lion for customs duty on merchandise unloaded from the galleys captained by Mr. Piero Chontarini, the value of which totals perperi 17816 as was agreed with Mr. Lion. The merchandise included:

—for tinware of about 75 cantars at perp. 26 per cantar	perp. 1898
—for 4 scarlet pieces of woolen cloth from Milan for the account of Mr. Piero Michiel	perp. 600
—for 40 green pieces of woolen cloth for the acount of Mr. Piero Michiel and Mr. Marin Barbo, valued	perp. 2800
—for one piece of woolen cloth imitation *vervi* for Mr. Piero Michiel	perp. 30
—for 10 scarlet pieces of woolen cloth from Mantoa for Mr. Piero Soranzo, valued	perp. 1000
—for 40 small boxes of crisp netting at perp. 50 per box	perp. 2000
—for 2 plain velvets and one satin and two gold satin brocades from Chologna for the account of Mr. Jachomo Bernabó valued in total	perp. 1266
—for 8 pieces of woolen cloth Fiorenza for my account	perp. 1040
—for 7 pieces of woolen cloth '60' from Mantoa for my account, valued	perp. 420
—for 60½ pieces of woolen cloth *loesti* at car. 22 per pic, with 50 pics per piece	perp. 2662
—for 25 pieces of woolen cloth *bresani* for the account of Mr. Antonio Chontarini and myself, valued	perp. 1250
—for 105 bundles of gold filaments for my account, but only 91 bundles were found, valued	perp. 800
—for 16 pieces of woolen cloth Fiorenza for the account of Marcho and Lunardo Justignano valued at perp. 150 per piece, total	perp. 2400
I made this entry to note that I was in accord with Mr. Lion	car. 1
30 October cash paid to Mr. Lion in part payment	perp. 100 car. 0
14 March 1437 cash payment to Mr. Lion for the balance due for customs on all merchandise unloaded from the galleys captained by Mr. Piero Chontarini	perp. 77 car. 0

FIGURE 3

CONSIGNMENT ACCOUNT

L F 11 1436

Woolen cloth *bresani* consisting of 25 pieces, for the account of Mr Antonio Chontarini, son of Mr Marin, and for myself, these are 3 scarlet, 9 azure, 7 gray-blues, 3 sky-blue, 3 medium gray, braza 1124 (†) q 3 (††) which were received from the galleys captained by Mr. Piero Chontarini, debit this 4th day of September for merchandising expenditures incurred at the unloading: for customs receipt and barge

....		perp 0 car 6
—for delivery to warehouse at duchatelli 4 per bale........		perp 0 car 18
—for delivery from warehouse to Piero's shop for measuring.		perp 0 car 9
—for pic (†††) measuring and taring		perp. 1 car 12
—for brokerage at perp j per piece		perp. 24 car. 0
—for warehousing at perp j per bale........................		perp. 3 car 0
Sum total..............	L 78	perp. 29 car 21
and for bailo's customs at j per c., valued at perp. 50 per piece	L.19	perp. 12 car. 12
and my sales commission at 2 per c........................	L.77	perp 24 car 0
On 19 October for Mr. Antonio Chontarini for one-half of the net balance................	L.47	perp. 574 car 12
On ditto date for one-half of the net balance................	L.6	perp. 574 car. 12

Total perp. 1215 car. 9

1436 L.F 11

Woolen cloth per contra credit this 20th day of September for the sale of 24 pieces of woolen cloth to Mr. Zorzi Chunba at perp. 51 per piece, totals perp. 1224, discount for shortage of 42 pics (††††) perp. 39 car. 16, and for an additional adjustment of car 9 per piece amounting to perp. 9 car. 0, net balance at payment, terms at the ships, broker Zorzi Chumano de Chandia L. perp. 1175 car. 8

On 19 October, 1437, for Mr Antonio Chontarini for one-half of one sky-blue woolen cloth divided between us, because it could not be sold, we priced provisionally at perp. 40 for the cloth...... L.47 perp. 20 car. 0

On ditto date for woolen cloth taken for myself Jachomo Badoer for the other half of the cloth .... L.11 perp. 20 car. 0

Total perp. 1215 car. 8

† Edler, 1934, p. 52. See 'braccio.' 'Braza' is braccio, a cloth measure of an arm's length, about ¾ of an English yard.

†† Dorini, 1956, preface p. XIII. 'q' is the equivalent of a quarter. Badoer also uses fractions, therefore 'q.3' stands for ¾. Badoer does not use decimals.

††† Edler, 1934, p. 213. See 'picco.' Pic, a cloth measure used in the Levant and is approximately equivalent to one Venetian braccio.

†††† Dorini, 1956, L.F.27. In Jael's account debit, Badoer gives sufficient data to determine that the regulation size of one piece of cloth is 54 pics.

It is merely a convenient device for recording expenditures to consignment accounts which involve significant time lags and the cash payment of these expenditures as they occur.

The bailo's customs duties are treated differently. These are payable periodically and a liability account (*Chomerchio del nostro bailo*, L.F.19), therefore, is necessary. For this reason, even though the customs tax is an unloading cost, it is not included in the merchandising expenditures.

The credits are rather straightforward. Twenty-four pieces of cloth are sold quickly at 51 perperi per piece; allowances are made for cloth shortages and other adjustments; the net balance is payable with credit terms to the arrival of the next ships (*termine a le nave*) and, of course, the broker is named. Badoer grants a variety of credit terms from one month (L.F.13) to one year or more (L.F.9), but the majority are directly related to the arrival or departure of ships, depending on the circumstances.

The one oddity is the disposal of the one remaining piece of woolen cloth. Since it could not be sold, it was decided, after 13 months, to divide it equally among themselves and it was valued at an arbitrary price of 40 perperi.

With the conclusion of this consignment, Badoer records his own commission of 2 percent of sales as agent and finally the net balance is allocated equally between Antonio Chontarini and himself. Badoer enters Chontarini's share in a liability account and his own share in his capital account on L.F.6.

Collection Services on Behalf of Clients

An important service which Badoer performed for his clients was as collector of delinquent accounts. Franzesco Zorzi, a client, assigned four such accounts to Badoer, who opened an account on L.F.37 with credits to "Debtors for the account of Mr. Franzesco Zorzi for his old account balances, . . . " and opened four account receivables for the delinquent debtors. The Debtors account was charged with all legal, notary and other collection expenditures. After repeated attempts, three accounts proved uncollectible, and they were simply written off by charging the Debtors account and crediting the delinquent receivables.

Badoer was successful in collecting one account in full. The debtor paid with a delivery of merchandise and cash for the balance, which were credited to his account. Cash and a new account for the merchandise were debited. Finally, Badoer charged his client a commission on collections and transferred the credit balance of the Debtors account to another account of his client as a liability, which eventually was satisfied with a delivery of merchandise for shipment to Venice.

Ventures for Badoer's Own Account:—Wares

A major interest of Badoer was trading in wares for his own account. Half of the merchandise he brought from Venice was his own or held in partnership with another merchant. The merchandise was quickly bartered or sold and the accounts, where partners were involved, were settled and the proceeds allocated. Whatever funds he was able to raise in this fashion and as a result of extensive trading in the Levant, in addition to his commissions and his other fees, he used to purchase merchandise for shipment back to Venice. His brother Jeronimo attended to the task of disposing of them in the Venetian market and periodically reported the results to his brother Jachomo.

Badoer recorded these transactions in a "Venetian Voyage" (*Viazo da Veniexia*) account. The term '*Viazo*' is not original with Badoer. It had been used for many years by merchants in maritime cities. A more appropriate term, perhaps, would be shipment or venture account [Lane, 1967, pp. 164–166].

The wares that Badoer shipped to Venice were varied. The most important were spices, which included cloves, ginger and pepper. Important also were incense, silk, leather, wool-fell, soiled wool and washed wool. Badoer also traded in slaves. The first such entry in the viazo account refers to a Turkish girl (*sciava tartara*) of about 20 years of age, darkskinned, with a scalded hand, named Madalena. She cost Badoer 102 perperi, including cost of boarding ship. The posting was made from a slave account titled "Heads for my account" (*Teste de mia raxon*).

Marine Insurance

Badoer, among other things, also ventured into marine insurance, which was a new industry in its initial phases of development (Astuti, 1968–69, pp. 68 and 110–115]. Badoer insured cargoes from Constantinople to all parts of the Mediterranean and the Black Sea. The first insurance he wrote was for a policy of 200 ducats for Aluvixe Arduine quoted below:

> Insurance contracted in Constantinople credit this 12th day of October for cash received from Aluvixe Arduini for an insurance of 200 ducats on his merchandise which was loaded on the ship of *patron* Mr. Piero di Belveder for the trip from Constantinople to Venice at a 6 percent premium, cash payment of 6 gold ducats and 21 perperi, the insurance, should anything occur, to be paid to Mr. Zuan di Priolli son of Mr. Nicholò.
>
> L.F.16 perp. 40 car. 12

Badoer charged Arduini an insurance premium of 6 percent. This premium, however, varied from 3 percent to 19 percent depending upon the risk factor, one being the Turkish peril (*pericholo de turchi*) which he mentions on L.F.248. Over a 3-year period, Badoer collected 548 perperi 16 carati in premiums and suffered only one insurance loss of 330 perperi, netting him a profit of 218 perperi 16 carati. This speaks well of the protection which the Venetian navy afforded its merchantmen.

Turkish Peril

An allusion has been made to the "Turkish peril." It was of serious concern to merchants and affected commerce in Constantinople in a variety of ways; however, it did not inhibit trading with the Turks. Badoer carried on an active trade with a number of Turkish merchants. Apparently, though, distrust and uneasiness did prevail as the following account seems to indicate:

> L.F.7 1436
>
> Saliet the Turk debit this September 10th for the sale of 7 small boxes of crisp netting from the account of Mr. Piero Soranzo at perp. 50 per box
>
> .... L.F.8 perp 350 car. 0

Badoer forgoes the amenities of titles in addressing the merchant and does not mention parental lineage, which he meticulously records when trading with Venetian merchants. He demands a 50 percent down payment on September 7 and on September 10, the day of the sale, he is paid in cash for the balance. Credit terms, where the Turks are concerned, are cash.

> 1436 L.F.7
>
> Saliet the Turk credit this Sept. 7 for a deposit of 2000 Turkish asperi to my account in Chaloiani Sufiano's bank.
>
> L.F.3 perp. 176 car. 2
>
> 10th ditto deposited to my account in Chaloiani's bank.
>
> L.F.3 perp. 173 car. 22

This nervousness about the "Turkish peril" is also reflected in the exchange rates for the aspero.[3] Badoer's ledger shows that the Venetian ducat and the Byzantine perpero remained fairly stable with only slight variations in their exchange rate. This was not the case with the aspero. When Saliet the Turk made his two deposits in Chaloiani's bank, they were converted at the exchange rate of 11 asperi 6 tornexi per perpero. But on November 10, just 2 months later, in the "Sinopoi and Trabexonda *Viazo*" account on L.F.7, 7482 asperi were converted at the rate of 33⅓ per perpero. This may be a reflection of the unstable conditions that most likely existed at Sinopoi and Trabexonda, which were two Venetian enclaves in Turkish territory on the Black Sea.

Return Shipments to Venice and Balancing of Accounts

The first two weeks of November 1436 were very busy ones for Badoer. The galley fleet commanded by Piero Contarini was preparing for its return trip to Venice. This was in compliance with a government timetable, whose purpose it was to assure a return of merchantmen at Christmas and in July for an orderly marketing of goods. Cargoes thus would

[3] The Turkish currency is composed of asperi and tornexi. There are 24 tornexi to one aspero.

be disposed of quickly, and return cargoes would be assured for the ships [Lane, 1973, p. 133].

Badoer would have disposed of all of the original merchandise which had been consigned to him, and liability accounts would have been set up for the proceeds realized. It was a question now of acquiring new merchandise for shipment to Venice. Generally Badoer would open new asset accounts for the merchandise purchased for each client or for himself, which would be charged with the invoice cost, the merchandising costs, brokerage fees and Badoer's purchase commission of one percent. When the merchandise was placed on board the galleys, the asset accounts would be closed and transferred to the clients' liability accounts, which generally would not balance. The difference, debit or credit, would be carried forward to be part of the next delivery of consignment goods or funds from Venetian clients. The Soranzo's account on L.F.1 (Figure 1) has such an entry on November 14. Badoer had purchased silk cloth for his client for a total cost of 424 perperi 3 carati. When it was loaded on the captain's galley, the previously opened asset account was closed and charged to this account, leaving a debit balance of 286 perperi 18 carati.

The evidence in Badoer's ledger indicates that the fleet sailed on November 18. No further entries of this nature are recorded for the rest of 1436. Badoer, during this period, essentially was concerned with bringing his ledger up to date. There is no formal balancing of accounts, but a balancing of sorts does occur. Small account balances were settled, cash payments and receipts were made and recorded and account adjustments, where required, were made. In four instances, statements from his Venetian clients, showing an accounting of transactions reported by Badoer, arrived in December with the ship of Todaro Vatazi. Badoer compared the statements with his accounts and recorded the balances, thus closing the accounts and forwarding the amounts to new accounts. Only in the Soranzo's account on L.F.1 (Figure 1) did the statement balance differ from the account balance. The correct debit balance of the account is 286 perperi 21 carati, but the client's statement balance showed 286 perperi 18 carati. Badoer takes the loss and enters the lower figure. This reconciliation of accounts with clients' statements occurs at varying intervals throughout the ledger.

Comments and Conclusion

The four months to the end of 1436 thus constituted a natural fiscal period. It was the time required to turn over the merchandise and prepare for shipment back to Venice and generally to adjust and bring the ledger up to date. Badoer now would have to wait for the outcome of sales on the Venetian market and for the arrival of new consignments from his clients to begin a new fiscal cycle.

It should be observed that a trial balance of Badoer's ledger would serve no useful purpose. Badoer was very accurate in his recording of transactions, but small differences, as for example the three carati in the Soranzo account (Figure 1) and the one carato in the "Woolen cloth bresani" account of Chontarini and Badoer (Figure 3), do occur in the ledger. These were of no consequence to Badoer, since the basic debtor and creditor relationships remained correct, but, as a consequence, the reason for taking a trial balance was invalidated.

This may raise a question of whether Badoer did, in fact, use a system of double entry. His ledger does not balance, at least not precisely, and it also is questionable whether a true accounting of his net income can be made. He records the initial merchandise he brought from Venice for his own account or in partnership with other merchants as a consignment, showing no costs other than those incurred in Contantinople. When sold, his share of the proceeds is credited to his capital account. Perhaps he considered the initial merchandise as his capital investment and, therefore, that it should be considered as such when converted to cash. His later acquisitions of merchandise are properly recorded at cost, and the net income or loss is properly closed to a profit and loss account.

Some questions also may be raised about the propriety of his commissions. He consistently takes a commission on purchases and sales of merchandise for his own account. Modern practice would chastise this as improper; nevertheless, the final net income is not distorted, only its composition. Despite the inaccuracies noted, the system Badoer uses is still basically double entry.

It was mentioned earlier that the ledger format used by Badoer did not readily lend itself to compound entries. Even where the more complete system of journal and ledger was used, at least in extant records, each entry consisted of one debit and one credit.

It is, therefore, remarkable that Badoer, in one instance at least and in an apparent effort to reduce the number of entries, should have devised a compound entry to record a purchase of silk for his own account, which involved more than two elements. The entry is awkwardly structured, but it is the first evidence that has surfaced so far of such a labor-saving device. On L.F.71 the purchase of silk is set up as follows:

Silk in '*scudelle*' for my account debit on day 6 June for Ramadan of Simiso for the purchase of Chant. 10 r. 57 of silk, tare for sacks and ropes r. 34 tare for waste at r 4½ per chanter. r 45. net balance chant 9 r 78. at perp 22½ per chanter. total. . . . . .perp. 219 car 18
and for the said Ramadan a cash payment in part . . . . L. F 48 perp 79 car 11
and a bank transfer from Mr Charlo Chapello's bank for the balance . L. F 36 perp. 140 car 7
in all. . perp 219 car 18

Ordinarily Badoer would record this purchase of silk, which was paid for partly with cash and the balance with a bank transfer, with three entries. One to record the purchase and set up the liability and two additional to record the payments. In this instance, Badoer records the whole transaction with one compound entry.

It would be difficult to say how widespread the use of compound entries was at that time, if, indeed, they were used at all. It is evident, however, how evolutionary changes in bookkeeping procedures occurred. The Renaissance bookkeeper, faced with an ever-growing volume of commerce which was increasing in complexity, was forced to devise ways to improve the bookkeeping system to make it more efficient. Only when the need for these changes became widespread would the improvements in bookkeeping gain general currency. The compound entry is not mentioned in accounting literature, which lagged behind practice, until the 17th century, when Simon Steven first described it in his treatise on "Mathematical Traditions" published in 1606.

The mosaic that emerges from the ledger is that of a man skilled and practiced in many phases of commerce. He is a merchant-entreprenuer who is engaged in varied complex ventures for his own account, financed with his own or borrowed capital or in partnership with others. He is quick to take advantage of commercial opportunities that present themselves, and his trading extends well beyond the confines of Constantinople to markets in the Black Sea area, the

Aegean islands, Asia Minor and Alexandria in Egypt. He is agent to resident Venetian merchants and to others and trades their wares and capital in the Byzantine market for a commission. In turn he is a provider of capital to other merchants and also ventures into marine insurance, a new emerging industry and, to some extent, also is an experimenter and innovator of new ideas in bookkeeping. Badoer is a multifaceted man, a Renaissance man of commerce.

REFERENCES

Austuti, G., "Le forme giuridiche della attività mercantile nel libro dei conti di Giacomo Badoer (1436–1440), *Annali di Storia del Dirito*, XII–XIII (1968–69).

Dorini, U. e T. Bertelè, eds. *Il libro dei conti di Giacomo Badoer, il Nuovo Ramusio*, raccolta di viaggi, testi e documenti relativi ai rapporti fra l'Europa e l'Oriente a cura dell'Istituto Italiano per il Medio ed Estremo Oriente, vol. III, pp. XV–857 (Libreria dello Stato, 1956).

Edler, F., Glossary of Medieval Terms (1934).

Lane, F. C., *Andrea Burgarigo, Merchant of Venice 1418–1449*, (1967, reprint).

———, *Venice, a Maritime Republic* (1973).

Jachomo Badoer, Renaissance Man of Commerce, and his Ledger

Edward Peragallo

Jachomo Badoer, a merchant of the Venetian nobility, spent more than three years trading in Constantinople. He is important because his ledger is the only record that survived, in its entirety, the sack of Constantinople by the Turks in 1453 [2]. Its value is unique as a source of the trade, financial and accounting practices of the Levant during the first half of the 15th century.

A previous paper [5] described Badoer's early efforts in establishing his trading contacts and practices in Constantinople. After two full years of operations, new insights into these practices and his personality emerge.

Badoer was a man of considerable wealth. He invested heavily in the Levantine venture in partnership with his brother Jeronimo, but still held extensive real estate in Venice and its environs. Reports from his brother (Ledger Folio 262) show rentals from mills in Mestre and from tenants in Venice, Treviso and Mestre; also trading in government bonds and collection of interest from loans and investments.

Interesting vignettes occur in the ledger that are revealing of Badoer's character, such as the care he takes of his apprentice, Antonio Bragadin, who is fatally ill (L.F. 26), his baptising of a Turkish slave boy, 15 years of age, and naming him Terzo (L.F. 45), and his anger at the swindle that Andrea de Stella perpetrated upon him (L.F. 149). All of these and others enliven the ledger and make it a very human document.

Badoer's *modus operandi*

Badoer's initial task upon the unloading of wares from the galleys for his own and his client's accounts was to organise a method of operations [5, pp. 885–8]. He managed his business affairs with the aid of an apprentice and depended upon brokers to consummate trades on the market in Constantinople and occasionally in Pera. He depended on their reported trades to record the details in the ledger.

At times, however, Badoer himself would sell certain wares at retail without the use of brokers. For instance, he sold 120 pieces of regulation size fustian cloth (L.F. 14, 71) and 169 butts of wine (L.F. 98), without use of brokers.

Badoer, however, also operated in other markets. Agents were employed either on a commission basis or in partnership. These ventures are recorded in voyage (*viazo*) accounts [5, p. 888] and are mostly for his own account. They range from Tana and Trabzon on the Black Sea, to Alexandria in Egypt and to Majorca and Zaragoza in Spain. Frequently these voyages represented shipments of goods for sale in those markets, the proceeds to be returned after expenses and commissions to agents were deducted or a share of the proceeds if the shipments were in partnership. Not all shipments were successful. In the Candia voyage account on L.F. 59, for example, a barrel of salted fish was shipped to the agent ser Marcho Filomati. The fish spoiled en route, the venture was a total loss. In some instances, funds would be sent to an agent to purchase wares in one market to sell in another market (Trabzon voyage, L.F. 152). A few times funds were provided agents for the purchase of goods for delivery to Constantinople, chiefly wool (Gallipoli voyage, L.F. 55) and oil (Modon voyage, L.F. 118).

The primary objective of most of these voyages was to provide Badoer with funds to purchase locally wares needed for shipment to Venice. Constantinople had a rich, diversified market of eastern wares. All trade routes from India, China, Russia and Turkey converged there. Badoer had little trouble purchasing most of the wares he needed. An important exception was the shipments from his agent ser Zacharia Chontarini in Alexandria of copper (L.F. 228), of silk (L.F. 179) and of cinnamon and brazilwood (L.F. 328). Entirely distinct from these accounts is the Venice voyage account, which represents shipments to Venice by Badoer for his own account.

Currencies—purchasing power of the perparo

The ledger is kept in perpari, the currency of Constantinople (Appendix A). To gain some measure of the value of wares and other transactions in the ledger, it might be useful to attempt to measure the purchasing power of the perparo by computing a per diem average of Badoer's personal expenditures. This would provide a rough standard of measurement. His personal expenditures from his departure from Venice on July 24, 1436, to February 15, 1440, total 1,743 perpari (L.F. 357). These include his travel expenses and his household and personal expenses at Pera and in Constantinople. These average to about 1 perparo 8 carati per day. Obviously, this reflects the cost of living of a Venetian merchant, a nobleman, accustomed to certain amenities, who is not extravagant and who is fully engaged in the trading activities of the market. The cost of living of the other classes would undoubtedly be lower. Nevertheless, Badoer's per diem expenditures may be used, within limits, as a rough measure of the value of transactions in his ledger.

Trading in currencies

Throughout the ledger there are entries indicating sales of heavy weighted coins that come into Badoer's possession. When this occurs he deposits the coins in a bank with the instruction that they be sold to the mint and the enhanced amount be credited to his account. The credit to cash on October 9, 1437, on L.F. 88, shows a deposit at the bank of

> ... ser Charlo Chapello of 10 pounds of heavy silver coins with the order that they be sold to Critopulo from the mint at 22 perpari 15 carati per pound ... they are charged to the account as 223 perpari 6 carati ... to L.F. 101 perp. 226 car. 6.

This shows a gain of 3 perpari, that Badoer leaves in the cash account. This, obviously, results in a cash overage, a fact that Badoer recognises when he attempts to reconcile cash.

Badoer also records losses on underweighted coins. The credit to the Gallipoli voyage account on L.F. 125 shows '... a loss for old asperi ...', and presumably underweighted, of 25 asperi (Appendix A), which is listed as one of the merchandising costs incurred in the sale of 8 boxes of crisp veils.

In a somewhat different situation, Badoer holds Turkish copper coins for sale for a Turkish client. In the account on L.F. 120 is recorded 'Copper in tornexi coins ... for the account of chir Jorgi Foti, 2 chanter 8 ruotoli [Appendix B] of copper net at perp. 17 per chanter, total perp. 47 car. 14'. The copper is later sold at 17½ perpari per chanter.

Exchange rates

The volume of trade between Venice and its foreign markets necessitated a large and active foreign exchange market to provide reliable exchange rates for the conversion of currencies. Such a market was located at the Rialto in Venice and Badoer availed himself of the information in the conversion of currencies (Appendix A).

The 'Turkish peril' was blamed for the difference in the rate of exchange of the Turkish aspero in Constantinople which traded at 11 asperi 6 tornexi per perparo as compared to the aspero in Trabzon which was convertible at 33⅓ per perparo [5, p. 889]. The Turkish peril was real, but it does not explain this difference. The Trabzon voyage account on L.F. 152 clarifies this point.

Badoer commissioned his agent Antonio de Negroponte to purchase certain wares in Simiso and to sell them in Trabzon, two Venetian trading centers on the Black Sea. In an abbreviated form the account contains the following:

L.F. 152 Debit

Voyage of Trabzon entrusted to Antonio de Negroponte, who reports purchases of the following wares in Simiso:

	asp.
Cost of 90 cordovan pelts at asp. 10¼ each	925
Cost of 304 hats at asp. 22 per dozen	680
Cost of 'chapizi of rexi' at asp.... per 'chapizo'	132
Cost of wheat 26 moza of Simiso, which is equivalent to 9 psomiarii per mozo in Trabzon, at asp. 85 per mozo [Appendix B]	2,210
etc.	etc.
Total	8,193

Total asperi 8,193 of Simiso values at asp. 19 per perparo, L.F.... perp. 431 car. 5.

L.F. 152 Credit

Voyage per contra, Antonio de Negroponte reports the following sales in Trabzon:

	asp.
Sale of 57 cordovan pelts at various prices	1,337
Sale of 304 hats	2,038
Sale of the 'rexi' which weighed 11 batimani at asp. 23 per batiman	257
Sale of 26 moza of wheat at asp. 24 per psmiaro	5,097
etc.	etc.
Total	17,850
Less merchandising costs	1,225
Net	16,625

Net balance asp. 16,625 valued at asp. 40 per perparo, L.F. . . . perp. 415 car. 15.

The account shows that the aspero of Simiso is an entirely different coin from the one of Trabzon and is twice as valuable. Badoer carefully differentiates these currencies by identifying them as the Simiso aspero, the Trabzon aspero, and the Turkish aspero which, according to Badoer's ledger, circulated in Constantinople at the exchange rate of 11¼ asperi per perparo. Obviously, these are three different currencies, all of them called asperi, and each divided into 24 tornexi.

Badoer's agent, Antonio de Negroponte, argues in the account on L.F. 166 '. . . that the perparo was valued at too high a price of 40 asperi and should be set at 36 . . .' asperi of Trabzon. Badoer agrees and makes the adjustment in the account.

An interesting aside is that wares, traded on the Levantine markets, tended to an equilibrium price. Despite the fact that the wares sold at twice the number of asperi they cost, when the Trabzon asperi are converted at the higher exchange rate into perpari, the net yield is practically zero.

Exchange rate interpolation

At times Badoer is faced with the problem of converting one foreign currency into another. Direct exchange rates between such currencies may not be available, but since he operates in Venetian trading centers, their currencies were traded on the market at the Rialto and their exchange rates into ducats were thus available. Badoer uses these rates to interpolate the exchange rates between such currencies. His agent ser Franzesco Chorner, who operates in Tana, purchased vitriol and other wares in Kaffa, both markets on the Black Sea, for delivery to Constantinople. The account on L.F. 307 shows a total cost of such wares of 6184 asperi of Kaffa

> . . . which are to be valued in the currency of Tana, setting the [Venetian] ducat in Kaffa at 66 asperi and equating it to the ducat in Tana at 13 bexanti and 2 tangi [Appendix A], which is the rate at which ser Franzesco Chorner purchased them, total 1,251 bexanti, which, valued at 4 bexanti per perparo, total 312 perpari 18 carati. . . .

The ratio yields an exchange rate of 4·95 bexanti of Tana for each Kaffa aspero, which converts the asperi into 1,251 bexanti.

Loans and interest payments

Badoer financed his operations with his own capital or in partnership with his clients, with funds provided by clients either by bills of exchange or by the sale of wares shipped from Venice, and occasionally by borrowing in the local market. Sarachaia Chomatiano counting-house was his principal source for such loans. In the account 'Copper for ser Piero Soranzo' on L.F. 83 is the following debit entry:

> . . . on day 18 July 1437 Sarachaia Chomatiano counting-house, for the interest on a loan of 800 perpari that I borrowed because of the greater advantage to borrow the money and pay cash than to purchase the copper on time, and this is not disobeying orders of ditto ser Piero Soranzo because I carried out his orders in the matter of price and in all else, the interest on the ditto loan for 4 months at the rate of 13 per cent, total . . . L.F. 80 perp. 34 car. 21.

It is apparent that Badoer had considerable discretion in the execution of his client's orders. Borrowed funds were cheaper than the credit terms offered on copper purchases, therefore he borrowed the money and charged the interest to his client's account. The interest paid by Badoer was usually at the rate of 13% per year, rising occasionally to 15%. This seems to be high in comparison with the rates prevailing in Venice where '. . . Venetian courts enforced collection (of contracts) so long as the rate of interest was moderate, 5 to 8 per cent' [4, p. 146]. However, they are not considered exorbitant when the risks and the possibility of greater profits in the Levantine trade are considered [1, p. 96].

There is no attempt to disguise interest payments as was common in Renaissance finance because of Church opposition to the practice. The Venetians considered it legitimate to borrow money at interest when it was determined by market conditions and it was openly practised.

Settlement of obligations

Account balances, in Renaissance trading, were settled by the use of bank transfers (*scritta di banco*) or cash, bills of exchange (*lettera di cambio*) [5, pp. 883-5], and by the offsetting of obligations, which Badoer uses throughout the ledger. The latter is the procedure of offsetting receivables and payables when Badoer is agent for both parties and both parties consent. Also, at the request of debtors, he accepts third party promises to pay as shown in the account on L.F. 259 when 'Chatalan Amidei... promised to give me as debtors for the said money ser Marcho Doria for part, and ser Franzesco di Drapieri for the balance....' Finally, at the request of creditors, Badoer promises to pay third parties. It was the practice in Renaissance settlement of obligations to offset receivables and payables wherever possible. This clearing operation was used extensively not only within the confines of one market, but also between markets. It minimised the transfer of money and at the same time assured prompt and safe payment of obligations [1, p. 101].

Verification procedures

Receivables and Payables

The accuracy of receivable and payable accounts was of paramount importance to Badoer. He not only took great pains to ensure their correctness, but periodically would submit statements to his clients for their verification and in turn would receive statements from them. Upon submission or receipt of such statements, he would invariably close the accounts and forward the verified balances to new accounts. This verification takes on added significance when one considers that Badoer's ledger does not balance [5, p. 890]. Small errors occur in the accounts and, occasionally, posting of entries is not completed, though corrections are made when errors are detected. These errors occur for the most part in the cash account, the merchandising account and in Badoer's own accounts. The confirmation of receivables and payables was thus a necessary procedure to insure their integrity.

Cash

After more than a year's operation, Badoer makes his first attempt to reconcile cash. On January 18, 1438, when forwarding the cash balance to the new account on L.F. 171, he says:

> ...on this day I counted the cash and found a shortage of 35 perpari besides the overage there should have been because of the profit of 18 perpari I made on the sale of the heavy perpari sold for their silver....

Badoer, as in the case of the profit on the sale of silver coins, does not adjust the cash account for the shortage.

Badoer, henceforth, reconciles his cash each time the balance is forwarded to a new account, but, alas! each time the shortage is increased. On July 10 it had increased to 120 perpari, on September 25 it was 204 perpari 7 carati, on December 4, 1438, it reached 240 perpari and when on February 17, 1439, the book balance forwarded was 233 perpari 15 carati, Badoer decided that the shortage could no longer be ignored. On February 28, 1439, he made the following credit entry to cash on L.F. 315:

> ...for the shortage I find in the cash count on this day, which I record as money spent for merchandising expenditures, but not recorded in the account... 170 perpari 10 carati.

The adjustment, obviously, is not supported by entries in his memorandum journal, but is solely an estimate and, furthermore, it does not fully account for the shortage. Therefore, one year later, when the ledger is closed on February 26, 1440, Badoer makes a final adjustment. The credit entry to the cash account on L.F. 391 says:

> ...for the closing of the cash account and on this day I find a cash shortage, which was spent for merchandising expenditures... 42 perpari 9 carati.

Badoer's contention that the shortage was caused by unrecorded payments of merchandising expenditures, undoubtedly correct in part, fails to account for the whole shortage, which seems to predicate that Badoer himself absorbed it. Furthermore, it ignores the errors made.

Bank Accounts

Badoer, during his stay in Constantinople, had accounts with eight bankers. Only two of these were of importance to him, the others were opened as a result of trades wherein a debtor would settle his account with a bank transfer made into his own bank. The balances in these accounts were not significant and Badoer, after a period of use, would close them.

At intervals, Badoer verifies the bank balances, which usually are in agreement with his accounts.

One small difference occurs in the bank account on L.F. 398:

> Ser Charlo Chapello banker debit on day 19 February 1440 for the balance brought forward which is in accord with the bank, save for a difference of 8 carati....

The shortage is written off as a loss when the account is closed on February 26, 1440.

Thefts and Shortages

Badoer seems to exercise adequate care and control of wares in his possession. All goods, upon unloading from ships or purchased in local markets, are placed in warehouses, which presumably are well guarded. Nevertheless, shortages and thefts do happen. On one occasion the account of ser Piero Michiel and ser Marin Barbo on L.F. 35 is charged with 16 pieces of silk cloth, but only '... 14 cloths of the ditto silk were loaded ... on the galley ... the other 2 pieces ... were stolen from my warehouse....' Again, in ser Nofri da Chalzi account on L.F. 117, '... one bale of pepper was stolen ... from the warehouse....' In all instances of thefts and shortages, the loss is charged to the clients' accounts.

Perhaps the most galling theft was committed by Andrea de Stella. In the account on L.F. 149 Badoer says that Andrea had stored

> ... one cask of gold tinsel, that he stole from me in the year of 1436 at the time of the galleys when he was staying with me, which robbery was discovered by Lucha who had rented him the warehouse, and who, with signs and gestures, conveyed to me that he had rented the warehouse to the ditto Andrea....

Badoer lost not only the gold tinsel, but had to pay 14 months rental for the warehouse. Furthermore, during Andrea's stay at his home, Badoer had loaned him '... two small silver cups with my coat of arms and two silver spoons, which I had in my house, and which he gave to Alesandro Zien upon his departure from here....' Badoer refers to him in the receivable account on L.F. 149 as 'Andrea de Stella bastard son of ser Zuan de Stela....'

Labour saving procedures

Handbooks

Badoer's bookkeeping entries involve just two elements, a debit and a credit [5, p. 883]. The task of recording complex transactions was a laborious one requiring multiple entries. With the heavy pressure of trading, Badoer found it imperative to seek ways to minimise the work of recording transactions. One device he used was the hand journal (*manoaleto, libereto di bazar, zornal*—L.F. 137), wherein he would record daily expenditures and periodically would make summary entries to the ledger. There are three categories of expenditures that Badoer handles in this fashion.

Cash payments for the unloading and selling of wares are charged to the clients' accounts and entered in the handbook as incurred, and when all are recorded the merchandising expenditures account is credited for the total. At intervals, Badoer summarises his handbook and debits merchandising expenditures and credits cash for the amount.

Brokerage fees are included in merchandising expenditures and initially are recorded as above, but are not immediately paid. Badoer had three or four regular brokers and he accumulated their fees in his handbook. He would then charge merchandising expenditures for the total and credit the details to the brokers' accounts. The liability would then be paid off in cash or in some other fashion (Pulixoto counting-house, broker, L.F. 124).

Badoer's personal expenditures are treated more directly. He accumulates them in his hand journal and a detailed summary is charged to his personal account and credited to cash.

Clearing and Barter Accounts

It was the practice of Badoer to set up accounts for each client for each consignment of goods, either received from Venice or purchased for shipment to Venice. On occasion he would vary this procedure when a number of clients requested the same merchandise. He would then record the acquisitions, either by purchase or barter, in one account. The group purchase of merchandise is a straightforward operation. The account on L.F. 200, 'Wax ... that I purchase for the account of several persons ...' is charged with the cost of wax purchased from various sources, and added are merchandising expenditures, cost of registering the wax and Badoer's commission for buying and for registering the wax. The total is then allocated pro rata among the clients, including himself and his brother, for shipment to Venice.

The barter transaction is more complex [1, p. 91]. Several clients of Badoer, including himself, barter their cloths for 'cremexe' and indigo provided by a local merchant. The account on L.F. 264 'Barter made with Josep Salia counting-house of cloths from several accounts in exchange for "cremexe" and indigo ...' is first charged with the cost of woollen cloths and silk draperies from the accounts of clients. It is then debited with the cost of 'cremexe' and indigo supplied by Josep Salia and his account, opened for this purpose, is credited. The barter account is now credited for the cloths and Salia's account is charged; a bank transfer in payment for the balance closes the latter account. Finally, the barter account is credited for the 'cremexe' and the indigo, which closes it, and new accounts for the clients are charged with the merchandise, which is to be shipped to Venice.

The assets exchanged total about 8,500 perpari, a considerable sum, and about two dozen entries were needed to effect the exchange over a period of more then one month. Nevertheless, a number of entries and accounts have been eliminated that would have been necessary if Badoer had attempted to barter for each client separately.

Compound Entries

In a further attempt to minimise entries, Badoer devised the compound entry. Awkwardly structured at first [5, p. 891] he succeeded in improving it. The credit entry in the account on L.F. 188 shows the following:

> Oils from Choron for my account credit on day 29 April 1438 for the sale of 4 butts of oil to ser Antonio Gara, 274½ laine, at 1 perparo 6 carati per laina total, discounted 8 carati per butt for customary tare, broker Alberto Faxuol, and for ser Tomà Spinola from the bank to ditto ser Antonio for a bank transfer of 200 perpari in part payment of ditto oil, and for ser Antonio and Zuan Gara from the bank to the ditto ser Antonio for a bank transfer of 142 perpari 7 carati in payment of the balance of the ditto oil, total in all, L.F. 88, L.F. 193, 342 perpari 7 carati.

Badoer sold the oil to the banker ser Antonio Gara who makes payment with two bank transfers, one in the bank of ser Tomà Spinola for 200 perpari and the other in his own bank for the balance. Three possible entries are combined in one compound entry. The format is an improvement over his earlier efforts. The two L.F. references indicate the location of the debit accounts.

Badoer appears to use compound entries only when bank and cash accounts are involved. However, he does use variations. One version appears in the account on L.F. 207: 'Tender caviar from Tana 6 kegs for the account of ser Bortolamio Roso....' Badoer disposes the caviar with three sales which are listed in the account separately and cash is charged for the total. There are other variations.

It would seem plausible to assume that other bookkeepers, just like Badoer, struggling to cope with the growing pressure of trade, would devise procedures to improve their bookkeeping. A study of bookkeeping records of the period would perhaps reveal that Badoer's use of the compound entry was not an isolated occurrence.

Marine insurance syndicate

Badoer, among his other activities, also insured cargoes destined to all ports in the Mediterranean and in the Black Sea [5, pp. 888–9]. The industry was still in its formative stage, so it is remarkable that Badoer, on one occasion, formed an insurance syndicate to spread the risk of a particularly valuable cargo. In a debit entry to the ser Nofri da Chalzi account on L.F. 164, Badoer provides him with a total insurance of 1,250 perpari for cargo on two ships. The insurance on the first ship is allocated among six co-insurers:

> ...and first cash payment of 8 perpari (premium) to miser Chora dal Pasto genoexe for insurance of 200 perpari on the galley Firentina, and to ser Zorzi da Quarto and Antonio da Chastro and Gotifreo insurance of 100 perpari each for a total premium of 12 perpari, and cash payment to Zulian Ziati firentino for insurance of 80 ducats, at 5 per cent, 12 perpari and 20 carati, and cash payment to Anzolo Azaiuoli, for insurance of 50 ducats (premium also at 5 per cent), and for customs and brokerage fee 3 perpari 8 carati, total 44 perpari 8 carati; and cash to Jachomo Badoer for insurance of 320 perpari on the ship of patron Jachomo Marzelo, at 6 per cent, 19 perpari 6 carati, total in all ... L.F. 131 (cash) 63 perpari 14 car.

The ducats are converted at 3 perpari 5 carati per ducat. The insurance issued totals 1,237 perpari, which is somewhat at variance with the 1,250 perpari mentioned earlier in the entry. Badoer charged the Nofri account with the total premium and credited cash for premiums paid to the co-insurers. For his own premium of 19 perpari 6 carati, which is included above, he makes an offsetting entry to his premium account, charging cash. Thus Badoer alone assumes the risk of insuring the ship of patron Jachomo Marzelo, whereas six co-insurers shared the risk of insuring the galley Firentina.

Shipments to Venice

Badoer's final task was the shipment of wares to Venice for his own, his brother's and his clients' accounts. Major shipments were scheduled in the fall of each year. In 1438 Badoer's preparations for such an operation began on October second with the arrival of the galleys captained by ser Lorenzo Minio. Consignments of 11,000 perpari (L.F. 272) were unloaded for Badoer and bills of exchange and statements from clients and from his brother were given to him by the captain.

Badoer now moved quickly to assemble the required wares [5, pp. 889–90]. Funds raised from the sale of goods and from the various voyages were utilised to acquire goods in the local market, mostly from counting-houses. Some were acquired in other markets through agents, such as wool from Adrianople (L.F. 292) and cinnamon and brazil-wood from Alexandria (L.F. 328). Indigo and 'cremexe' were acquired in a barter exchange of woollen cloths and silk draperies (L.F. 264). Loading began on November 20, upon the return of the galleys from the Black Sea ports of Tana and Trabzon, and were not completed until December 17. The shipment was a valuable one of some 21,500 perpari and its cargo varied (Appendix C). Badoer's own wares were substantial, upward of 6,100 perpari. Badoer also entrusted captain Lorenzo Minio with a number of bills of exchange and account statements for delivery to clients and to his brother in Venice. The fleet sailed shortly afterwards and Badoer attended to the task of bringing his ledger up to date.

Comments and conclusion

It might not be amiss to mention that Badoer was not troubled by problems of valuation. Market value is the one he used, though at times he is called upon to estimate the value of wares subject to customs duties (L.F. 19), which was determined in accord with customs officials. The intent, of course, was to estimate the market value of the merchandise at the time of the tax.

Badoer also uses estimated values when transactions cannot be consummated in the market. For instance, in the account 'Woollen cloth bresani for the account of Antonio Chontarini and Badoer ...' on L.F. 11, Badoer, unable to sell a blue cloth, decides, with the assent of his partner after a period of 13 months, to divide it equally between themselves and values it at an estimated price.

The disquieting fact about Badoer's ledger is that it does not balance. Small differences of a few carati occur in some accounts, but these do not bother Badoer, because they do not affect the basic correctness of the accounts (L.F. 1, 11). However, a number of postings are incomplete. Most of these are credits to merchandising expenditures. This is not surprising when it is recalled that these credits are not entered until the consignment accounts are fully charged with these costs, a process that at times may take months to complete. This peculiar practice was also a factor in Badoer's inability to reconcile cash. However, he also omitted some postings to his commission account (L.F. 286), to profit and loss (L.F. 209) and to cash (L.F. 221). Offsetting this is the evidence that Badoer corrected errors when detected.

The ledger clearly shows that Badoer was fully conversant with the duality of entries. One wonders, therefore, if he might not have been acquainted with the trial balance. The correctness of debtor and creditor accounts was of the utmost importance to Badoer and since this was ensured by the confirmation of these accounts, the precise equality of debits and credits may have been of secondary importance to him.

Badoer's analysis of transactions was sound. He correctly recorded complex trades, such as barter, partnerships, ventures, and foreign exchange. One may challenge his taking of commissions on purchases and sales for his own account, but the distortion is not of total income, but only of its allocation. Badoer was also an innovator. He developed and perfected the compound entry and was instrumental in working out a plan for the sharing of marine insurance risks in a new developing industry. Clearly, Badoer was a bold, experienced and versatile merchant operating for his own account and for the account of others, who did not hesitate to take advantage of all trading opportunities open to him, no matter how diverse or complex their nature. His activities, centred in Constantinople, reached markets throughout the Levant, Black Sea and the Mediterranean basin.

References

[1] Astuti, G., 'Le forme giuridiche della attività mercantile nel libro dei conti di Giacomo Badoer (1436–1440)', *Annali di Storia del Diritto*, XII–XIII (1968–69).

[2] Dorini, U e Bertelè, T. (eds), *Il libro dei conti di Giacomo Badoer, il Nuovo Ramusio, raccolta di viaggi, testi e documenti relativi ai rapporti fra l'Europa e l'Oriente a cura dell'Istituto Italiano per il Medio ed Estremo Oriente*, vol III, pp. XV 857 (Libreria dello Stato, 1956)

[3] Edler, F, *Glossary of Medieval Terms* (1934)

[4] Lane, F C, *Venice, a Maritime Republic* (1973)

[5] Peragallo, E, 'The ledger of Jachomo Badoer. Constantinople September 2, 1436 to February 26, 1440', *Accounting Review*, October 1977

Appendix A

Currencies used in Badoer's ledger. Exchange rates are those prevailing in 1438.

Constantinople

The ledger is maintained in the currency of Constantinople, which is composed of perpari, carati and duchateli, with 24 carati to a perparo and 1½ carati to a duchatelo.

Venice

Badoer was constantly confronted with the problem of conversion into currencies of those countries with which he traded. The foremost, of course, was the Venetian. The money generally used was the ducat, with 24 grossi to a ducat and 32 piccioli to a grosso. Occasionally, he used the lira de grossi (L.F. 305) divided into 20 soldi with 12 danari to a soldo and 32 piccioli to a danaro. The lira de grossi was equivalent to 10 ducats. The basic exchange rate was 3 perpari to a ducat. This was the rate Badoer always used in transactions with his brother. With other parties he used the market rate, which averaged about 3 perpari 2–4 carati per ducat and occasionally went as high as 3 perpari 8 carati.

Turkish currencies

The aspero was the currency used and it was divided into 24 tornexi. However, the aspero circulating in Constantinople seems to have differed from the aspero of Trabzon and both of these from the one in Simiso. The Turkish aspero in Constantinople exchanged at 11 asperi less 1 tornexe (L.F. 167) per perparo and fluctuated as high as 11 asperi 6 tornexi (L.F. 3). The Simiso aspero was valued at 19 asperi to the perparo (L.F. 44, 152), whereas the Trabzon aspero (L.F. 152, 166) exchanged at 40 asperi to the perparo. This suggests that the aspero in these three cities were coins of different weights.

Candia

The perparo was the currency used in Candia and it was divided into 12 grossi and 32 piccoli per grosso. Its exchange rate was 1½ perpari of Candia for one perparo of Constantinople (L.F. 198, 187).

Tana

The currency was composed of somi, bexanti and tangi. The bexant seems to have been divided into 6 tangi (L.F. 283). The bexant exchanged at the rate of 13 for each Venetian ducat and 4 for each perparo of Constantinople. In the ledger account on p. 307 the rate was 13 bexanti 2 tangi per Venetian ducat. In the Kaffa voyage account (L.F. 176), the somo was valued at 9 perpari 13 carati. This would seem to indicate that the somo was divided into approximately 2 bexanti.

Kaffa

The aspero was used in Kaffa and was valued at 66 asperi per Venetian ducat (L.F. 307) and 20 to 22 asperi per perparo.

Alexandria

The ducat was the currency of Alexandria and it was divided into 230 diremi (L.F. 299, 56). It exchanged at the rate of 2 perpari 10 carati of Constantinople.

Messina

The onza was the currency of Messina (L.F. 94) and it was divided into 30 tarì and each tarì in turn was divided into 20 grane. The exchange rate was 1 onza for 13 perpari of Constantinople.

Modon

The perparo was used and was divided into 20 soldi and each soldo into 4 tornexi (L.F. 188). One perparo of Constantinople exchanged for 2¼ perpari of Modon.

Appendix B

Weights and measures used in Badoer's ledger

Weights

Chanter or cantaro—cantar, this was the basic weight used by Badoer. It was 150 pounds and was divided into 100 ruotoli.

Livra or libbra—pound, divided into 12 ounces and the ounce into 6 sazi or saggi.

Ziurlo—112 pounds, a Turkish weight (L.F. 264, 26).

Butimano—equivalent to 15 ruotoli, weight used in Kaffa (L.F. 226, 219).

Mena—a weight of a few pounds (2–8, for spices, silks, corals, etc., in Egypt, Syria, Persia, Turkey). (L.F. 299) [3, p 175].

Linear measures

Picho or picco—pic, about ¾ of a yard. The regulation size of a piece (*pezza*) of cloth in Badoer's ledger was 54 pics.

Braza or braccio—one pic, about ¾ of a yard.

Dry measures

Mozo or moggio—Badoer does not mention its capacity. Edler (1934, p. 318) says it varied from 4 to 52 Florentine bushels depending on the location (Italy, S. France, Turkey, the Levant); in Florence it was 24 bushels. Badoer used it for grains (wheat, millet, etc. L.F. 51).

Pisomiaro or psomiaro—used in Trabzon, 12 pisomiari equalled 1 mozo (L.F. 51). 1 mozo of simiso equalled 9 pisomiarii of Trabzon, (L.F. 152).

Liquid measures

Bota or botte—butt, a wine measure (about 100 gallons).

Charatello or caratello—cask or keg (2 charatelli equalled 1 botte, L.F. 98).

Mitro or metro—about $\frac{1}{10}$ of a butt (L.F. 98).

Laina or saina—oil measure used in Constantinople; 76 saine equalled 1 botte di mena (Naples), which equalled about 100 gallons, therefore 1 saina was about 1½ gallons [3, pp. 319–20].

Appendix C

Shipments to Venice 1438.

Loading date		Client	perp.	car
Nov. 20	L.F. 63	Agency—Jachomo Dolfin; 3 loaves of wax; galley Minio . .	163	12
Nov. 21	L.F. 273	Piero Michiel and Marin Barbo for 2/3, Jeronimo and myself 1/6 each; 3 packs of indigo; galley Minio	1,089	3
Nov. 24	L.F. 150	Piero Soranzo; 1 cask of 'cremexe savaxi'; galley Minio . . .	435	1
Nov. 24	L.F. 150	Piero Soranzo: 1 cask of 'cremexe of wine'; galley Minio . .	414	23
Nov. 26	L.F. 275	Piero Michiel and Marin Barbo for 2/3, Jeronimo and myself 1/6 each; 1 barrel of 'cremexe savaxi'; galley Minio	863	18

Loading date		Client	perp	car
Nov 26	L.F. 274	Piero Michiel and Marin Barbo for 2/3, Jeronimo and myself 1/6 each, one barrel of 'cremexe of wine', galley Minio	665	11
Nov 26	L.F. 278	Venice voyage, my account, 1 bale of silk, 126 lbs. shipped from Alexandria and transferred to a galley at Modon	425	21
Nov. 26	L.F. 278	Venice voyage—my account, chant. 49 r. 61 of copper; ship of patron Manoli Vergizi	865	22
Nov 26	L.F. 282	Jeronimo and myself; share equally 2 sacks of santonin seed; galley Minio	564	7
Nov. 26	L.F. 216	Jeronimo and myself; share equally 341 white wether pelts; ship of Zuan Chontarini	86	0
Nov. 26	L.F. 268	Piero Michiel and Marin Barbo; 3 loaves of registered wax; galley Duoda	183	3
Nov. 26	L.F. 268	Piero Michiel and Marin Barbo; 25 loaves of wax, 10 on galley Duoda and 15 on galley Minio	1,337	22
Nov. 26	L.F. 268	Piero Michiel and Marin Barbo; 3 'fasi of verzi'; galley Duoda	682	18
Nov. 28	L.F. 150	Piero Soranzo; 3 'fasi of verzi'; galley Duoda	725	10
Nov. 29	L.F. 151	Piero Michiel and Antonio da la Cholona; 6 loaves of wax; galley Minio	411	8
Dec. 1	L.F. 298	Piero Michiel, Jeronimo and myself; 3 packs of indigo; galley Duoda	1,160	3
Dec. 3	L.F. 140	Piero Soranzo and Zuan Musolini; 5 bales of pepper; galley Minio	754	1
Dec. 8	L.F. 292	Piero Michiel and Marin Barbo for 2/3, Jeronimo and myself 1/6 each; 14 sacks of wool from Adrianople; ship of Zuan Chontarini	410	5
Dec. 8	L.F. 278	Venice voyage—my account; 3 sacks of wax from Trabzon; galley Tiepola	186	0
Dec. 12	L.F. 204	Piero Michiel; 8 bales of ginger; galley Tiepola	551	5
Dec. 12	L.F. 296	Piero Michiel; 2 female slaves; ship Chontarini	245	0
Dec. 12	L.F. 296	Piero Michiel; 2 loaves of wax, weight chant. 3 r. 79; galley Tiepola	110	20
Dec. 12	L.F. 269	Zuan Trivixan; 22 loaves of wax, 16 on galley Minio and 6 on galley Tiepola	1,403	0
Dec. 13	L.F. 295	Piero Michiel and Marin Barbo; 4 bales of pepper, net weight chant. 9 r. 60; galley Tiepola	497	22
Dec 13	L.F. 303	Piero Michiel and Marin Barbo for 2/3, Jeronimo and myself 1/6 each, 1 box of incense, weight 2 chanter 60½ ruotoli; galley Tiepola	80	6
Dec 13	L.F. 303	Piero Michiel and Marin Barbo for 2/3, Jeronimo and myself 1/6 each; 3 bales of ginger in salt, weight chant 5, galley Tiepola	156	7
Dec. 14	L.F. 299	Venice voyage—my account, 2 boxes of incense, weight chant 4 r. 76½; galley Tiepola	146	12
Dec. 14	L.F. 298	Piero Soranzo; 1 keg of reddish 'cremexe', weight 405 pounds 11 ounces; galley Tiepola	929	9
Dec 14	L.F. 277	Jeronimo my brother; 10 loaves of wax, 6 loaded on captain's galley and 4 on galley Tiepola	541	14
Dec. 14	L.F. 283	Jeronimo and myself; 11½ pounds of rhubarb seeds; galley Minio	27	18
Dec 14	L.F. 299	Venice voyage—my account; 5 ziurli of indigo in 2 packs, galley Duoda	541	12
Dec. 16	L.F. 299	Venice voyage—my account; 1 small sack of zedoary packed with the rhubarb, weight r. 22½; galley Minio	14	18
Dec. 15	L.F. 298	Piero Soranzo; 2 ziurli of indigo; galley Minio	217	0
Dec. 16	L.F. 295	Piero Michiel and Marin Barbo; 6 bales of pepper; galley Tiepola	1,042	18
Dec. 16	L.F. 302	Antonio Marzelo; 1 bale of pepper; galley Tiepola.	173	15
Dec. 17	L.F. 311	Franzesco di Garzon; 1 slave 13 years old of the Rosa nation to be delivered to his uncles in Venice; ship of Zuan Chontarini	84	0
Dec. 17	L.F. 180	Marin Barbo; 1 girl slave 12 years old of the Rosa nation; ship of Zuan Chontarini	76	0
Nov. 4	L.F. 266	Jeronimo and myself; 5 bales of woolfell from Adrianople, 584 pelts per count; ship of Zuan Chontarini	223	0
Nov. 4	L.F. 216	Jeronimo and myself; 610 woolfells; ship of Zuan Chontarini	241	9
Dec. 28	L.F. 299	Venice voyage for my account; 10 'fasi' of cinnamon and 4 'fasi' of brazil-wood weighed in Alexandria 1712½ mene, and the brazil-wood weighed chant. 24 r. 21; shipped separately from Alexandria to Candia and there transferred to a galley bound for Venice	2,856	8
		Total shipments	21,584	21

The Accounts of the Corporation of Bristol: 1532 to 1835

D. M. LIVOCK*

This paper deals with the form of the accounts of the City of Bristol from 1532 to the reform of the Corporation in 1835. It is concerned primarily with the accounting methods employed, that is, the form and content of the account books and any indication there may be of the use to which they were put, and only incidentally with the sources of income and the purposes of expenditure.[1]

The main accounting records of the Corporation of Bristol for this period fall into two series. The first, from 1532 to 1785, known as the Mayor's or Great Audits, provided the means whereby the chamberlain accounted to the mayor and those members of common council who were elected as auditors, for the money which he should have received during the year. The form of the Audit changed little, but subsidiary records and books of account, which begin in 1615, increased and improved with the growth of financial business until, in 1698, a new accounting system including cash book, journal, and ledger was introduced. Even then the form of the Mayor's Audit remained unchanged. The second series, on a full double-entry basis, begun in 1786, continued in more or less the same form for many years and was used after 1835 by the reformed body.

1532 to 1698

The early financial records of the Corporation have disappeared. From the time that the town first obtained the lease of the fee farm

* Fellow of St. Anne's College, Oxford. P. D. Leake Research Fellow in Accounting, 1960–62.

[1] An extended discussion of sources and purposes is to be included in a study of the financial history of Bristol; a P. D. Leake Research Fellowship for the study was awarded for 1960–62, and it is being completed with the support of a grant by the Houblon-Norman Fund.

(1224), and from the time that King Henry III first granted the right to tax incoming goods for murage, quayage, and pavage (1232), some accounts must have been necessary. An Inquisition of 1339 refers to the amounts raised by these taxes and to the expenditure from them on the repair of the walls, the quays, and the streets; but though accounts may still be found of the customs taken by the king there is no record of more local transactions. Even later, the accounts of the sheriffs who accounted for the fee farm, and of those burgesses who were charged, under the charter of 1499 with the collection of tallages for town purposes have been lost.

THE MAYOR'S AUDITS

The earliest account book still in existence is the Mayor's Audit[2] for 1532; it is the first of a nearly unbroken series continuing until 1785. The object of the Audit was to enable the chamberlain to account to the mayor and commonalty for that part of the Corporation's money which he should have received and to present an account which the auditors could examine and, if necessary, amend.

The office of chamberlain was formally set up by a charter of 1499; he was to be elected by the mayor and common council in Guildhall and to hold office at their pleasure. His duties and authority were to be the same as those of the chamberlain of the city of London. He was to have a seal and to have "the right to appear before the King, the King in Chancery, the Justices of the Common Bench, the Treasurer and Barons of the Exchequer and before all Judges and Justices in whatsoever courts to sue and be sued, to answer and be answered in all actions, suits, plaints and claims, real personal and mixed."[3] In the sixteenth century, he was the chief executive officer of the Corporation. He was to receive all revenues, income, profits, and emoluments for the use of the mayor and commonalty, to make necessary payments and to keep all the muniments. He was to render account annually within one month of the feast of St. Luke the Evangelist (18th October) before the mayor and aldermen, or before two burgesses appointed by the mayor. When he resigned or was removed from office he was to render an account within one month.

Before 1640 the Audits are limited in their content. They do not include either the income from, or the expenditure of, any rates which may have been raised. They do not show loan transactions, the purchase of estates not financed from revenue, or the money held on behalf of orphans for whom the mayor acted as ward. Their main purpose was accountability and their general form varies little throughout the

[2] It must be emphasised that "Audit" was the name given to the account book prepared by the chamberlain to enable the auditors to check his accounts.

[3] *Bristol Charters, 1378–1499*, ed. H. A. Cronne (Bristol Records Society, 1946), p. 165.

series.[4] That 1532 is not the first Audit is most probable; in the summary at its end, the balance of the previous year is brought forward. It is likely that a series of accounts began following the charter of 1499. Each year's account, made at first by the chamberlain "with his owne hande" and written on paper, was originally bound in a limp vellum cover, sometimes the leaves of service books torn up at the Reformation.[5] Up to 1640 Roman numerals were used, though from 1586 a note of the total of each page in Arabic figures appears in the left-hand margin.[6]

Each account begins with the rentals of city lands and country estates. The rent due for each property is shown and an indication made of empty houses and unlet land. At the bottom of each page, in the middle, a total is given from which a deduction is shown for vacancies. At the end of each section there is a "sum total." The chamberlain is thus charged with all rents due to the Corporation during the financial year. Next appears a list of new burgesses with the fees paid by them and finally a section for "Fines and casualties." In the early years this was small, but as the custom grew of charging fines for renewal of leases and when, after 1640, money taken up at interest was also included under this heading, it grew to a considerable size. The chamberlain then lists his "discharge." First are the Quarterly Payments for the day-to-day expenditure of the Corporation, including the repair of municipal property and city estates, the entertainment of the judge of assize and the recorder, the journeys to London of the chamberlain and the town clerk, law charges, and, at the end of each quarter, a list of officers' fees. After the four quarters, ending always with the Michaelmas quarter, are shown "General and ordinary payments," which include any fixed charges on city and country estates and charity lands, the repair of country estates, the cost of holding manorial courts, and, latterly, payments to the sheriffs in respect of the fee farm and tolls. As the business of the Corporation grew, interest on loans and orphan money, and repayment of them, are shown separately. Each page is added and a total stated at the end of each section. On the final two pages of the Audit appears a summary (Plate 1), the left-hand page showing the income due for the year and the right-hand page what the chamberlain has spent. The balance due to or by the chamberlain at the commencement of the year is generally shown as a receipt or a payment, as the case may be, and the final difference between the totals of the two pages is the amount due to or by the chamberlain at the end of the year. This summary is signed by the mayor and auditors.

[4] A series of Little Audits (1561–1654) in a similar form, containing the accounts of a part of the corporate estates, were, in 1655, incorporated in the Mayor's Audits.

[5] The books were later rebound, often several to a volume.

[6] The Arabic figures are probably a later addition.

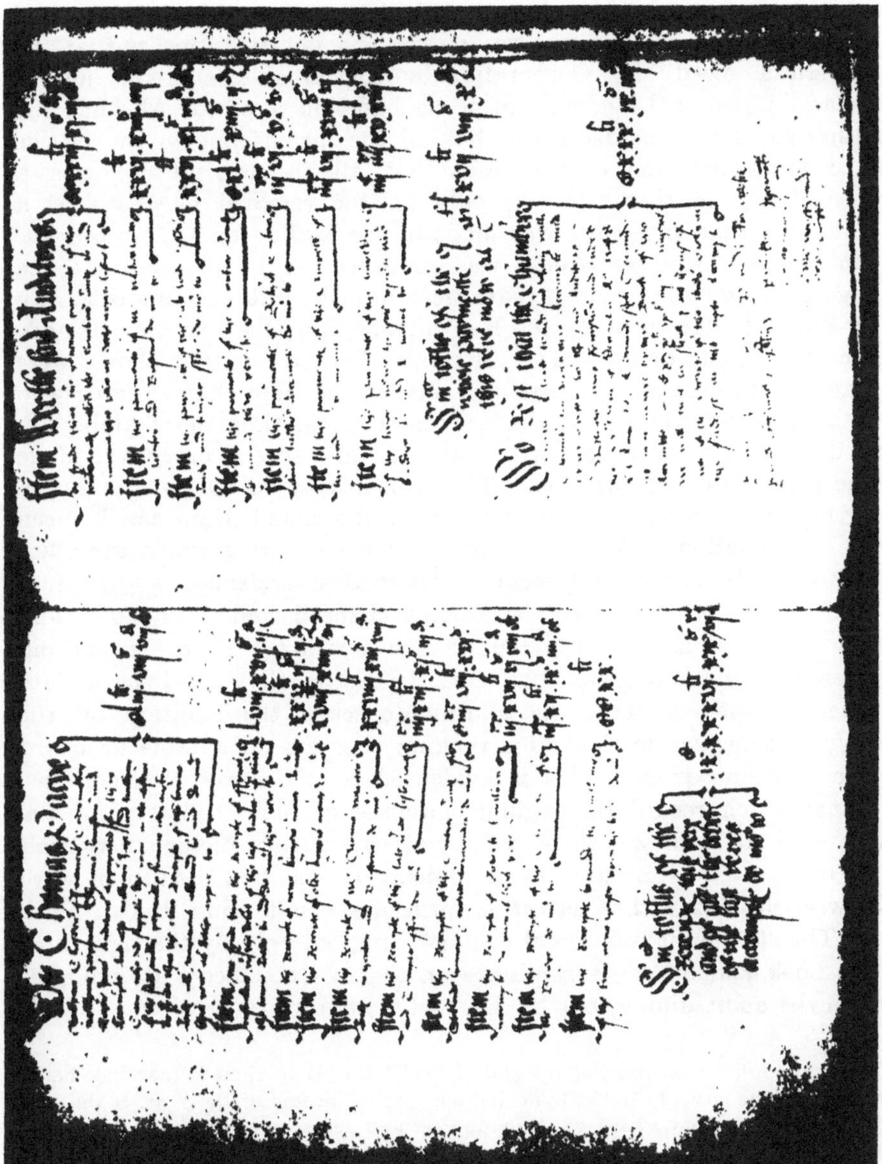

Summary of the Mayor's Audit 1547/48

By kind permission of Bristol Corporation

In some years after 1550, lists follow of amounts due to and by the Corporation at the end of the year and of arrears of rents.

But though the purpose of the Audit was accountability, the closing balance was not cash in hand as no adjustment was made at the end of the financial year for the arrears of rent, and it often appears that the chamberlain owed the Corporation a considerable sum of money whereas, in fact, a large part of it he had not received. All that the auditors could do was ascertain that all the income due to the mayor and commonalty was entered and that all the expenditure was a proper charge to them. It was only on the removal or death of a chamberlain that any entry was made in the Audits for arrears of rent. When this occurred an Audit was prepared up to the date of the change of chamberlain and arrears were brought into account with any other amounts due to or by the last chamberlain; the resulting balance was cash owing to or by him or his estate. The arrears then shown were charged as income in the first account of the new chamberlain, who thus became responsible for them. From time to time the chamberlain craved allowance for arrears irrecoverable and a special entry was made in the expenditure of that year. The difficulties involved in attempting to arrive at the actual cash due to or by the chamberlain can be seen by an examination of the split Audits for years during which the office changed hands, and would seem to be further evidenced by the fact that between 1534 and 1651 the office changed hands 12 times and for 9 of these changes the Audits are missing![7] There is nothing to show how the audit was conducted. In Newcastle-upon-Tyne as late as the sixteenth century, the auditors checked the addition by the medieval exchequer method of arranging counters on a table or board marked out in squares. This is evidenced by the early chamberlains' accounts which record the regular purchase of plain counters for the purpose (in 1562 they cost 1*s.* 8*d.* a pound).[8] Such a method may well have been used in Bristol. It is difficult to see how additions were otherwise checked with a narrative form of account using Roman numerals. That the audit was a real one is shown, not only by the signatures in the book and by the expenditure on the fees of officers attending it and on the audit dinner, but by the fact that from time to time altera-

---

[7] To quote a later example, at the end of 1748/9 the Audit showed that the chamberlain owed the city £2,661 13*s.* 3¼*d.* for the surplus income of the year. It did not show that of this sum £2,589 2*s.* 4½*d.* represented rents with which he had been charged, but which he had not received. The balance of moneys received on behalf of the Corporation should, therefore, have been £72 10*s.* 10¾*d.*, a much more likely figure.

[8] E. Halcrow, *Mr. Treasurer—Newcastle-upon-Tyne before 1835* (*Local Government Finance* referred to in subsequent notes as L.G.F.—July and September, 1953), p. 2.

tions were made. It is seldom that any comment is made, but one item[9] at least shows that the summary was not prepared until after the audit had taken place as, though the totals of the section of the account containing that item are altered, the summary shows the amended figure. In the early accounts there is little indication of the formality of the audit[10] but the ordinances of the Corporation show the importance attached to the need for it. Auditors were elected for the various schools and almshouses administered by the Corporation and for all money in the care of members of the common council, such as the money collected for the purchase of corn for the poor in 1585. Those accounts which have survived are all in the same form.

Another problem was the custody of account books and of money and deeds. In 1572 it was agreed that these books of accounts "which he [the chamberlain] shall yearlye make being subscribed with his owne hande shall remayne in a chest with three lockes whereof Mr. Maior for the tyme being to kepe one keye and one of the Aldermen another keye and the thirde keye to be kepte by one other of the common counsell that shalbe appoynted for that purpose and that the Chambleyne shall kepe a booke conteyning the foote of his yearlie accompte for his remembraynce whereunto the Auditores for the tyme being yearlie shall sette their handes at the tyme of delivyring uppe of the said bookes." [11] This ordinance was repeated in 1702. One or more chests were kept in a chapel adjoining the Guildhall and numerous ordinances deal with their contents.[12] They included all corporate deeds and, in

[9] In 1539/40 there is a note at the bottom of one page of expenditure "ffor so muche the xx[li] chargid in this side paid to the Lorde of Essex late recorder of this towne for his fee dew to him at the fest of the Natyvite of our lorde god in anno 1540 whiche acustomablye was usde to be paid at won tyme and for that this said. Lorde of Essex was behedid before the seid fest in the seid yere of anno 1540 which the Auditores fynde that the parcell of xx[li] awght not to be allowed in this accompt." The symbol xx[li] means (in 16th century English) twenty pounds, using the Roman numerals for twenty and the Latin libra for pounds.

[10] How an audit was conducted in the fifteenth century is recorded by Ricart, a town clerk of Bristol, in his Kalendar started in 1479. He writes that "the morowe vpon All Sowlen day, the Maire is vsid to walk to Redclyff, and the Toune clerk with him; there to sytte in Audite vpon William Canynges ij chauntryes, and the vicorye and the propters with them. And aftir the seide Audyte is fynesshid, the Towne clerk to entre thaccompte of the same in a boke there, callid Canynges liger, and there the Maire to receyve 1 noble, the towne clerk xx d., the swerdberer viij d., and the four Sergeauntez of the Maire xvi d." *The Maire of Bristowe is Kalendar*, ed. L. Toulmin Smith (Camden Society, 1872), p. 79.

[11] Book of ordinances (Bristol Archives Office—referred to in subsequent notes as B.A.O.—04272).

[12] As early as 1446 an ordinance copied into the *Great Red Book* commands that certain monies be paid out by the holders of the four keyes of "Barstaples cofre with Inne the Chapell of Saint George in the Yeldhalle" (*G.R.B.* text I p. 127). In 1543 the money bequeathed by Nicholas Thorne for loans to young clothmakers was also to be kept in Barstaple's chest (Book of ordinances, B.A.O. 04272, p. 30) and in 1583

1625, it was decided that one of the aldermen, certain members of the council, and the town clerk should meet at the chapel, remove all writings and evidences into the Armory House, and order sufficient presses and boxes for placing them in St. George's Chapel again when they should be sorted out "Devided in competent boxes and chests appart."[13] No cash is mentioned, but the custody of money must still have been important.

BOOKS OF ORIGINAL ENTRY SUBSIDIARY TO THE AUDITS

An examination of the Audits shows that they were written up after the end of the accounting period. Not only is the handwriting the same throughout (apart from the final summary which was done at the time of the audit) but the form used made it impossible for the account to be compiled from day to day. Therefore, there must have been books of original entry; there must also have been some record of the funds not contained in the Mayor's Audits. None of these before 1615 remains. After that it is possible to trace the efforts of the mayor and commonalty to obtain effective financial control. What was needed was a method of accounting for rents due, for daily receipts and payments, and for the transactions which were not financed from the annual revenue of the Corporation and, in the early years, were not the responsibility of the chamberlain. The books used for these purposes were—

(i) *Rents.* The first surviving accounting record for the Corporation's estates is a Rental in which properties are listed with, in both margins, a horizontal line, which is crossed by vertical ones to indicate that the money has been received. When a volume covers several years the marginal markings are extended. These rentals continued until 1605; it is not known how the rents were recorded between then and 1640, when a ledger with personal accounts was started.

(ii) *The chamberlain's daily income and expenditure.* Separate day books showing receipts and expenditure have survived from 1658, but in 1668 an attempt was made to improve the form by starting "A Jornall or day Book," on the left-hand page of which all receipts are recorded under the heading of "Rents, ffines, and cassualties," and on the right-hand page all payments under the heading of "Generall and ordinary payments." A column on the left is used for the date, the middle of the page for narrative, with a single cash column on the right. The narrative is detailed and after each item its destination in Ledger or Audit is indicated. It is a pity that day books and ledgers have not generally survived for the same period, but it is possible to follow the entries through for a few overlapping years.

---

an ordinance decrees that the deeds of the Hospital of the Three Kings of Cologne and Trinity Hospital are to be kept in the chest appointed for the poor with four locks and names four persons to be keyholders (B.A.O. 04272, p. 51).

[13] City of Bristol Common Council Proceedings, 16th March 1625, p. 136.

(iii) *Other corporate transactions.* The first attempt to gather together into one list the balances of the Mayor's and Little Audits, of city bonds and of orphan money appears in the annual lists of such items given in the Bargain Books from 1610 to 1630. The purpose of these books was to record leases of property, and the inclusion of financial matter is unusual.

In 1613 a new chamberlain saw the need to provide a comprehensive account, and, in 1615, started a "Booke of the Citties Accomptes for monies due to the Maior and Cominaltie of Bristoll and what orphantes monie is in the custody of the Chamber." In it is listed for each year to 1639:

1. An inventory of bonds and other specialties.
2. The accompt of moneys received for interest and otherwise upon bonds for the use of the mayor and commonalty.
3. The accompt of moneys disposed of and let out at interest for the use of the mayor and commonalty.

A summary account follows, much in the form of the summary in the Audits. It is signed by the auditors. Through this account may be traced the purchase of estates. The first half of the book is devoted to these annual statements and the second half is a personal ledger covering the capital transactions in bonds and the interest thereon. In 1621 a second book was started entitled "Civitas Bristol The state Book of the Mayor and Cominalty." For the first time all the transactions of the Corporation are shown as a whole. For example, on 22nd August, 1635, all amounts due to the Corporation are listed, including the balance of the Mayor's Audit, the stock of butter purchased for sale to the commons but still unsold, the stock of gunpowder, and the stock for putting the poor to work in the bridewell (house of correction). The total is £9,102 19*s.* 4¾*d.* On the other side is shown that £3,885 3*s.* 4*d.* was owing by the mayor and commonalty unto orphans and others. There remained in "Stock to Ballance £5,217 16*s.* 0¾*d.*"

In 1639 these books ceased to be kept. A personal ledger was opened in 1640, and succeeded the ledger in the second part of the Book of City Accounts. In the front of the ledger are the rent accounts, and in the back are those for amounts owing for orphans' money and for seals. The ledger was at no time an integral part of the accounting system, but only a memorandum, and the cash transactions in respect of orphan money and seals are from this date included in the Audits.

It is impossible to know whether the gaps in the series of account books are due to the destruction or loss of the books or whether, in fact, the chamberlain failed to keep them. That this is possible is shown by the efforts of the common council to insist on an adequate system of bookkeeping, which finally led to a new set of books being started in 1698. But as early as 1669 the council "ordered and agreed that the Chamberlin doe forthwith provide and constantly keepe a ledger booke and cash book."[14] It seems that little happened for, in 1670 and 1685, the chamberlain again was ordered to make a cash book. Common council had realised the necessity for some record which would show how much cash there should be. In 1687 it was agreed that "the Chamberlaine doe begin the Auditt of his Accounts at the Counsell Chamber att nine of the clocke on the 7th November next and that the Chamberlaine henceforward keepe a cash booke from Michaelmas last upon pain of forfeiteinge his office."[15] In fact, the office was not forfeited until 1698, but in 1692 a committee was set up to go into the question of the city accounts which in 1693 "ordered that a Journal Ledger and Cash booke be bought at the City's charge and delivered to Mr. Chamberlain to keep the Citys accounts therein. . . ."[16] Common council was doing its best to enforce financial control and had realised that the Mayor's Audits were not enough. Finally, in 1698, the chamberlain was charged for injustice, negligence, and unfitness for his office and was dismissed.[17]

(iv) *Vouchers*. The need for vouchers and other records which could be examined by the auditors when verifying income or expenditure must have been apparent from the beginning, but nothing is in existence until after the end of the sixteenth century. The Bargain Books, which record leases, begin in 1604 and continue until after 1835. They deal with the whole of the estates administered by the Corporation whether as corporate property or on behalf of the schools, almshouses, and other charities managed by them. In 1652 a series of Bond Books begin which give details of bonds issued for loans raised by the Corporation. From 1651 Receipt Books remain which contain signed receipts for payments made by the chamberlain. In the earlier books the receipt was written in the book, but later it was written on a loose piece of paper and pasted in the book. In addition to the receipt books the chamberlain's vouchers remain from 1600. These consist largely of tradesmen's bills, and a detailed study of them would give a continuous record, not only of prices and wages, but also of the methods used in building and in the repair of sewers and water pipes.

1698 to 1785

The series of account books which began in 1698 continued until 1785, when the common council felt again the need for revision. The main improvements were the institution of a cash book and the incorporation of personal accounts for rents as a part of the accounting system. The Mayor's Audits appear to continue in an unbroken series,

[14] *Ibid.*, 1669, p. 193

[15] *Ibid.*, 13th October, 1687, p. 1.

[16] *Ibid.*, 27th September, 1692, p. 87.

[17] *Ibid.*, 11th November, 1698, p. 169.

though the Audit was now an exact copy of the journal, which acted in effect as an impersonal ledger.[18] The form was little changed. It started with the rentals of town and country lands. Then followed sections for the receipt of burgess money, fines and casualties, money taken up at interest and income from the new market. Next, payments are listed under headings similar to those used in the past—quarterly payments including officers' fees, general and ordinary payments out of the city and country lands, payments of principal, interest and annuities, and payments on account of the exchange and market. The total of each section is carried to a final summary account which begins with the previous year's balance. The Audit was doubtless written out for the mayor and for signature by the auditors. It may well have been retained by them as the official record, the chamberlain keeping the journal.

The first cash book shows receipts on the left-hand page and payments on the right-hand. No opening balance is shown. Each page is added and the balance carried forward. A small cross in the date margin seems to indicate that the item has been posted, but no folio is given. After 1739, totals are carried forward and a monthly balance made and the journal folio (except for rents received) is given in the date margin. By 1758 a folio column has appeared beside the cash column. The folio shown for rent received is not that of the personal account in the ledger and some intermediate book must have been used. The ledgers contain only personal accounts. They were debited on the left-hand side with the rent due (which was credited to the journal or Audit), and credited on the right-hand side with cash received. These accounts formed an integral part of the accounting system. Some ledgers had also personal accounts for city seals and orphan money, but these were only a memorandum as all capital and interest receipts and payments were entered in the journal from the cash book.

Accountability was the primary object of the new system, and there was still no way of seeing at a glance the state of the city's finances. The balance appearing at the end of each financial year as being due from the chamberlain was still based on the income which should have been received. It was, therefore, represented by arrears of rent and cash. In most accounts on a charge and discharge basis, arrears of rent at the beginning and end of the accounting period are included in the summary, but this was never done in Bristol. By 1780, however, if the total arrears of rent are deducted from the amount said to be due from the chamberlain the result is the balance as shown by the cash book. A system of accountability based on a modified form of double-entry bookkeeping had been achieved.

[18] The earliest surviving journal is for 1777 and is marked 'D.16' indicating the loss of 15 volumes, but as the Audits are still in existence and they are replicas of the journals the continuity of the accounts is unbroken.

1785 to 1835

Whether inefficiency of chamberlains, a desire to bring the Corporation's accounts into line with current accounting practices, or a need for more knowledge of its financial position, led the common council to take further action, is not known, but on 8th December, 1784, it was unanimously agreed that a Committee should be set up for one year to "inspect correct and improve the manner in which the City accounts are now kept and to form some more perfect mode of keeping the same in future." [19] In December, 1785, it was reported that the Committee had not been able as yet to digest and settle a plan to be offered for the consideration of the council and it was agreed that it should be continued another year. (That the Committee and the common council had confidence in the chamberlain is shown by the fact that he was reappointed for another year and was declared, as usual, receiver of the rents and profits of the several hospitals and charities under the order and control of the Corporation.)[20] On 29th October, 1787, the Committee reported that they had not only directed that a different mode of accounts should be adopted but that it had been carried out for the year ended the 29th September, 1786, and was ready for inspection and audit. They also recommended that a committee should continue to watch over the "Improvements of the City Stock" and that proper offices and repositories should be erected for the transaction of corporate business and the safekeeping of papers.[21]

The new accounting system began on the 1st October, 1785, and a new set of cash books and journals starts from this date. Impersonal accounts were opened at the back of the existing ledger. A full double-entry form of accounts was adopted which attempted to set out the whole financial transactions of the Corporation, including a valuation of its estates.[22] The first entry in the journal lists the assets of the Cor-

[19] City of Bristol Common Council Proceedings, 8th December, 1784, p. 71.

[20] *Ibid.*, 14th December, 1785, p. 103.

[21] *Ibid.*, 29th October, 1787, p. 182.

[22] In the first journal the basis of this valuation is set out and the opening inscription reads—

Mr. Chamberlain,

We the Committee appointed by an order of the Common Council, 8 December, 1784 to inspect, correct and improve the manner in which the City Accounts are now kept and to form some more perfect mode for keeping the same in future, Do hereby direct that a Stock Account be forthwith made of all the property belonging to the Mayor Burgesses and Commonalty of this City, And that the Interest of this Corporation in Estate Lands and Houses be valued by you in such Stock Account agreeable to the following Rules, viz.—

Houses in Bristol on Leases for Lives

If 3 Lives in being 2 Years Rack Rent and 12 Years Chief Rent.
If 2 Lives ——— 4 Years Rack Rent and 10 Years Chief Rent.
If 1 Life ——— 8 Years Rack Rent and 6 Years Chief Rent.

Houses on Leases for 40 years, renewable

poration which totalled to £137,960 4*s*. 10¾*d*. (Cash was £1,250 7*s*. 7¾*d*., sundry debtors £4,399 11*s*. 11½*d*. and the rest the value of corporate estates.) The total was credited to stock account and debited to the respective impersonal accounts. The second entry debited to stock account the various liabilities of the Corporation amounting to £77,210 2*s*. 5¼*d*.

The cash book was of a simple form with receipts on the left-hand side and payments on the right-hand.[23] It was balanced monthly and a journal entry made for the items on each side, and from those entries the ledger was posted. The posting folio in the cash book was the journal folio. The full detail was copied from the cash book into the journal, but for ease of posting the items were grouped under the appropriate ledger headings. At the end of the financial year rents payable were debited to the personal accounts and interest on loans credited to them by journal entry, with a corresponding total in the respective impersonal accounts. Finally, the balances of the impersonal accounts were carried to Stock Account, which thus showed the income for the year, the payments from it, the capital value of property, and the total debts. The balance of this account was carried forward to the next year and underneath an explanation was given, showing the increase or decrease in stock which had taken place. The Stock Account for the first year is given in Table 1.

After 1785 the Mayor's Audits were no longer written up. A summary of receipts and payments was given in the journal and below the Stock Account in the ledger, and this was signed by the auditors. All remaining balances in the ledgers of personal and impersonal accounts were listed in a balance book and this, too, was signed by the auditors. It proved the arithmetical accuracy of the accounts, as the separate

Two Years Rack Rent and 13 Chief Rent.

Houses on Rack Rents

Fourteen Years Rack Rent.

Houses in Bristol renewable at a fix'd fine

If 3 Lives in being--Double the fine and 14 Years Chief Rent

If only 2 Lives, to be valued as if no fix'd fine.

Estates in the Country on Leases for Lives

If 3 Lives in being 11 Years Rack Rent and 14 Years Chief Rent.

If 2 Lives -- - ---- 13 Years Rack Rent and 12 Years Chief Rent

If 1 Life ——- -- -- 18 Years Rack Rent and 7 Years Chief Rent

Estates Let at Rack Rents 25 Years Purchase.

[23] As the financial business of the Corporation grew, especially in the collection of various dues from shipping, subsidiary cash books were necessary at the point of collection and those concerned with markets, town dues, the mayor's dues and the quay warden have survived. The form varies with the information needed For example, the collector of mayor's dues recorded the date, the name of the vessel, the tonnage, the master's name and where it came from, with a single cash column for the amount received for dues. Similarly, appropriate detail was entered in the market books, but each was, in effect, a simple cash received book.

TABLE 1

STOCK ACCOUNT—1st October, 1785 to 29th September, 1786

			£	s.	d.				£	s.	d.
1785 Oct. 1	To Sundries—[Valuation of payments out and loans, etc.] Stock	24 and 32	77,210.	2.	5¼	*1785* Oct. 1	By Sundries	23	137,960.	4.	10¾
	" Bailiff of Portishead		7.	10.	4.		" Renewals on Dr. Owen's and Bartholomew's Lands	37	2,334.	18.	2.
1786 Sept. 29	" Sundries—[Interest on City Seals, Annuities and gifts and payments]	120	3,148.	10.	1.	*1786* Sept. 29	" Rents General Account	128	2,411.	8.	10¼
	" Fee Farm and Quit rents for 13/4d. per annum payable by Christ Church Churchwardens	127	20.	0.	0.		" Sundries [Income from Markets, gifts, gains on Renewals of Leases, etc.]	129	2,444.	15.	7.
	" Sundries [transferred expenditure and loss on property]	131	9,924.	8.	6.		" Sir Thomas White's gifts gained on them.	132	67.	5.	0½
	" Ald. Robert Kitchen's gift, for loss thereon	132	3.	10.	0.		" Mr. Thomas White's gifts gained on them.	132	24.	7.	10.
	" Mr. Thomas Chester's gift, for loss thereon	133	1.	0.	0.		" Bailiff of Portishead year's rent of Fishing Stages, there due 29th September, 1786	133	2.	10.	3.
	" Rents payable by the Chamber	133	159.	4.	5.						
			90,474.	5.	9¼						
	" Balance carried to next years account to folio	346	54,771.	4.	10¼						
			145,245.	10.	7½				145,245.	10.	7½
Explanation of the above Account											
	Balance to the Credit of Stock 1st October, 1785, was		63,077.	10.	3½						
	Balance to the Credit of Stock 1st October, 1786, is		54,771.	4.	10¼						
	Stock decreased		8,306.	5.	5¼						

columns for debit and credit balances had to show identical totals, but there was no attempt to produce a balance sheet. A much more extensive analysis of expenditure was now possible, although unanalysed "Quarterly payment" accounted, in the first years, for 25 per cent of the total.

This bookkeeping system continued unaltered up to 1835, and for many years after the Corporation had been reformed. Only one change of importance was made. Another set of books began in 1817, and in the front of the new journal a recommendation of the surveyors of city lands is inscribed which directed the chamberlain to close every account which originated from an estimated value of the property of the Corporation; the surveyors were fully confirmed in their former opinion that "such valuations are merely visionary." This was done, and, until after 1890 when the first balance sheet was produced, there were no capital accounts for corporate property. Between 1785 and 1835 there was a considerable increase in both income and expenditure, and the new system did at least show, in far greater detail than the Mayor's Audits had done, how the income arose and on what it had been spent. The annual charge for loan interest was the amount due irrespective of payment and the annual income was based, as it had been throughout the whole period, on rents receivable, not on rents received, but sales of property and expenditure on new buildings were included in the annual account, which thus gave no clear indication of the revenue position. It is hard to assess how useful it was as a means of efficient financial control. On the death of a chamberlain in 1815 there was a deficiency of £3,600, and the following chamberlain was dismissed in 1822 for the misuse of charitable funds, but history does not record whether these misdemeanours became apparent because of, or in spite of, the accounting system. The efficient audit of an enterprise of this size would need a considerable amount of time and experience. It was still being carried out by elected members of the common council and may have become a somewhat formal procedure.

Towards the end of the eighteenth century, and in the early years of the nineteenth century, reform was in the air and there was a growing demand for the publication of accounts to show how money received from the public in rates and tolls had been spent. In Nottingham, before 1795, the bellman gave notice that the accounts were to be submitted to the council and freemen were allowed to inspect them.[24] In 1793 the accounts of Glamorgan were ordered to be printed in the *Bristol Gazette*.[25] The County of Middlesex printed its accounts under an

[24] V. W. Walker, *Mr. Treasurer, Nottingham—before 1835* (L.G.F., April, 1957), p. 85.

[25] M. Elsas, *Mr. Treasurer, Glamorgan—before 1889* (L.G.F., November, 1957), p. 262.

Act of 1815.[26] In 1810 a petition to have the accounts of Newcastle-upon-Tyne printed and made public was rejected, but authorised later, and publication started in 1818.[27] As a result of popular agitation, a regular printed series of accounts started in Liverpool from 1816.[28] In Bristol the accounts of the Corporation of the Poor appeared in local papers from 1823, and the act of 1806 setting up paving commissioners contained a regulation that the accounts should be audited and published in two or more papers, but the common council of Bristol, a closed corporation raising no rates and spending the income of property which it regarded as its own, was not inclined to make public any financial information and it was not until after the reform of that Corporation in 1835 that accounts were printed and published.

Comparison with Other Accounts of the Period

Professor Yamey has written "the origins of accounting and indeed of written records are probably to be found in the need of an 'accounting' officer to render a statement of money and other assets received in his charge on behalf of an employer or disbursed on his behalf." [29] The accounting methods in use in Bristol up to 1785 had this as their sole objective and it is not, therefore, possible or profitable to compare them with accounting methods used by the merchants of the sixteenth and seventeenth centuries. As first known in 1532, they were similar to that in use by other towns and for estate accounting. Dr. Oschinsky, in her study of *Medieval Treatises on Estate Accounting*, found that the accounts, whether on rolls or in books, usually ran from Michaelmas to Michaelmas and were "a record on which the accountant stated all the goods both in kind and in money which had been received by him or had been paid out by him during the period of account, together with his liabilities at the beginning and at the end of the period. Thus it was essentially a statement of the receipts and expenses of the accountant and not of the manor." [30] The same system was used for the Cromwell household accounts for 1417-1476 and there was no attempt to arrive at the profit or loss for the estate.[31]

[26] Staff of the County Record Office, *Mr Treasurer—Middlesex—before 1889* (L.G.F., December, 1952), p. 277.

[27] E. Halerow, *Mr. Treasurer—Newcastle-upon-Tyne before 1935* (L.G.F., September, 1953), p. 1.

[28] Dr. George Chandler, *Mr. Treasurer—Liverpool* (L.G.F., July, 1951), p. 151.

[29] B. S. Yamey, "*Some Topics in the History of Financial Accounting in England, 1500-1900*," *Studies in Accounting Theory*, eds. W. T. Baxter and S. Davidson (London: Sweet & Maxwell, 1962), p. 15.

[30] D. Oschinsky, "*Medieval Treatises on Estate Accounting*," *Studies in the History of Accounting*, eds A. C. Littleton and B. S. Yamey (London: Sweet & Maxwell, 1956), p. 91

[31] E. M. Myatt-Price, *Cromwell Household Accounts, 1417-1476*, *ibid.*, p. 107.

From 1306 the Mayor's accounts of the city of Leicester, though using a more narrative form, follow the same basic system. They start with income from tallages and fines and then set out in detail the payments, and, when in 1375 chamberlains were appointed, their accounts followed the same pattern.[32] Gradually the narrative form was superseded by the more modern columnar account and the income and expenditure was grouped under broad headings, but the basic objective of accountability remained unchanged, and, as late as 1800–1801, the account headings in use gave little indication of the purposes of expenditure. Unfortunately, the great fire destroyed early financial records of the city of London and the first one remaining is City Cash for 1632. This is very much in the same form as the Mayor's Audits. It starts with the income due from rents, casual receipts, extraordinary income, debts and orphans' money. This is followed by payments divided into inward fees, outward fees, weekly wages and materials bought for reparations, loans made and orphan money repaid. A final summary shows what is due from the chamberlain and is audited and signed by eight auditors. Thus, in London, the corporate account books in 1632 included loan transactions and orphan money, whereas in Bristol these were shown in subsidiary books until after 1640. In London, as in Leicester and Bristol, subsidiary books must have been kept, but the first one remaining is the City Cash's Cash for 1962. Receipts of money are on the left and payments on the right. It starts with an opening balance and each page is added and the balance carried forward. Folio numbers in the margin show that each item was posted to some other book of account. In Bristol a cash book was not started until 1698.

Before 1785 there was no attempt in Bristol to show the true annual expenditure or to arrive at the annual financial position. Professor Yamey found this to be the case in a number of seventeenth and eighteenth century double-entry ledgers and he says "the neglect of what today is called accrual accounting is evident in the treatment of interest on debts. . . . There is no thorough-going attempt in any of the ledgers to make allowance for accrued interest at balancing dates."[33] In this, commercial and corporate accounting were alike.

After 1785 accrual accounting began, but, until the end of the nineteenth century, no balance sheet was produced. Nevertheless, the accounting system in Bristol was well up to contemporary standards and ahead of some other corporate bodies. A petition in 1810 that the accounts of Newcastle-upon-Tyne should be broken up under additional headings was rejected, although in 1813 the common council ordered

[32] *Records of the Borough of Leicester*, ed. Mary Bateson (1899), Vol. 1, p. 232 and Vol. 11, pp. 154 157.

[33] B. S. Yamey, "Some Seventeenth and Eighteenth Century Double-Entry Ledgers, *Accounting Review*, October 1959.

that a new and improved method of accounting should be devised and adopted, but a further analysis was only just developing in 1835.[34] In 1824 a specially appointed Finance Committee of the city of Nottingham deplored the condition of the Cash Book which was seldom cast up or balanced and whose general appearance was confused and unsatisfactory.[35] The account books of the Corporation of Bristol, on the other hand, were well kept and the system provided all that was thought necessary when, after 1835, the Corporation was empowered to raise a Borough Rate and the era of local government finance began.

[34] E. Halcrow, *Mr. Treasurer—Newcastle-upon-Tyne before 1835* (L.G.F., September, 1953), p. 4.

[35] V. W. Walker, *op. cit.*

Sixteenth-century Accounting

The Ledger of John Smythe, Merchant of Bristol

by JEAN VANES, B.A.

DISCUSSION of early accounting methods in England has been based very largely on the textbooks published in the second half of the sixteenth century. The few account books surviving from the early part of the century have not been subjected to detailed analysis and the general impression has been that, though they might be in bilateral form, the methods of book-keeping employed were both primitive and careless. A study of the ledger of the Bristol merchant, John Smythe, who traded to Spain and Gascony and whose account book spans the years 1538–1550, has shown that he was using a system of venture accounting very similar to that used in fifteenth-century Italy.[1]

Until comparatively recently little has been known about the lives of provincial merchants in England in the sixteenth century and, since few of their records remain for study, almost nothing was known of their business methods. It is generally accepted that England – most of Europe in fact – was about two hundred years behind Italy in the techniques of accountancy and banking. However, as Professor Lane found in Venice, 'mercantile practice was far better and far more varied than is indicated by the treatises published in the sixteenth century'.[2] That this was true for Italy, France, the Netherlands and Spain has long been obvious. It may be that, with further study of the records, we shall find that it is true also in England.

The few remaining English account books suggest that, though English merchants occasionally had difficulty with Arabic numerals and with alphabetical order, they well understood the basic principles of accountancy. If they did not use full double-entry book-keeping, it was not for lack of the opportunity to learn it but because the scale and nature of their trade made such detailed and accurate book-keeping not only 'to painfull and busy', but possibly unnecessary and uneconomic. When the merchant was his own accountant it was less likely that 'so many daungers and discomodities' would come 'of the negligent kepyng of reconynges'.[3]

John Smythe's ledger

The John Smythe ledger is a large, leather-bound volume, originally fastened with a strong buckle and strap. The leather has an all-over pattern of tooled rectangles and diamonds, the pattern larger on the front than on the back. It is in excellent condition, though it has been repaired at some time and some of the pages restitched out of order. It has three hundred folios of 13 in. × 8½ in., with the watermark 'J. Nivelle' which shows that the paper was manufactured at Troyes in north-eastern France where the ledger may have been made and then exported to England. It covers the years 1538 to 1550 and is apparently one of a series though it seems to bear no distinguishing letter A, B or C, as one might expect. Most of the earlier accounts were brought forward from an 'old boke w^{c} began in *anno* 1533' and many accounts end with 'This cownt is passed into my newe booke fo.——— the ij^{de} day of July *anno* 1550'.

The first folio records only that 'This boke of accowmpt*es* ap*er*teynith to J*o*hn Smythe, m*a*rchant of Bristowe' and carries one of Smythe's merchant marks. Each folio is headed with a cross and, occasionally, having dispatched a particularly valuable consignment of goods, Smythe adds, 'God send hit saff'. However, 'God and profit'[4] were already beginning to part company. There is no long prayer like that in the 1436 Borromeo ledger 'to the salvation of our souls and with honour and profit to our bodies,[5] nor a petition like Ympyn's, 'Please it God, our merciful Lord, to grant me grace to earn and gain and may He preserve me from adversity'; nor when he notes his profits does Smythe add, 'Praise and honour to Almighty God who granted me this. Amen.'[6] By 1779 a merchant who kept his books carefully was said to 'walk in the paths of *moral rectitude*.'[7] God had already begun to help only those who helped themselves.

Pages of the ledger are given up to the enumeration of Smythe's plate in 1539, 1542 and that which was in his 'powar' in May 1549, some of it possibly as pledges for debts. When his mother died in 1546 he made a list of her possessions and a note of the legacies he must pay according to her will. There is, however, no attempt to estimate the value of all his possessions, such as Mellis suggests there should be in a 'solempne Inventorie'. It is possible that such an inventory would be in a 'Secreat greate Boke'. Similarly, the 'Kalendar', 'Abecedario' or table of contents was often a separate sheet or separately bound pages in the front of a

[1] Bristol Archives AC/B63, to be published jointly by the Historical Manuscripts Commission and the Bristol Records Society.

[2] F. C. Lane, 'Andrea Barbarigo, Merchant of Venice 1418–1449'. *Johns Hopkins University Studies in Historical and Political Science*, Series LXII, No. 1 (Baltimore 1944), page 154 n. 1.

[3] Ympyn, *A Notable . . . Woorke . . .*, Chapter 29, quoted Yamey, Edey and Thomson, *Accounting in England and Scotland 1543–1800*, (London 1963), pages 6–7.

[4] I. Origo, *The Merchant of Prato* (London 1957), page 114.

[5] P. Kats, 'Double entry Book-keeping in England before Hugh Oldcastle', *The Accountant*, LXXIV (1926), page 92.

[6] P. Kats, 'The "Nouvelle Instruction" of Jehan Ympyn Christophle', *The Accountant*, LXXVII (1927), pages 267 and 269.

[7] Quin, *Rudiments of Book-keeping*, quoted in Yamey and others, page 11 (author's italics).

ledger[8] and, if Smythe kept one, it has been lost. The entries are not in alphabetical or date order and when a page was full the balance of the account was simply transferred to the next empty page. It is not unusual to find an account of 1549 or 1550 pushed in between two earlier accounts.

Smythe sets out his accounts clearly in correct bilateral form; the folios numbered across the double page from 1 to 300, the left-hand side for debit, the right-hand side for credit. However, although his accounts are set out 'alla veneziana'[9] and in many ways they resemble those of Andrea Barbarigo, accountancy was for Smythe almost certainly the 'Reconynge*s* of Spayne' learned from the kind of apprenticeship described in *The Marchants Avizo*[10] with several years spent in Spain. His own apprentices travelled a great deal. At one time, in 1546, while Henry Setterford was at Bordeaux, Hugh Hammond was in Andalusia and Robert Tyndall carried money from one to the other. Tyndall, particularly, seems to have spent many years at San Sebastian.[11]

Such experience must have enabled the apprentice to gain a good knowledge of Spanish business methods. In addition, several other Bristol merchants lived for some time in Spain. Robert Thorne and his brother Nicholas, Thomas Howell, Roger Barlow, Thomas Batcock and Hugh Tipton all lived in Spain during the first half of the sixteenth century and all were Bristolians or had strong ties with the town. Smythe had dealings with most of them as well as with William Ostriche, the London merchant who was the Governor of the English merchants at San Lucar near Seville. Edward Pryn with whom Smythe and some Portuguese merchants formed a company in 1540 spent many years in Portugal and must have had a good knowledge of accounts to be 'admyttyd for mynester' of the company 'here in Ynglonde'.[12]

Early manuals of accountancy are lacking in Spain as in England, but it is possible that such business techniques were introduced into southern Spain from Italy. As early as 1390 Italian firms like that of Datini had factors in Catalonia who kept their books in double entry,[13] but it was the presence of an important colony of Genoese at Seville from the thirteenth century[14] which may provide the link through which Bristol merchants learned Italian techniques. That these methods were well understood in Spain by the mid-sixteenth century is shown by the ledgers of Simon Ruiz, which begin in 1551.[15]

Smythe's daily purchases and sales were recorded in a 'shop-boke', though, unfortunately, none of the shop books has survived. The sixteenth-century manuals recommend that three books should normally be kept, the shop book or Memorial, the Journal and the 'Leager' or 'Quaterne' – the 'great boke of accompts.'[16] However, they admit that 'howe be it, some marchauntes there be, that use but small feate of marchandise, which do occupie but onely the Journall and Leager'.[17] A 'jornal' is mentioned once by Smythe but as there are no other references to it, this would seem to be an error for the shop book.

In the shop book – only once called 'my memoryall' – every transaction was noted in detail by himself, his family his apprentices and servants and this daily information was later transferred to the ledger. This was often done much later and not within the prescribed five or six days. Ympyn comments that 'a right Marchant of Italy will not faile to write at after none all thynges that he did in the forenone'. Smythe frequently seems to have left it for two or three months and this may account for some of the mistakes in the ledger. On one occasion he was forced to write on an account for iron, 'Itm. j ton xij C w^{t} I do fynde lackyng by this cow*nt*, whe*ther* it be stolen or forgoten to be sett apo*n* my shop boke when it was solld I can not well say'.

Although Smythe does not strictly follow the instruction that 'in the Journall or Leiger book there may not be any alteration of Cyphers, blotting (nor places left in blanke in the Journal) . . . otherwise the books are of no credit in Law',[18] his corrections are usually carefully made. The wrong figure is erased and the correct one inserted and at the end of the entry it is often repeated – 'I sey vj^{li}'. For a whole incorrect entry he writes, 'I arryd in settyng this itm. and therefore wryte it discowntid in a newe cow*nt*'. Sometimes he was in a hurry and merely crossed out and there are many blank spaces, but the constant naming of sureties and witnesses in his various transactions would seem to indicate that the books themselves were not yet sufficient evidence in the Bristol courts of Staple and Tolzey.

Model of venture accounting

From a study of the John Smythe ledger it seems clear that Smythe was using a system of venture accounting similar to that described by Professor Lane from the account books of Andrea Barbarigo of Venice. The main characteristics of venture accounting have been found in all the surviving Venetian account books as well as those of Ragusa.[19] This

[8] Ympyn, Chapter III, quoted P. Kats, *The Accountant*, LXXVII (1927), page 266. In 1522 Thomas Howell, the London draper, paid 3*s* 4*d* for his ledger and 8*d* for a Kalendar. (I owe this reference to the kindness of Mr J. Brierley who is editing the ledger.)

[9] R. de Roover, 'The Development of Accounting Prior to Luca Pacioli' in Littleton and Yamey, eds. *Studies in the History of Accounting* (London 1956) page 139, quotes this description of bilateral form from a Florentine, Paliano di Falco Palliani, 1382.

[10] P. McGrath (ed.) *The Marchants Avizo* (Harvard, Cambridge, Massachusetts, 1957), pages xvi–xxiii.

[11] J. Alban Fraser, *Spain and the West Country* (London 1935), pages 92–96. Bristol Archives, St John Baptist Misc. Papers 178.

[12] F. W. Weaver, *Visitations of the County of Somerset 1531 and 1573* (Exeter, 1885), pages 125–126. Pryn's nephew married a Portuguese lady and became aide to Don Antonio, the Portuguese Pretender. B. M. Lansdowne MSS. LIII 24, LIV 74.

[13] I. Origo, *The Merchant of Prato*, page 114. R. de Roover in Littleton and Yamey, pages 138 and 141, gives an example of Italian venture accounting in Spain.

[14] J. Lynch, *Spain under the Hapsburgs*, Volume I (Oxford 1964), page 103. R. Pike, 'The Genoese in Seville and the opening of the New World', *Journal of Economic History*, Volume XXII (1962), pages 348–378. A. Girard, 'Les étrangers dans la vie économique de l'Espagne au XVIe et XVIIe siècles', *Annales d'histoire économique et sociale* (1933), pages 567–578.

[15] H. Lapeyre, *Une Famille des Marchands: Les Ruiz* (Paris 1955) pages 339–345

[16] J. Peele, *The Maner and fourme* . . ., (Richard Grafton, London 1553) Chapter V.

[17] J. Mellis, *A Briefe Instruction* . . ., (John Winder, London 1588) Chapter V.

[18] Malynes, *Lex Mercatoria 1656*, quoted *Yamey and others*, page 49. In the Chancery Court in the sixteenth century the account books of the London merchants seem to have been accepted in evidence. Public Record Office, Early Chancery Proceedings, Ci 589/43, 'theire bookes of theire owne wrytyng to be of lyke forsse as is a specialtie'. A speciality is a legally enforceable deed or contract – F. Pollock and F. W. Maitland, *The History of English Law* (Cambridge, 1911), Volume II, page 220.

[19] F. C. Lane, 'Venture Accounting in Medieval Business Management', *Bulletin of the Business Historical Society*, XIX (1945), page 168.

system which was the 'most practical form for merchants much of whose wealth was coming and going on the seas' enabled Smythe to keep account of his obligations and claims through the various personal accounts which include also family and household expenses.

In addition, by means of the 'voyage' accounts, he could compare, year by year, the relative profitability of the various overseas markets to which he sent his goods. Accounts for apprentices and factors abroad would enable him to correlate his accounts with theirs, while commodity import accounts showed clearly the amount of profit recently received on iron, the various kinds of wine, fruit, woad and oil. If he needed to do so, Smythe could calculate his total profit over any given period in a profit and loss account to which he closed the voyage and imported commodity accounts.

The complete system is shown below. When Smythe bought leather from Thomas Machin in 1540 he credited Machin's account and debited the accounts for calf skins and hides. His payment for the leather appears but there is in the ledger no cash account to be credited. When the skins were laden in his ship, the *Trinity* in February 1541, the leather accounts were credited and a voyage account – 'Viag*es* to Biscay in este Spayne (Robert Tyndal my prent*es* being my ffactor there)' was debited. When Tyndall's account came in to his master, Smythe credited the voyage account with the selling price of the goods and debited Tyndall's account. Unfortunately, Smythe often did not bother to copy into the ledger the account he received from his factor, so the accounts from Tyndall mentioned do not appear, though there are other examples of accounts from factors in the ledger.

The credit side of a factor's account showed the total of the purchases he had made for his principal and his own expenses. The purchases were then debited to an imported commodity account, such as that for wool oil. When William Pickes bought oil on May 22nd, 1542, his account was debited and the oil account was credited. Pickes did not pay any money in 1542 but is credited with canvas for sails and with candles and timber purchased by Smythe for his ship. Smythe started an account for the ship but crossed it through and it seems possible from the large number of entries for stores and for payments for freight from other merchants that he may have kept a separate book for the ship. Similarly, the system as set out is not completed in the ledger because there is no cash account.

MODEL OF VENTURE ACCOUNTING USED BY SMYTHE

DEBIT (L)	*CREDIT* (R)
'owithe –'	'– is dewe to have –'
1. *Personal account of supplier*	
cash *or* goods	cloth *or* wheat, leather, lead, etc.
2. *Export Commodity Account*	
cloth *or* wheat, leather, lead } from 1 R.	consignments to ships
3. *Voyage Account*	
detail of consignment from 2 R to factor with all costs 'Clere aborde', names of ships, masters, merchant marks	factor's account of sales
PROFIT *or*	*LOSS*
4. *Factor's Account*	
factor's account of sales from 3 R, cash sent to him or bills of exchange	factor's account of purchases, costs 'clere aborde' - tax, freight, insurance, factor's expenses
5. *Import Commodity Account*	
factor's account of purchases and costs from 4 R	detailed list of sales to customers
PROFIT *or*	*LOSS*
6. *Personal Account of Customer*	
Wine *or* oil, iron, woad, etc. as in 5 R	cash *or* goods
7. *Cash*	
from customer	to supplier
8. *Profit and loss*	
'Gaynes for my owne acownt ow*ith* –'	'Gaynes is dewe to have –'

Many of the sixteenth-century manuals advise the merchant to keep a separate cash-book and this was often done in order to keep the exact details of the master's wealth secret from the apprentices and servants. However, in the absence of any references to a separate cash-book, it is impossible to be sure that Smythe kept one. Thus, with no cash account, no account for the ship and no accounts for expenses or for the profits of money-lending, as well as Smythe's occasional failure to copy factors' accounts and commodity accounts in full, there are a great many entries in the ledger for which it is impossible to trace a corresponding debit or credit.

Profits and losses from voyage accounts and imported commodity accounts were carried to a profit and loss account. This was closed at the end of January 1544 (the date in the ledger is given as January 1543 because in the old calendar the year began in March), but the total profit of £1,427 16*s* 0½*d* was not transferred to a capital account nor was there any attempt, at least in this ledger, to estimate the total value of the merchant's assets at this time. A second profit and loss account, like many of the accounts in the second half of the ledger, was never completed.

Personal accounts

There are necessarily a large number of personal accounts in the ledger. These are clearly set out and in the accepted form, though the pages are not ruled into columns. Most items are carefully dated and the exact amount and type of commodity is specified. The cost and total value of each purchase is stated, often in Arabic numerals, sometimes in a mixture of Arabic and Roman, and then set out, usually in Roman numerals in the final column, these being regarded as less liable to error or falsification. Generally all foreign currency is changed into sterling in the totals column, though on one occasion the whole of Thomas Shipman's account from Biscay was copied into the ledger in maravedis. It is noticeable that Smythe always uses Arabic numerals when dealing with maravedis.[20]

[20] A maravedi was a coin of Moorish origin.

A Personal Account

248 L. anno 1546.			
Edward Rowley of Kingsnorton owithe the 14 day of July xviij^{li} ij^{d} ob. w^{c} is for the rest & closyng up of his acowmpt fo. 167	xviij^{li}		ij^{d}½
Itm. the 15 day of July 57^{li} 11^{s} 4^{d} & is for viij tons, pipe, j qr. iij li. Rendry iren at vj^{li} the ton & j ton, j qr. xxiij li. S.S.[21] iren at xix nobles the ton, to be paide at all tymes requyrid	lvij^{li}	xj^{s}	iiij^{d}
etc.			
anno 1546.			248 R.
Edward Rowley *per* contra is dewe to have the [22] of December xviij^{li} r. by Grevys	xviij^{li}		
Itm. the 21 day of Jenyver r. by Letes father	xvij^{li}	x^{s}	
Itm. the 25 day of May *anno* 1547 r. of hym at Bristowe xl^{li} & I rebate to hym xviij^{d} ob. mont*ith* all	xl^{li}	j^{s}	vj^{d} ob.
Itm. the 8 day of Augost r. of hym at Bristowe xxxvij^{li}	xxxvij^{li}		
etc.			

Other personal accounts include freight charges, house rents, purchases of victuals and stores for his ship, expenses connected with his civic duties and accounts of money-lending. Although valuables, such as 'a flat cup & a smawle standyng cup of sylver' were often taken as pledges for loans, no profit is shown from these transactions, since to take interest on a loan was for most of this time illegal. Only once does he write,

> Itm. for *Master* Bowen 5 nobles *the* prinsypall & the cost*es* 3s 7d [23]

as though interest of approximately 10 per cent was being taken. It seems probable that the money-lender found some way when interest was forbidden to take a concealed profit. Professor de Roover has suggested that in Italy the borrower actually received something less than the sum recorded in the ledger.

Very rarely was anything paid for in ready money. Apart from 'barter' agreements, 'three monthes and three monthes' was usual, or 'half in hand and half at *Owr* Lady Day' or at one of the local fairs. The amount owing was recorded on a bill stating the agreed days of payment. As payments were made, they were recorded on the back of the bill and when all was paid the bill was returned. Payments rarely seem to have been made on time. Smythe recorded all the details of his own bills in the ledger and often crossed off the amounts owing as he paid them, a practice which drew the censure of a seventeenth-century writer who complained that thereby 'the Beauty of their Books is turned to Deformity.'[24]

Prices vary a great deal but one can only suppose that the price was lowered on the unusual occasion when someone paid cash. There are times when so much is 'discowntid' or 'rebatid' in the price but whether this is the result of prompt payment or poor quality is difficult to discover. Payment was sometimes by a 'circular' or 'giro' method,[25] a well established practice by the fifteenth and sixteenth centuries. It was quite usual for Smythe to supply wine to William North or Stevyn Chick who then paid John Yerbery for the cloth he had sent to Smythe. With some of his customers Smythe waited years for payment and there is a formidable list of debts and desperate debts in the inventory taken at his death.

Voyage and factor accounts

Some of the more interesting accounts in the ledger are the voyage accounts which correspond exactly to the 'Viazo' accounts of Andrea Barbarigo and which are described by Mellis in his Chapter XV on 'Viages'. A merchant regularly concerned with exporting to various overseas markets wished to compare their relative profitability each year as well as to be able to check the accounts of his agents or factors abroad. Each time he sent a large consignment, usually in a particular ship or fleet of ships, he opened a new account. This contained on the debit side full details of all the goods sent; their cost and quality; how they were packed and sometimes their merchant marks, and the names of the ships and their masters. All the costs and expenses were added here, including the carriage to Bristol, the dyeing and finishing of cloth and licences and insurance. The credit side was completed when accounts were received from the factor or when the whole consignment was sold.

If the account was closed before all the goods were sold those remaining were debited to the following year's account at their cost price. The debit side, or sometimes both sides of an account had left-hand columns in which the goods were listed so that none was forgotten when the account was closed. Any profit or loss was then posted to the profit and loss account. In Smythe's ledger there are accounts of voyages to Bordeaux, Biscay, Lisbon and Andalusia.

An account was opened for the apprentice or factor who was then debited with the value of goods sold and any money sent to him and credited with the purchases he made on his master's behalf. It usually seems to have been necessary to export gold in order to complete the purchases for the year. In 1539 Francis Codryngton carried 110 Crowns of the sun by land to Tyndall at Bordeaux while 196 ducats and 97 Crowns went by sea. In 1546 Edward Pryn as 'taker' made Smythe as 'remitter' a Bill of Exchange which the purser of the *Trinity* of Wales carried to Hugh Hammond in Andalusia so that Hammond as 'payee' was able to obtain £25 from Pryn's agent, Hugh Tipton. This was money Pryn owed Smythe from the profits of the company importing woad.

In 1547 when Hugh Hammond sent money from Andalusia to Bilbao he sent 600 ducats in cash carried by Tyndall and 200 ducats in a bill made by John Swetynge of Cadiz to be paid to Henry Setterford at Bilbao by Robert Jeffarson, merchant of London. These are the only occasions when bills of exchange are mentioned, though Smythe sometimes notes a loss on the exchange of gold. He obviously followed Weddington's advice with his factor's accounts, first to 'peruse diligentlie and se yf in all thingis they be just'[26] because he sometimes notes an alteration.

> Itm. more j d*ucat* w^{c} he r. of the purs*er* of the Pr*i*mros & gave me no cowmpt of hit .. .. .. v^{s}

Professor Lane found in the Venetian merchant's accounts that factors were very slow to send in their accounts, possibly from negligence but also possibly because of delays

[21] 'Rendry' is Renteria in Northern Spain, 'S.S.' is San Sebastian.

[22] Blank in MS.

[23] This entry is dated 1548. During the years 1545–1553 interest of 10 per cent was legal in England.

[24] Monteage, *Debtor and Creditor*, 1675 preface, quoted in Yamey and others, page 12.

[25] P. Kats, 'Double-entry book-keeping in England before Hugh Oldcastle', *The Accountant*, LXXIV (1926), page 95.

[26] Weddington *Breffe Instruction* . . . ' quoted by Yamey and others, page 97.

in settling local expenses, taxation and freight charges. This may be one of the reasons why so many of the voyage accounts in the second part of the Smythe ledger have no credit entries and the second profit and loss account on folio 200 is incomplete. On the other hand, the war with France may have caused losses at this time and Smythe was granted a licence to import Bordeaux wine in 1545 because of the great losses he had sustained 'by serving his Majeste this sommer upon the see'. It may have been that some of these consignments were lost but he makes no note of it. Only one brief account for salmon from Ireland carries the note, 'My foreseid cabow (cargo, merchandise) being employed was taken w^t Scott*es*'.

Commodity accounts

Occasionally accounts were opened for the main exports – cloth, wheat, leather and lead – as these commodities were purchased and recorded in various personal accounts. However, this was by no means general and where no commodity account exists it is very difficult to trace an individual purchase of cloth, for example, from the supplier's account straight to the debit side of a particular voyage account. In the second part of the ledger, even where they exist, these commodity export accounts are often not complete.

Commodity accounts for imports were usually very detailed. Separate accounts were opened for the various types of wine; Gascon, sack, bastards, taynts, osseys. There are many accounts for iron and for wool oil, as well as those for woad, soap, raisins and figs and salt. The debit side of such an account gives the price of the goods 'clere aborde' the ship, then all the expenses of freight, taxes, insurance, windage, hauling and stowing.

The credit side usually gives a detailed list of purchasers with dates of purchase, amount and total cost and the folio reference of the customer's account. Both sides of the account have left-hand columns in which the quantity is recorded so that Smythe could be sure that the total amount on each page coincided. A typical entry on folio 84 R., for wool oil reads,

> 8 Itm. the 22 of May 52^{li} for iiij tons to
> W*illia*m Pik*es* fo. 97. .. .. .. lij^{li}

The credit sides of the iron accounts were often summarized unlike the others,

> anno 1542 153 R.
> Iren p*er* contra is dewe to have the 19 day
> of Augost 405^{li} 7^{s} that is ffor 67 tons,
> 7 C, j qr. ll li. iren *con*teyning 6451
> end*es* solld from the 7 day of Aprill
> last past untyll this day at divers
> pr*ises* as by my shop boke more largely
> may apere, mon*tith* as aforesseid .. iiij^{c}v^{li} vij^{s}
> etc.

When these commodity accounts were closed, it was often necessary to value the remaining stock to carry forward to a new account. The basis for this valuation was usually the cost price, sometimes a possible selling price and sometimes something between the two. There is on one occasion the possibility that an allowance was made for deterioration in quality in his stock of woad, but this is impossible to prove.

From odd papers found in the ledger it would seem that it was often the task of one of the apprentices to descend to the cellar and make an inventory of the stock when such a valuation was needed. Finally, any profit or loss on the imported commodity account was carried to the profit and loss account.

Profit and loss account

Since profits and losses were carried to the profit and loss account as soon as the voyage and imported commodity accounts were completed, Smythe could at any time roughly calculate his profit or loss over a given period without actually closing the account in the ledger. The account on folio 92 was closed when he reached the bottom of the page in January 1544 to show a profit of £1,427 16*s* 0½*d*. This includes only the voyage and commodity profits and the profit on a licence. No account is taken here of profits on the ship, from the company importing woad or from money-lending since none of these accounts appears in the ledger. A second profit and loss account was opened on folio 200 but was never completed.

In these accounts, Smythe was in fact including as 'profits' a lot of money which he had not yet received. Folio 43 gives a list of 'dessperid dett*es*' from his old book which totals over £76 and a study of the ledger shows that a very large number of his customers were very slow in paying. However, only a token amount of £60 'lost by dett*ers* & *other*wise' is included here and no provision is made for the other sums not paid.

Conclusion

The ledger was not checked and balanced when it was full. It seems as though Smythe sat down quietly in his 'cownter' on the first few days of July 1550 and transferred each account separately into his new book, noting at the end of each account in the old book the new folio number. Very few fifteenth- and sixteenth-century merchants balanced their books each year as the manuals advised. Andrea Barbarigo made trial balances in 1431, 1435 and 1440 and then let it run until his death in 1449.[37] For such men who well knew the whole state of their trade, accountancy was still used mainly to record transactions. It was not yet 'the glasse of a mannes state wherein all men maie se clerely in what case thei stande.'[38]

By 1547 Smythe was a busy man, alderman and mayor, and concerned more perhaps with the affairs of the city as well as his own extensive land purchases and the exploits of his sons at Oxford and in London than with a too exact concentration on the details of his own business records. In any case, if it is the business of the accountant to supply important information to management, no doubt many company directors might prefer the 'Receypt for to make one gallon of good ypocras' which graces Smythe's last page to the more doubtful delights of a balance sheet.

A RECEYPT FOR TO MAKE ONE GALLON OF GOOD YPOCRAS.

> Yow must take iij ownc*es* of synamon or ij ownces if hit be very good
> Itm. of gyng*er* hallf an ownce
> Itm. of galyngale hallf an ownce
> Itm. of clovys a quarter of an ownce
> Itm. of long pep*er* a quarter of an ownce
> Itm. of graynes hallf a quarter of an ownce
> Itm. of shewg*er* iij li. & if the wyne be dowzet ij li. wyll serve
> Itm. of good red wyne one gallon.

[37] F. C. Lane, *Andrea Barbarigo*, page 180. B. S. Yamey, 'Scientific Book-keeping and the Rise of Capitalism', *Economic History Review*, 2nd Series I (1949) page 106, states that many books were not balanced regularly even in the seventeenth century.

[38] Ympyn, *A Notable*. . .'*Woork* . . .,'Chapter 29, quoted in *Yamey and others*, page 7. A. C. Littleton, 'Social Origins of Modern Accountancy', *Journal of Accountancy*, LVI (1933), page 267.

SELECTIONS FROM A PRE-REVOLUTIONARY ACCOUNTING RECORD

ROBERT M. JENNINGS
Assistant Professor, Colorado State University

IN RECENT random reading the author encountered a reference to a Rhode Island firm with copies of business records dating to the early 1700's. The firm is The John Stevens Shop of Newport, Rhode Island. Upon inquiry, a photo-offset copy of the original account book was obtained from the present proprietor, and an interesting investigation was underway.

One of the first obvious accounting facts to present itself is the debit and credit notation. This particular individual used the present style of debits as left-side entries, and credits as right-side entries, as indicated by a number of pages in which individuals are charged on the left pages of the book and credited on the right pages. With the customary English practice of presenting balance sheets with the items reversed from American practice,[1] there is some uncertainty regarding this method of presentation. Regardless of the reason, the record keeper consistently maintained this separation.

There is some evidence to support the contention that this must have been one of the earliest uses of the double entry bookkeeping method in America. One transaction with a Mr. John Record shows a debit of 16 pounds and 4 shillings in 1717 (no month or day reference). On May ye 14, 1724, Mr. John Gidby was debited for various work done and the records indicate a contra credit in partial settlement on June ye 12, 1724. Supporting this recording as a very early American use of double entry bookkeeping is the recent Fortune Magazine article by Mr. John Chamberlain stating, "the Browns of Providence . . . Obadiah, who took over the business when James died in 1739, owned an early business textbook, *A Guide to Book Keepers According to the Italian Manner* (and presumably inaugurated the art of double entry bookkeeping in America)."[2]

Many of the transactions, although reduced to the pound, shilling, pence, and monetary equivalents, are the clear result of barter transactions. In the permissive orthography of this period, notice how Ebenezer Godard settled his account in 1728 and 1729:

"By one peace of garlick	5–18–00
By one bushel of Lime	0–01– 3
By a note to Tillinghast's Shop for One Thousand of Board Nails & Tho^nd & ½ of Shingle Nailes....	1–17– 6
By 6 yards of (oran Brigs)[3]	0–16– 0
By a noate to James Sheffield	10–00– 0
By Goods of Samuel Holmes	11–14– 0
By 28 pound of Shuger	1– 2– 0
	31– 9– 9"[4]

This list of credits to Godard's account also indicates the prevalence of transferring obligations.

The phrasing from Godard's account (and other information) indicates the customary practice of showing credits to the account with the designation "By" indicating the mode of account settlement. The same account on the facing page indicates the various debits with the designation "to" which indicates the reason for the charge to the customer's account.

[1] See the 1857 balance sheet of Deloitte and Greenwood. James Kilpatrick, Deloitte, Plender, Griffiths and Company, p. 19.

[2] John Chamberlain, "A History of American Business—Part I," Fortune, May 1961, p. 133.

[3] Because of other information drawn from "John Stevens—His Book" the present author feels that this phrase may be "oven bricks"; however, if this is true then the 6 yards apparently refers to cubic yards and, if so, the 16 shilling amount seems unreasonably small.

[4] Photo-offset copy of "John Stevens—His Book" p. 18.

Certain debits from Godard's account are as follows (again in the orthography of the period):

"June ye 28th, 1728 to Building your seller Wall 36 Perch att 6ˢ p perch 10—16—0
. . .
to one stak of chimeys & sollid foundation 19—00—0
to Laying 2 harths and mending one 0—10—0"[5]

When the reader views the prices of this period of two and one-half centuries ago, he might well apply the encomium of "the good old days." From various pages random items show, "Bushels of corn—6 shillings, 10 gallons of Syder (cider)—10 shillings, one gallon of Molases (sic)—2 shillings."[6] But, as might be expected, the wage picture does not appear particularly bright. For example, from the record appear such references

"Robert Hart 1726—
Dʳ to Schooling your child 8 weeks att 6 p week 0— 4—0"[7] . . .
Cʳ. Sep. 21—By 2 Days Works (sic) att Brayton's 0—12—0"[8] . . .
Cʳ—By one years Rent of your chamber 9—00—0"[9] . . .
to 9 Days work of Marcy quilting 00—18—0"[10] . . .

The records of the business were often kept in sufficient detail to construct a profit and loss statement for, at least, certain phases of the varied business operation. Reconstructing from given data (with allowances for the author's assumptions), an income statement regarding fowl dealings (fowl in present day orthography) reveals a "clear gain of 36 pounds and 13 shillings." This "clear gain" was the result of combining as income items three classifications, 40 pounds and 2 shillings, gote (sic) to sell, 18 pounds—9 shillings sold, and 4 pounds—no shillings gaine (sic).[11] The deductions from income were placed in two categories—bought consisting of 21 pounds and 13 shillings, and Loste consisting of 3 pounds and 15 shillings.[12] The listed items then total 62 pounds 11 shillings of "income" items and 25 pounds and 18 shillings of income deductions resulting in the clear gain of 36 pounds 13 shillings.[13]

Included in the accounting records are certain transactions with various individuals named Brown. This famous merchant family and their dealings with John Stevens provide an interesting exercise in critical historical analysis. "In Rhode Island, the Browns of Providence, a family dynasty like the Hancocks of Boston and the Derbys of Salem, had been doing business as merchants for a half-century before the Revolution. Captain James Brown ran a general merchandise shop, operated rum distilleries, owned a slaughterhouse and ships, acted as a banker, and traded with South Carolina, where he bartered for rice with Rhode Island cattle. His younger brother Obadiah . . . undertook to rear James Brown's sons—and the quartet of 'Nicky, Josey, John and Mosey' Brown was to dominate Rhode Island trade and commerce for a long generation."[14] On page 15 of "John Stevens—His Book" appears a debit account to a Mr. John Brown in October of 1727. Included in the numerous transactions were two billings for a pair of shoes for Josiah—5 shillings 6 pence and a pair (of shoes) for John—5 shillings. Although there is considerable name similarity these transactions were rejected as

---

[5] Op. cit., p. 17. The reader should be able to reconcile most of the spelling of the period with present mode of spelling, i.e., seller—cellar, stak—stack, etc.
A perch is a measure of stone work comprising about 25 cubic yards.
[6] Ibidem—at random.
[7] Note that 8 weeks schooling cost 4 shillings.
[8] Indicating a daily wage rate of 6 shillings.
[9] Indicating 9 pounds as annual rent.
[10] Marcy was apparently John Steven's wife Her daily wage rate if the above description is correct was 2 shillings per day. Compare with Robert Hart's wages in footnote 8
[11] The author assumes as follows: gote to sell infers inventory at either cost or selling price (uncertain), sold is obvious and gaine refers to appreciation either through growth or procreation.
[12] Bought here is self explanatory, loste is presumed to be through death or wandering off of identified fowl.
[13] All data from photo-offset copy of "John Stevens—His Book" p. 54.
[14] John Chamberlain, ibidem.

not being with the dynastic Browns. The reasons for the rejection were; 1. the dissimilarity of the parent names of James and John, 2. the chronological discrepancy from the material in footnotes 2 and 14. On page 65 of John Stevens record appears the following,

Major James Brown of Newport		--- Dr. ---
		£--------
Decem^r ye 2^d 1729	to one Tomb Stone	13—00—00
	to 260 Bricks at 5^s p. hundred	00—13—00
	to geting ye Stuff togather & Building ye Bases	1—15— 0
	to Cuting 160 Letters at 2^d p. Letter	1— 6— 8
		16—14— 8"

This record is believed to be with the Brown family referred to in Chamberlain's article. The reasons for acceptance of this transaction are; 1. the approximate chronological agreement, 2. the closeness of military rank and, 3. the amount of the billing to Major James Brown of almost 17 pounds, which in terms of the magnitude of transactions of this time period would have been more than a month's wages for an average person indicating strongly that credit for this amount would hardly have been granted to anyone who did not possess an exceptional credit standing.

Should the question of American dollars and English pounds and their conversion ratios in 1727 arise, John Steven's record provides the answer. "George Anon's Treasurs that he tuck in the South Sea concis of 1,326,175··2··10½ pounds Sterling or 5,842,787 Dollors."[15] If the reader substitutes took and consist in their proper places and then makes the indicated calculation the apparent rate of exchange was 1 pound sterling was equivalent to $4.40 in American money.

John Stevens was also engaged in a partnership arrangement with John Sims during the 1730's. Most of the work was of a construction nature and performed jointly. The partnership was conducted simply on a ½ and ½ basis with each recording time worked, settlements in produce, and similar information. Upon settlement date, all transactions were footed and the necessary additions and deductions made. Upon eventual completion of the settlement both partners signed the record book "Decem ye 17th Then Ballanced Theas accounts & made Even on Boath Sides {John Stevens / John Sims"[16]

As the accounting profession continues to grow and develop, the discovery, retention and preservation of such records as "John Stevens —His Book" should become a major objective of the profession. The information available from such records far transcends the accounting information revealed. Historians, economists and other social scientists could extract much information that would benefit their own lines of endeavor.

[15] Op. cit. p. 6.
[16] Op. cit. p. 67.

accounting in colonial Virginia: a case study

by Almand R. Coleman, William G. Shenkir and Williard E. Stone*

Occasionally, we find business records from a previous era sufficiently complete to allow the accounting historian to undertake an analysis of the then existing accounting and management practices. Such is the case with the records of William Prentis and Company, a leading colonial store in eighteenth century Williamsburg, Virginia. This store has been described as the "most solvent and most respected business in Williamsburg, if not in the entire colony."[1] Though the store's journals and ledgers have been lost, its annual reports with balance sheet and supplementary information permit speculation concerning the development of accounting during the colonial era.[2]

The store operated under the name of William Prentis and Company from 1733 to 1765. Its beginning can be traced to about 1701 when two brothers, Dr. Archibald Blair and the Reverend James Blair,[3] and a mutual friend, Colonel Philip Ludwell, opened a general merchandise store in the home of the Reverend Blair. In 1719, the store

Almand R. Coleman, *CPA, is Charles C. Abbott professor of business administration in the graduate school of the University of Virginia in Charlottesville. He is a member of the AICPA and the Financial Executives Institute and is a past vice president of the American Accounting Association. Mr. Coleman is the author of* Financial Accounting: A General Management Approach. **William G. Shenkir**, *CPA, Ph.D., currently serves as a project director with the Financial Accounting Standards Board. A member of the AICPA, the AAA and the Virginia Society of CPAs, Mr. Shenkir has made frequent contributions to professional publications and coauthored, with Glenn A. Welsch and James A. Bear, Jr., "Thomas Jefferson: Management Accountant," which appeared in the April 1972* Journal of Accountancy. **Williard E. Stone**, *CPA, Ph.D., professor of accounting at the University of Florida, Gainesville, is the author of approximately 60 articles dealing with accounting. He is a member of the AICPA's education executive committee and of the Florida and Pennsylvania Institutes of CPAs and is a former vice president of the AAA.*

*The research for and writing of this article were completed while Mr. Shenkir was professor of accounting and director of the graduate accounting program at the University of Virginia's McIntire School of Commerce. (The Financial Accounting Standards Board, as a matter of policy, disclaims responsibility for any publications by any of its individual members or staff.)

[1] Mary R. M. Goodwin, *The Colonial Store* (Colonial Williamsburg Research Report, March 1966), typescript, p. iii.

[2] The authors are indebted to Edward M. Riley, director of research of colonial Williamsburg for information concerning the store's early history. (See Edward M. Riley, "William Prentis & Co.," *Financial Executive*, April 1968, pp. 33-41.)

[3] The Reverend James Blair, 1655-1743, obtained the charter for the College of William and Mary from the King and was the college's first president. He also served as commissary, or deputy, in Virginia for the Bishop of London. Concerning his half interest in the store, Parke Rouse, Jr., in his *James Blair of Virginia* (The University of North Carolina Press, 1971) observes, p. 176: "The commissary's silent partnership in Doctor Blair's store was to be a source of considerable wealth, as well as of whispered criticism that a clergyman should engage in trade."

The accounting practices of William Prentis and Company from 1733 to 1779 seemed to meet the requirements of the economic environment of the period.

was relocated on the Duke of Gloucester Street, in Williamsburg, where it remained until 1740 when expanding operations required greater space, and a brick building was constructed on the same site. This building exists today in restored colonial Williamsburg.

The Blair-Ludwell partnership controlled and managed the store until sometime before Ludwell's death in 1727, when the Blair brothers bought Ludwell's interest. The next owner-manager change took place in 1733, when Archibald Blair died and the firm's organization changed from a simple partnership to a business operated by a professional manager, William Prentis. From 1733 the store was operated under the name of the owner-manager:

- ☐ William Prentis and Company—1733 to 1765.
- ☐ John Prentis and Company—1765 to 1775.
- ☐ Robert Prentis and Company—1775 to 1779.

The business imported and sold goods from England as well as merchandise purchased locally. The company also acted as an exporter, and the 1733 balance sheet disclosed that two hogsheads of tobacco were awaiting shipment to England and a quantity of pork and corn, costing £56.4.0, was en route to Jamaica. Undoubtedly the trade with Jamaica included imports of sugar and rum.

The events leading to the Revolutionary War, and the war itself, brought the business to an end in 1779. Disruptions in trade abroad are indicated in the store's annual reports beginning in 1773. At the end of that year, the store's report showed inventory of imported goods at £4,476, the largest in the store's history. Imported goods inventory declined to £2,623 in 1774, to £1,560 in 1775, and to £280 on February 4, 1777, when the store's operations were suspended. Thereafter, Robert Prentis stayed on, at half salary, until 1780 to liquidate the assets of the business.

In summary, the business was in existence from 1701 to 1779, almost 80 years in the formative period of this country's economic and political development.

Analysis of accounting records

For the period of William Prentis's tenure as professional manager, 1733-1765, and thereafter from 1765-1779, there were annual or biennial meetings of the owners. At these meetings, a financial statement was presented and attested to by the subscribers. These statements, fortunately preserved for us,[4] serve as the basis for inquiry into the fol-

[4] The original Webb-Prentis Papers (1733-1780) are owned by the Alderman Library of the University of Virginia and are quoted from with permission. Each annual (or biennial) report is on one page of paper 15 inches long and 12 inches wide. On one side the report is signed under seal by the owners or their representatives. On the other side of the page is the financial statement(s).

lowing aspects of the business: business organization, annual reporting format and disclosure, statement periods, accounting system, accounting principles, translation adjustments and management compensation.

Business organization

The owners of William Prentis and Company were designated subscribers and their proportionate ownership, which changed many times due to inheritance or sale of ownership shares, was disclosed in each of the reports accompanying the financial statements. The company was set up as a partnership, and ownership equity was not evidenced by formal certificates but stated in fractional proportions, e.g., 1/6, 9/24.

Although limited liability was not available to the owners, the organization had characteristics suggestive of a corporation:

1 It had a life independent of its owners, and owners' shares were transferable.

2 The managing owner had the autonomy usually associated with professional management and was paid a salary.

3 Owners' withdrawals were called dividends and were proportionate to the amount of each owner's capital account.

4 The company in 1759 repurchased the interests of two subscribers (similar to a corporation's buying its own stock) and adjusted the remaining owners' capital accounts accordingly.

5 Annual reports were provided for each owner, or his representative, just as today a stockholder is given a copy of a corporation's annual report.

> The accounting books purchased must have been carefully kept since there is evidence that the company was a fiscal agent for the Virginia Colony, making payments for materials and work performed by individuals for the colony.

Annual reporting format and disclosure

Each yearend balance sheet was accompanied by a formally signed and witnessed report indicating the subscribers' "audit" of the company's accounts and their satisfaction with its owner-manager. The report began as follows:

"We the Subscribers having Examined and Audited the Accounts of William Prentis under the Name of himself and Company to the 25th of November last do find the same rightly Stated, and that the Stock of said Company has been well and truly Managed by him the said William Prentis and therefore we acquit and discharge him, his Heirs, Executors and Administrators of all his past Intromissions[5] with the said stock."

A typical report continued by disclosing the respective interest of each owner. From 1733 to 1742 the report also gave the formula for calculating the manager's compensation and stated that he was to manage the stock[6] according to "instructions agreed upon by himself and said Company." The financial statement accompanying the report was an English form of balance sheet with the liabilities and owners' equity listed on the left side (marked "dr.") and the assets on the right (marked "cr."). The financial statement for August 31, 1733, is shown in Exhibit 1, page 35.

In an ingenious method of meeting an awkward monetary problem, three variations of statement presentation were used. The first method, shown in Exhibit 1, used from 1733 to 1742, presented two balance sheets, one entitled "Stock in current money" (i.e., Virginia currency) and the other "Stock in sterling" and a separate schedule containing the translation adjustment and summarizing the owners' total equity. A second statement presentation, used from 1745 to 1753, was in the form of a single balance sheet. The sterling assets were listed first, followed by the translation adjustment, and the remaining assets were shown in Virginia currency. Total assets and the sum of the liabilities and owners' equity ("ballance") were stated in Virginia currency.

During the period 1755-1779, a two-statement presentation was again used. However, this time the sterling balance sheet appeared first, followed by one in Virginia currency. The first item shown on the asset side of the Virginia currency statement was the owners' equity "ballance," in sterling from the prior statement, followed by the translation adjustment.

The annual reports never included an income statement and there is incomplete information about the company's operations, particularly after 1742, when the manager received a fixed salary. Prior to that date, the sales volume for both domestic and imported goods appears parenthetically to explain the amount of the liability for the manager's commission. Otherwise statement disclosure is remarkably complete. Cash on hand was stated in Virginia pounds although undoubtedly composed of coins and bills of different countries and

5 "Intromission" is defined in the *Shorter Oxford English Dictionary* as "2. Intermeddling, interference; esp., in or from Scotch Law, intermeddling with the effects of another, either with or without legal authority. . . .

6 The word "stock" as used repeatedly in these reports refers to all the company's assets, "after all Debts, Salaries, and just Demands being paid and allowed." In other words, "stock" refers to owners' equity—assets less liabilities.

Exhibit 1

Stock in current money

1733 Aug. 31	*Dr.*			
To Sundry Creditors as Per List	£541	19	5¾	
To Commission Allowed Dr. Blair's Est. & William Prentis on £1,284 . 17 . 1¾	64	4	10¼	
To the Dividend Agreed to be Made at the Settlement	413	11	4½	
Due to Ballance	3,807		7¼	
	£4,826	16	3¾	
Cr.				
By the Storehouses & Lotts	£ 150			*
By Goods Bought in the Country	587	12	7	*
By the Houses & Lotts of Levingston	200			*
By Cash in Hand	607	8		*
By Sundry Debts as per List	3,210	4	10¾	
By 2 h.hds. Tobacco Which Cost	15	6	10	
By Pork & Corn Sent to Jamaica Which Cost	56	4		
	£4,826	16	3¾	

*Figures for four asset items supplied by researcher since these were missing from torn orginal document.

Stock in sterling

1733 Aug. 31	*Dr.*		
To Commission Allowed Dr. Blair's Est. & William Prentis on £1,624 . 8 . 7	£ 81	4	5
Due to Ballance	2,660	16	2
	£2,742		7
Cr.			
By Bills of Exchange in Hand	£ 70		
By Protested Bills in Hand	378	4	4
By Goods Imported without Shipping Charges	848	5	6½
By Sundry Debts as Per List	1,445	10	8½
	£2,742		7
Ballance in Sterling	£2,660	16	2
20% on Ditto	532	3	2¾
Ballance in Current Money	3,807		7¼
	£7,000		

(Signed)
James Blair
Wilson Cary
For Mrs. Ann Whiting
John Blair
William Prentis

other currency items.[7] For two years (1735 and 1740), accounts receivable were valued net with the amount of bad debts disclosed parenthetically. For example, this item in the 1740 balance sheet reads: "By Sundry debtors as (per) list deducting for bad debts . . . £194.5.2." For these same two years, protested bills of exchange were reported separately from current bills of exchange and were shown "net of bad ones" in the 1735 statement.

Inventories were segregated into imported goods and domestic goods ("Goods Bought in the Country"). The cost basis of imported goods inventory was consistently disclosed with the notation "without Shipping Charges." Fixed assets were presented as the "Storehouses & Lotts." The recurring liabilities were debts payable in sterling, "Sundry Creditors as Per List," accrual of the manager's compensation and the accrual of the dividend agreed to be paid. Owners' equity, as noted previously, was the balancing item on the statement's left side.

Statement periods

From 1733 to 1743 annual statements were prepared. Thereafter, until 1774, biennial statements

[7] Since the Virginia Colony minted no money, the term "Virginia currency" or "current money" had reference to such circulating medium as treasury notes, tobacco notes, bills of exchange and some specie of several foreign origins. (Robert Polk Thompson, *The Merchant in Virginia 1700-1755* (unpublished Ph.D. dissertation, University of Wisconsin, 1955), p. 239.) Examples of foreign coins circulating and their rating in Virginia currency were as follows: the Spanish half dollar (3 shillings), Spanish pistorean (1 shilling 6 pence), Portuguese "joe" (96 shillings) and French pistol (23-24 shillings). (James H. Soltow, *The Economic Role of Williamsburg* (Colonial Williamsburg Research Studies, 1965), p. 111.)

were prepared except for annual statements for the years 1746, 1748 and 1751, and a four-year statement for the period preceding William Prentis's death, 1762-1765. The August 31 yearend date in use from 1733 was changed to November 25 in 1740 and was used from 1740 until 1763 except for 1745 (September 17) and 1748 (December 21). The date was changed in 1765 to August 4, the day William Prentis died. Again, this yearend date was changed to November 4, 1775, when John Prentis died and changed to February 4 in 1777, the date that normal operations were discontinued. The statement dated May 4, 1779, was the last manager-owner report.

Thus, over a period of 47 years seven changes were made in the closing dates. All appear to have coincided with changes of management rather than with changes of owners. Ownership changes occurring as the result of death bequests, sales from one owner to another and repurchase of ownership interests were either effected on regular statement dates or adjusted between the parties based upon the last regular statement.

Accounting system

The audit report of August 31, 1733, discloses the existence of a formal bookkeeping system when it notes that the subscribers purchased "all the Goods and Books of Accts." The accounting books purchased must have been carefully kept since there is evidence that the company was a fiscal agent for the Virginia Colony, making payments for materials and work performed by individuals for the colony. During the period from 1726 to 1733, such payments amounted to £394.10.4, for which the company received a commission of about 2½%.[8]

The bookkeeping system must also have been efficient to cope with the problems of recording transactions in different currencies and yet provide the internally consistent financial information contained in the reports for the 47-year period 1733-1779. Careful records of the owners' capital must have been maintained, because the capital of August 31, 1733, can be reconciled with that of May 4, 1779, by the sum of the reported profits less the dividends and shares repurchased. Appendix A, page 41, shows such a reconciliation for the 1733-1765 period, covering the tenure of William Prentis as manager.

The maintenance of an efficient bookkeeping system was a necessity to achieve profitable mercantile operations. A liberal credit policy existed both from suppliers and to customers. Currency was in short supply, and trade was, therefore, based on bookkeeping barter, tobacco notes and bills of exchange. Tobacco notes were, in effect, warehouse receipts for harvested crops in Virginia warehouses. Crops were subsequently shipped to Britain and credit given the planter. Payments by colonial merchants to English suppliers were generally in the form of bills of exchange drawn upon these credits. During the long period between the sales of merchandise, the accounts of customers were carried by the merchants as open accounts. Evidence of these long credit terms exists in the amount of the receivables in the Prentis statements. From 1733 through 1742, the years for which the statements disclose the necessary data, accounts receivable balances at the end of each year averaged 150% of annual sales.

> The calculation of managers' commissions and the translation of sterling to Virginia currency only at yearend indicate that accruals and adjustments were recognized only at statement time.

Other evidence of the dependability of the bookkeeping records of eighteenth century Virginia was the reliance placed by the law upon such records when disputes occurred between debtors and creditors. A merchant, when bringing suit against a creditor and being unable to present a document attesting to the amount due, was permitted to swear:

"That the matter in dispute is a store account, and that he hath no means to prove the delivery of such articles therein contained . . . but by his store book; in that case such book shall and may be given in evidence at the trial, if he shall make out by his own oath or affirmation, that such book doth contain a true account of all the dealings, or the last settlement of accounts between them, and that all articles therein contained were *bona fide* delivered, and that he hath given all just credits due to the defendant, in such account; and such book and oath or affirmation, shall be admitted and received as evidence. . . ."[9]

Accounting principles

The Prentis statements appear to have been prepared from records maintained on a modified cash

[8] For this reference, the authors are indebted to William G. Keener, *Blair–Prentis–Cary Partnership: The Store and Its Operations* (Colonial Williamsburg Research Report, April 1957, Typescript; p. 12). The original source cited was reviewed by the authors: *Executive Journals of the Council of Colonial Virginia* (Virginia State Library, 1930), Vol. IV, p. 101 ff.

[9] William W. Hening (editor), *The Statutes at Large: Being a Collection of All the Laws of Virginia* (Richmond, 1819), Vol. VI, p. 54.

basis. Continuous accounting for individual receivables and payables is indicated by the notation "as per list" used on the statements. A careful recording process is further indicated in the separate sales figures for domestic goods and imported goods used in calculating the manager's commission from 1733-1742. The calculation of managers' commissions and the translation of sterling to Virginia currency only at yearend indicate that accruals and adjustments were recognized only at statement time.

The cost basis was used in stating assets (see Exhibit 1). The expression "without Shipping Charges" used in valuing inventory of "Goods Imported" can be viewed as an early form of conservatism, since sizable transportation charges were expensed when incurred rather than allocated between cost of goods sold and cost of goods in inventory at yearend.

Uncollectible accounts were accounted for on the direct writeoff basis in the 1735 and 1740 statements. There is no indication that an allowance was ever in use. Uncollectible protested notes were also directly written off in the 1735 statement.

Fixed assets ("Storehouses & Lotts") appear on the statements at acquisition cost. In 1733, this asset account carried a value of £150, representing the cost of the store and the warehouse on two separate lots. The account was increased to £350 in 1740 when a red brick building was constructed on the Duke of Gloucester Street. The exact location of "the other lot and frame building" has not been determined by recent research efforts,[10] but it must have had a value of £60 because it was apparently sold in 1741 and the balance sheet asset reduced to £290. Depreciation was never recorded, and the £290 figure continued to be reported on the statements until the company's liquidation in 1779. In 1778 two Williamsburg newspapers carried advertisements for the sale of the store and lot; in November 1779, they were sold to Robert Prentis for £1,000.[11] No figure ever appeared in the statements for store equipment, so a consistent practice of expensing these relatively minor expenditures must have been followed through the years.

> Transactions of William Prentis and Company were recorded in either English shillings (sterling) or current money (Virginia currency). At yearend, a translation adjustment was required. . . .

The 1737 statement contains the following item: "By 2/3 of £250 the purchase of houses bought of Col. Thomas Jones . . . £166.13.4." This represented a loan to Colonel Jones for two-thirds the purchase price of the Raleigh Tavern in Williamsburg. In the statements for 1738 through 1741, the cumulative rent received was disclosed parenthetically and deducted from the original loan balance of £166.13.4, with the net figure extended. However, the 1742 statement reverted to the original figure of £166.13.4. The entire accumulated rent was taken into income in 1742. The £166.13.4 does not appear in the 1743 statement, so a disposition of the investment is indicated, although no disclosure is made of such an occurrence or of whether a gain or loss was incurred.

The gains from currency exchange translations of sterling to current money were always included in owners' equity. Further, a sale of "Houses & Lotts of Levingston" appears to have been made in 1736, but no indication of a gain or loss was given.

Translation adjustments

The lack of a uniform currency created an accounting problem for the colonial merchant. Transactions of William Prentis and Company were recorded in either English shillings (sterling) or current money (Virginia currency). At yearend, a translation adjustment was required, as the annual reports indicate.

The exchange rate over the 47 years of the Prentis statements varied from a sterling premium of 15% to 30%. Virginia law established an exchange premium of 25% in 1728,[12] but the rate appears to have fluctuated somewhat as indicated in the Prentis statements from 1733 to 1751. After 1751, the statements consistently used the 25% legal premium in translating sterling to Virginia money. It seems unlikely that the actual exchange rate remained unchanged over this period, especially in the troubled years preceding the Revolutionary War.

Another intriguing currency matter was the use of different exchange rates in the same statement. As an example, in the 1745 statement the total sterling assets were £2,443.16.11. The translated amount was disclosed parenthetically as

£ 586	sterling at 130%
196	sterling at 125%
1,661.16.11	sterling at 120%

[10] Goodwin, *op. cit.*, pp. 269-70.
[11] Keener, *op. cit.*, p. 61
[12] Riley, *op. cit.*, p. 41

The total value of the sterling balance was accounted for, but there was no explanation for the amounts translated at the different rates. Some breakdown must have been made of the balance in imported goods inventory since the only other sterling asset (notes receivable) was not as great as any one of the specific amounts.

Management compensation

When William Prentis became manager, the report of August 31, 1733, stated his compensation to be

". . . five percent of the selling price for all goods by him Sold when the said price is paid and recovered in this country, and likewise five percent for all goods bought in this country when sold again or Shipped off and Exported, the said five percent to be reckoned out of the nett proceeds of the selling price in this or any other country and likewise five percent on the damage of all Protested bills of Exchange negotiated and recovered by him on Account of said Company as also his Traveling Expenses in recovering any Debts or Protested Bills due to the Company."

This agreement was stated in each report from 1733 to 1742. In the 1743 report, the compensation was changed to a fixed annual salary of £200, which in 1752 was increased to £250, and in 1759 to £300.[13] In addition, William Prentis received a share of the profits of the company proportionate to his interest, which, by the time of his death, had grown to 9 of the total of 22 shares.[14]

> The change in dividend policy gave William Prentis considerably more scope to exercise his management talents than the restrictive practice in effect from 1733 to 1742.

Evaluation of management performance

An analysis of the Prentis statements gives us some clues as to the management performance of William Prentis and his successors. For the purpose of such an analysis, we have chosen to break the period of the statements, 1733-1779, into four segments:

☐ 1733-1742—Management by William Prentis under the restraint of 100% "payout" of earnings.
☐ 1742-1765—Continued management by William Prentis during a period of internally financed growth through partial retention of earnings.
☐ 1765-1774—Management by successors of William Prentis.
☐ 1774-1779—Liquidation brought on by Revolutionary War.

1733-1742

In the 10-year period 1733-1742, net income totaled £4,821. At each yearend, dividends equal to net income for the year were declared so no earnings were retained in the business. During this period, the return on owners' equity approximated 7½% a year.

In 1735, large writeoffs of uncollectible accounts (£419) reduced net income to £107. At that yearend, a "liquidating dividend" of £1,000 was declared, in addition to the operating dividend of £107, reducing owners' equity from £7,000 to £6,000.

This reduction in operating capital imposed considerable restraint upon William Prentis in his position as manager. How he managed changes in the firm's assets is indicated in Appendix B (the statement of changes in financial position), page 42, for the period August 31, 1733, to November 25, 1742.

The major sources of funds were

1 A reduction in receivables and bills of exchange	£1,519
2 A reduction in inventory of domestic goods	580
	£2,099

Funds obtained from these sources were used in the following manner:

1 To increase the inventory of imported goods	£ 996
2 To pay the liquidating dividend in 1735	1,000
3 To cover sundry items	103
	£2,099

Using the yearend calculation of commissions, annual sales can be approximated as follows: £2,500 and £2,300 in 1734 and 1735 increasing to the £3,000 level from 1736 to 1741.

In summary, William Prentis managed the business in such fashion that, despite a 100% payout of earnings and the £1,000 reduction in owners' equity, sales volume increased, approximately 7½% was earned (and paid) on equity and the proportion of imported goods to domestic goods in the yearend inventory was changed from 60-to-40 to 96-to-4. An ownership philosophy in which payment of cash dividends exceeded earnings

[13]This appears to have been a substantial salary, for in 1772 a salaried manager of a Culpepper, Virginia, store received £60 sterling per annum and an "experienced storekeeper" in Petersburg received £80 for the first year, £90 for the second and £100 for the remaining three years of a five-year term (Soltow, *op. cit.*, pp. 52-53).

[14]Interestingly, he also received an additional £50 in 1746 "for his expenses in a Voyage to England."

probably served to somewhat limit William Prentis in the exercise of his management talents.

1742-1765

During this period (1742-1765), the Reverend James Blair, owner of a half interest in the firm, died. The annual report of November 25, 1743, signed by the subscribers on December 12, said:

". . . We do likewise find that the stock of the said company then left in the hands of the said William Prentis after all Debts, Salaries and Just demands being paid and Allowed amounts to the Sum of six thousand Pounds Current money according to an account on the other side, one half part of which Stock was the share of the Reverend Mr. James Blair deceased and is now under the Management of John Blair Esq. acting Executor of the said James. One sixth part more is the share of Major Wilson Cary, one sixth part more the share of Sarah Mary Ann and Elizabeth daughters of the said William Cary and the remaining one sixth part is the share of . . . William Prentis. . . ."

In the years following 1744, the owners adopted a more aggressive business philosophy, one directed at growth, by changing the company's dividend policy. The 1744-45 biennial report shows net income of £1,036 for the two years, dividends of £420 for 1744, but none in 1745, so the addition to the owners' equity of £616. Increases in owners' equity, November 25, 1742, to August 4, 1765, through retention of earnings were

September 17, 1745	£ 616
November 25, 1746	(16)
December 21, 1748	1,400
November 25, 1749	500
November 25, 1750	500
November 25, 1751	800
November 25, 1753	1,200
November 25, 1755	1,000
November 25, 1757	1,000
November 25, 1759	1,097
November 25, 1761	2,000
November 25, 1763 (dividend)	(2,200)
August 9, 1765	4,591
Total	£12,488

These figures can be deduced from a comparison of net income and operating dividends (Appendix A). In 1759, the 1/24th share of Bryan Fairfax and the 1/24th share of George Wm Fairfax were reacquired for a total of £1,097. A summary statement of owners' equity, 1742-1765, would show

Owners' Equity, November 25, 1742	£ 6,000
Add Net Income, 1742-1765	30,086
Total	36,086
Less Dividends Declared	17,598
Balance	18,488
Less Shares Repurchased in 1759	1,097
Owners' Equity, August 4, 1765	£17,391

This indicates that the firm tripled in size through internally financed growth. For this 23-year period, the return on equity was approximately 11½% per year.

The change in dividend policy gave William Prentis considerably more scope to exercise his management talents than the restrictive practice in effect from 1733 to 1742. How he managed changes in the firm's assets, liabilities and equity is indicated in Appendix B (the statement of changes in financial position) for the period November 25, 1742, to August 4, 1765.

The major sources of funds were

1 Net income	£30,086
2 Increases in payables due suppliers	1,166
	£31,252

Funds obtained from these sources were used

1 To pay cash dividends (£17,598 declared less £1,111 adjustment for unpaid dividends accrued at 11/25/42 and 8/4/65)	£16,487
2 To purchase ownership interests of Messrs. Fairfax	1,097
3 To increase receivables	10,982
4 To increase inventories (imported goods £2,240 and domestic goods £168)	2,408
5 To cover sundry items	278
	£31,252

These changes are typical of growth companies today in that the net income earned was not matched by a corresponding increase in cash internally generated. To illustrate, the firm reported net income for the 23-year period of £30,086 and there would have been an inflow of cash in this amount if the firm had collected exactly what it billed customers and had bought and entirely paid for the cost of goods sold. However, these conditions did not prevail as the following facts indicate:

1 The firm collected less than it billed customers	(£10,982)
2 The firm bought more goods than it sold	(2,408)
3 The firm paid suppliers less than the cost of goods bought	1,166
The net of these items being	£12,224

So cash "internally generated" was the £30,086 net income less £12,224, or £17,862.

In summary, the change in dividend policy freed William Prentis from the growth-stifling requirement of having to generate cash equal to net income. Under his able management, the firm tripled in size and level of earnings. Annual return on equity increased from approximately 7½% for the 10-year period, 1733-1742, to 11½% for the 23-year period, 1742-1765. William Prentis also provided for management succession. At his death on August 4, 1765, he was succeeded as manager by his eldest son, John.

1765-1774

The reports from August 4, 1767, to August 4, 1774, indicate a "caretaker" management performance by John Prentis. For the biennium ending August 4, 1767, net income of £2,891 was earned, dividends of £2,282 were declared, and the balance of £609 was added to owners' equity. Thereafter, the owners returned to the 1733-1744 practice of declaring dividends equal to earnings, and owners' equity remained unchanged at £18,000. Dividends equal to earnings were declared: 8/4/69, £2,706; 8/4/71, £2,175; 8/4/72, £1,800; and 8/4/74, £1,646. Return on equity approximated 7% a year as contrasted with the 11½% realized during the preceding "growth" period.

> Complicated financial problems—such as operating with many kinds of currency and accounting for investment and debt in both English and Virginia moneys with fluctuations suggestive of today's dollar situation—were met and solved.

Since there was little change in the size of the firm as measured by owners' equity, one would expect to see little change in the size of individual assets and liabilities. This fact is borne out in Appendix B (the statement of changes in financial position) for the period August 4, 1765, to August 4, 1774. The major change was the £2,170 increase in receivables which was financed, in part, by (1) the £609 retention of earnings and (2) the £976 decrease in inventory of imported goods.

1774-1779

It is inappropriate to attempt any evaluation of management performance during this five-year period. Economic and political conditions were abnormal and management's primary concern was liquidation.

Accounting—a record of commercial history

A clear picture of a well-managed and successful colonial business emerges from the accounting statements of William Prentis and Company for the period 1733 to 1779. Each of the owner-managers left a distinct and individual imprint on the enterprise. William Prentis was an able manager under the supervision of James Blair. With the handicap of a fixed amount of capital, he successfully operated the business with a fair return to the owners on their capital. Upon the death of James Blair, he increased invested capital, business volume and the return on invested capital. His son John, although not innovative, continued a well-managed business as did Cousin Robert, but the period of growth was over with the passing of the William Prentis management. The business could not survive the difficult Revolutionary War period and was liquidated in 1779.

Throughout the entire period 1733 to 1779, the accounting system appeared adequate to the needs of management and for trusteeship reporting. Complicated financial problems—such as operating with many kinds of currency and accounting for investment and debt in both English and Virginia moneys with fluctuations suggestive of today's dollar situation—were met and solved. For the entire 79-year period, the several partner-subscribers displayed a high degree of confidence in the accounting system, for there is no evidence of any dispute among them or with the owner-managers. The accounting principles in use, as evidenced by disclosure in the statements, lacked some of today's refinements, such as depreciation and the recording of capital gains and losses. However, some of our now generally accepted accounting principles, such as the cost basis and accrual accounting, were in use. The accounting practices of the period seemed to meet the requirements of the economic environment in which the business operated. ■

Appendix A

William Prentis and Company
Statement of changes in owners' equity
1733-1765
(In pounds in Virginia currency)

Owners' Equity Balance, August 31, 1732			£ 7,000
Net Income for 47 years, 1733-1765, Inclusive			34,907
Total			£41,907
Deductions:			
Operating Dividends, 1733-1765, Inclusive		£22,419	
Liquidating Dividend in 1735		1,000	
Repurchase of Ownership Shares in 1759:			
Bryan Fairfax (1/24th)	£ 542		
George Wm. Fairfax (1/24th)	555		
		1,097	
Total Deductions			24,516
Owners' Equity Balance, August 4, 1765			£17,391

Note: Net Income and operating dividends, by years, were:

Year	Net Income	Operating Dividends	Year	Net Income	Operating Dividends
1733	£ 414	£ 414	1750	£1,005	£ 505
1734	511	511	1751	1,519	719
1735	107	107	1752	—	—
1736	317	317	1753	3,244	2,044
1737	619	619	1754	—	—
1738	636	636	1755	2,951	1,951
1739	529	529	1756	—	—
1740	703	703	1757	3,428	2,428
1741	505	505	1758	—	—
1742	480	480	1759	3,054	1,957
1743	485	485	1760	—	—
1744	—	420	1761	4,391	2,391
1745	1,036	—	1762	—	—
1746	358	374	1763	—	2,200
1747	—	—	1764	—	—
1748	1,650	250	1765	6,182	1,591
1749	783	283	Totals	£34,907	£22,419

Appendix B

William Prentis and Company
Statement of changes in financial position
1733 to 1774
(In pounds in Virginia currency)

	8/31/33 to 11/25/42	*11/25/42 to 8/4/65*	*8/4/65 to 8/4/74*
Source of Funds			
Net Income	£ 4,821	£30,086	£11,138
Decrease in Sterling Bills of Exchange	226	312	—
Increase (decrease) in payables	(270)	1,166	119
Increase (decrease) in Due to Manager	(53)	100	92
Disposition of Houses & Lotts of Levingston	200	—	—
Total Sources of Funds	£ 4,924	£31,664	£11,349
Application of Funds			
Payment of Dividends Declared (adjusted for accrual at beginning and end of period)	£ 4,755	£16,487	£10,474
Reduction of Ownership Interest	1,000	1,097	—
Increase (decrease) in Receivables	(1,293)	10,982	2,170
Increase (decrease) in Inventories:			
Goods bought in the Country	(580)	168	(161)
Imported Goods	996	2,240	(976)
Increase in Storehouses & Lotts	140	—	—
Increase (decrease) in Houses Bought of Col. Jones (2/3 interest)	167	(167)	—
Increase (decrease) in Cash on Hand	(261)	857	(158)
Total Uses of Funds	£ 4,924	£31,664	£11,349

Source: Appendix C, page 43, and supplementary information on net income, dividends and reduction of ownership interest

Appendix C

William Prentis and Company
Comparative balance sheets
1733 to 1774
(in pounds in Virginia currency)

	8/31/33	*11/25/42*	*8/4/65*	*8/4/74*
Cash on Hand	£ 607	£ 346	£ 1,203	£ 1,045
Sterling Bills of Exchange	538	312	—	—
Receivables:				
Trade—In Va. Currency	3,210	2,205	11,241	11,926
Trade—In Sterling	1,735	1,447	3,393	4,878
Inventories:				
Goods Bought in the Country	659	79	247	86
Imported Goods (w/o shipping chgs.)	1,018	2,014	4,254	3,278
Storehouses & Lotts	150	290	290	290
Houses & Lotts of Levingston	200	—	—	—
Houses Bought of Col. Jones (2/3 interest)	—	167	—	—
Total Assets	£ 8,117	£ 6,860	£20,628	£21,503
Payables:				
To Sundry Creditors—Va. Currency	£ 542	£ 272	£ 593	£ 353
To Sundry Creditors—Sterling	—	—	845	1,204
Due to Manager—For Commission or Salary	161	108	208	300
Dividends Payable	414	480	1,591	1,646
Balance	7,000	6,000	17,391	18,000
Total Equities	£ 8,117	£ 6,860	£20,628	£21,503

A Note on Papers concerning the Causes and Effects of Double Entry

The causes of the evolution of double entry are discussed in passing in several of the papers in this anthology; and they are the main subject of the final two papers. Other papers would have been included if they had not been printed elsewhere; for example :

B S Yamey, "Notes on the Origin of Double-Entry Bookkeeping", Accounting Review, XXII, 1947, pp 263-273, reprinted in B S Yamey, Essays on the History of Accounting, New York, Arno Press, 1978.

R de Roover, "The Development of Accounting Prior to Luca Pacioli According to the Account Books of Medieval Merchants" in A C Littleton and B S Yamey, Studies in the History of Accounting, New York, Arno Press, 1978.

As to its effects, several views may be found in the following works :

W Sombart, Der Moderne Kapitalismus, 6th edition, Munich and Leipzig, 1924, vol 2.1, pp 118-119.

B S Yamey, "Accounting and the Rise of Capitalism: Some Further Notes on a Theme by Sombart", Journal of Accounting Research, II, 1964, pp 117-136.

B S Yamey, "Scientific Bookkeeping and the Rise of Capitalism", Economic History Review, 2nd Ser I, 1949, pp 99-113.

J O Winjum, "Accounting and the Rise of Capitalism: An Accountant's View", Journal of Accounting Research, IX, 1971, pp 333-350.

THE FUNCTIONAL DEVELOPMENT OF DOUBLE-ENTRY BOOKKEEPING

by B. S. Yamey

(Reproduced by permission of the Accounting Research Association)

The Committee of the Association does not necessarily endorse the views expressed in papers published under the auspices of the Association

Introduction

It is a widely accepted view that accounting practice has, in the course of its evolution, been determined by the business requirements it has had to satisfy.* Accounting is regarded as pragmatic in the sense that at all times it has been adapted to assist the business man in the solution of some of his business problems.

Accepting this view of the *functional* nature of accounting development it should be possible to explain every change in accounting practice or technique and the emergence of the double-entry bookkeeping system by indicating the new business requirement which called forth each advance. In this paper the functions of accounting in the period before the coming of the joint stock company will be discussed, and the attempt will be made to discover which actual need(s) caused the first appearance and subsequent adoption of double-entry bookkeeping.

The Origins of Bookkeeping

The opinion that double-entry bookkeeping is the final and perfected stage in the evolution of systematic accounting from disorderly and unclassified entries in diaries or memorials is sometimes expressed.† However true this may be, as an explanation of the evolution it is unsatisfactory because it does not explain, in the first place, why business entries were made in diaries, and secondly, why a method of recording simple, incomplete entries gradually become transformed into a completely unified system of bookkeeping. An answer to the first question will be hazarded in this section. The word "hazarded" is used purposely, because owing to the paucity and incomplete nature of the evidence regarding accounting practice before 1494, any explanation must of necessity be hypothetical. The history of accounting before double-entry will first be constructed synthetically on the basis of the "pragmatic" nature of accounting, and then checked with the available evidence.

In the most simple conditions the periodic inventory of his possessions would be all that the trader would require to assist him in the administration of his resources. The inventory would serve as a control over his various resources, and would at the same time enable him to gauge his wealth and any increase or decrease it has experienced since the last inventory. The control provided by the inventory is very necessary to ascertain whether those assets, which the trader thinks he has, are actually in his possession; and whether they are in good order and condition.

Before credit transactions are introduced into trade the periodic inventory can be made without the assistance of any bookkeeping records. The trader can compile an inventory merely by surveying the various articles in his possession. His goods will be in the warehouse, his cash in the strong-box, and his house, land, &c. will be at hand for enumeration.

Some writers* employing the above approach to the study of the history of bookkeeping have regarded the inventory as the first form of bookkeeping record. It is most probable that the trader would make a memorandum of the result of the inventory, though from the point of view of the control of his resources such a record would not be necessary. For the same reason the view† that the private ownership by individuals of property in itself proves the existence of some form of bookkeeping appears to be erroneous. The ownership of property entails some form of control, but not necessarily a form of accounting control. The process of taking inventories, without any records, will suffice in the simplest circumstances.

As soon as a merchant grants or receives credit in the course of his business the need for accounting records becomes urgent. Debts payable or debts receivable represent negative or positive items of wealth, and as such must figure in a complete inventory of a trader's possessions. If a trader has not kept any records of his credit transactions he is unable to place a reliable valuation on his liability to others, or his due from debtors. The existence of a debt cannot be ascertained other than by means of some form of record, because as a rule evidence of debt is not afforded by the nature of the right itself, which is intangible. There is therefore an adequate and compelling reason for keeping records of credit dealings, because without them the inventory will

* Thus Row Fogo: Bookkeeping "is neither a discovery or a science, nor the inspiration of a happy moment, but the outcome of continued efforts to meet the necessities of trade as they gradually developed." (In R. Brown: *A History of Accounting and Accountants*, 1905, p. 93.)

See also A. C. Littleton: *Accounting Evolution to 1900*, 1933, p. 362. R. A. Bryant in *Accounting Review*, Vol. X (1935), p. 411. R. de Roover: "Characteristics of Bookkeeping before Paciolo," in *Accounting Review*, Vol. XIII (1938), p. 144.

† See H. Sieveking: *Aus Venetianischen Handlungsbüchern*, 1901, p. 301.

* See J. Hagers in *Maandblad voor het Boekhouding*, 1896-7, p. 19; B. Zieger in *Deutsche Handelsschul-Lehrer Zeitung*, 1905, p. 2.

† See E. Peragallo: *Origin and Evolution of Double-Entry Bookkeeping*, 1938, p. 16 (note 1).

lose its value as a means of control. More important, however, than the indirect control provided by the inventory is the direct control which records afford over the administration of credit. Unless he has records of his dealings the trader would be subject to the deceit of his debtors and creditors and the failings of his memory in the collection and payment of debts. The trader's vigilant eye is insufficient to safeguard that part of his wealth bound up with credit transactions.

The recording of debts has its aggressive aspect, too. Sir Roger de Coverley was unkind enough to raise the matter in an argument with a trader : "And indeed what is the whole business of the Trader's Accompt, but to over-reach him who trusts to his Memory."* But as Stephen Monteage pointed out in his *Debtor and Creditor made Easie* (1682) the deliberate failure to keep accounts could have the same effect : " I have likewise heard of some that in policy keep no Books of Accounts, that they may the better make large reckonings to their Correspondents."

The next development in accounting must presuppose a change in the nature of the trading unit from a single proprietorship with an active proprietor controlling the entire business to a form of trading where the separation of the ownership and its control enters the picture. The most elementary form of such absenteeism arises where the proprietor relinquishes direct control over some part of his wealth, either because the business has increased in size or complexity beyond the capabilities of one man, or because the owner chooses not to devote all his energies to the business.

A servant may be appointed to manage the warehouse. This does not make the compilation of the inventory more difficult, but the inventory alone is no longer useful in the control of the warehouse assets. The figure for merchandise which appears in the inventory must itself be controlled. It is not sufficient that the records show how much merchandise is on hand ; it is more important to know from the records how much ought to be on hand. The latter question can best be answered by compelling the servant to account for the final figure by keeping records of every incoming or outgoing of goods. One would expect that such records would be quantitative only.

In a similar way cash, bills of exchange, and other assets, when their control goes out of the hands of the owner, become the objects of accounting records.

We have now reached a stage in the complexity of business organisation where records of all assets and liabilities would be useful. It is appropriate to consider why these records should be kept in the form of *accounts*.

When the number of transactions affecting the same debtor, parcel of goods, &c. is small, a chronological list of these events in the form of a diary or memorial would be capable of supplying information on any point with the minimum of effort. But when the firm's dealings with any individual become more frequent, it is very cumbersome to ascertain from a mere list the firm's position as against that debtor or creditor. Some classification of the memorial entries becomes imperative in the interests of clarity. Hence we get the beginnings of accounts in which the memorial entries are inserted according to the nature of the transaction. From this advance it is a short step to the sub-classification of the entries in each account according to whether they are incomings or outgoings. The incomings and outgoings may be placed either next to each other, or one above the other in the accounts.* In some old account books the incomings were placed in the first section of the ledger, and the outgoings in the rear.†

While the keeping of records in the form of accounts may be ascribed to the usefulness of the method, it is not easy to explain why the procedure for recording entries in accounts should be followed consistently for all transactions. It is difficult to comprehend why receipts of cash or goods, the granting of credit to a debtor, and the extinction of a debt payable should all be entered on the debit side of their respective accounts. This procedure is logical in the sense that all these entries represent the same type of occurrence : an increase in the property of the owner. But there is no reason why, at the stage of development now under discussion, such a logical procedure should have been followed. There is evidence that the less logical procedure was adopted by some merchants. M. de Roover found an example of what " seems illogical and inconsistent with established ideas " in the books of the Flemish merchant, Guillaume Ruyelle (1369).‡ Also in the works of the German writers Schreiber (1518), Kaltenbrunner (1565), and Schultz (1611) one finds this " irrationality," though these authors followed the basic ideas of double-entry.

Bookkeeping Prior to the Appearance of Double-Entry

The actual development of bookkeeping, as revealed by those account books which have been made accessible by the researches of continental scholars, will now be sketched in order to see whether it confirms the hypothetical reconstruction outlined above.

The evidence afforded by the actual business records preserved must be accepted with some reservation, because it is very likely that the account books discovered are not complete.§ Also, there is some difficulty in advancing the discovered facts as evidence to substantiate the theory sketched above. That theory attempted to correlate accounting changes to changing business needs. As changing needs can as a rule only be the result of changes in the nature of business organisation, the important data is not so

* *The Spectator*, No. 174 (1713).

* See Peragallo *op. cit.* p. 19.

† See de Roover *op. cit.* p. 146.

‡ See L. Carman : " Researches of Raymond de Roover in Flemish Accounting " in *Journal of Accountancy*, Vol. LX (1935), p. 116.

§ See B. Penndorf : *Geschichte der Buchhaltung in Deutschland*, 1913, p. 36.

much when accounting changes occurred, but whether the passage of time brought with it more problems to be solved by accounting. On this point the evidence is meagre. Nevertheless, it will be interesting to note the chief facts.

The earliest business records found in most countries consist of entries made in books which can best be described as diaries. The entries were both of a private and commercial nature. In an account book dating from 1475 to 1483 found in Utrecht there are pious mottoes, rules for moral conduct, and treatments for coughs and other ailments.* The Hanseatic partnership of the Wittenborgs (circa 1310) kept records of their credit dealings only† ; and this is characteristic of all early account books. Whenever settlement was made the entries were crossed out. Entries were not made in chronological order, the costliness of paper inducing the use of any empty space sooner or later. " The recording of the transactions was so simple in those days that the mere ability to write was all that was necessary."‡

Fairly early, it would appear, the credit transactions were classified in account form. In Germany Penndorf found examples of accounts in the books of the Runtingers (1383-1407) and Johan Pisz (1421).§

Support for our theory of accounting development was found in the work of Daniel Defoe, who described bookkeeping for shopkeepers in very simple conditions. He says : " He that gives no trust, and takes no trust, either by wholesale or retail, and keeps his cash all himself, may indeed go on without keeping any books at all, and has nothing to do, when he would know his estate, but to cast up his shop and his cash, and see how much they amount to, and that is his whole and neat estate."¶ If there are credit transactions, a ledger must be kept, and he says : " All the tradesman has in the world must be found in these three articles, or some of them :—Goods in the shop ; money in cash ; debts abroad. The shop will at any time show the first of these, upon a small stop to cast it up ; the cash-chest and bill-box will show the second at demand ; and the ledger, when posted, will show the last."‖ He also realises the use of an account as a check or control over an inventory item : " The keeping a cash book is one of the nicest parts of a tradesman's business, because there is always the bag and the book to be brought together ; and if they do not exactly speak the same language, even to a farthing, there must be some omission."** Business complexity had apparently not created serious accounting problems for many eighteenth century English traders.

It is interesting to trace the effect of absentee ownership on accounting in this early period. In antiquity the administrators of the Babylonian temple-banks, of the Ptolemaic treasury, and of the revenues of Imperial Rome made periodic abstracts from their records to account for their management.* The municipalities of the early Italian city-states kept comprehensive records of their affairs. The Teutonic Orders in Germany had some form of account-keeping, and accounts were drawn up to facilitate the handing over of control by a leader to his successor in office.† In purely trading concerns the same influence is discernible. Penndorf shows that the accounts of the Toelner partnership in Germany (1345-50) were much more complete than those of the contemporary single proprietorships.‡ Mickwitz has shown that the early records of partnerships of Reval include both cash and credit transactions, while those of single proprietorships did not include cash items till a late date.§

There is little reason to believe that the early records were inadequate in the circumstances. As de Roover says : " Nothing could be further from the truth than to pretend as Werner Sombart has done that the medieval merchant's accounts were in such a state of muddle that it was impossible for him to tell how he stood."‖ Even to-day many small business firms would find the early type of accounting sufficient for their needs. Hagers, who found a memorial of a sixteenth century shoemaker, remarks : " This book displays a remarkable similarity with the bookkeeping which some members of the cobbling craft practise to-day."¶

The Appearance of Double-Entry Bookkeeping

The first set of accounts kept in double-entry form which we know about are those of the *massari* or officials responsible for the administration of the finances of the town of Genoa dating from 1340. It is significant that the first example of double-entry bookkeeping is to be found in the accounts of an organisation where the ownership of the property and its control are sharply divorced.

Double-entry bookkeeping did not at once appear in its present-day form. The profit and loss account was seldom used by the German merchants of the sixteenth century.** The profit balances on individual ventures or lots of goods were carried directly to the capital account. In Italy, however, the profit and loss account appears to have been used before the capital account was introduced.††

After the introduction of double-entry bookkeeping there appears to have been little further development in accounting until the adoption of the principle of limited liability in company legislation during the

* See J. Hagers : *Maandblad voor het Boekhouding*, 1901-2, p. 161.
† Penndorf *op. cit.* p. 3.
‡ Zieger *op. cit.* p. 2.
§ Penndorf *op. cit.* p. 23.
¶ Defoe : *The Complete English Tradesman*, 1745 (Quotations from the 1841 reprint), p. 311.
‖ *ibid.* p. 310.
** *ibid.* p. 317.

* See Leyerer : *Theorie und Geschichte der Buchhaltung*, 1919, p. 25.
† Penndorf *op. cit.* p. 18.
‡ *ibid.* p. 9.
§ G. Mickwitz : *Aus Revaler Handelsbüchern*, 1938, p. 189.
‖ de Roover : *La Formation et l'Expansion de la Comptabilité à Partie Double*, 1937. Translation by Cosmo Gordon in his review *A.R.A. Review Supplement*, No. 2, p. 20.
¶ Hagers *op. cit.* p. 162.
** Penndorf *op. cit.* p. 185.
†† Sieveking *op. cit.* p. 318.

nineteenth century. The one significant advance was the use of the double-entry system to show the internal movement and transformation of assets within an enterprise. As this development is of more inportance to the history of cost accounting, which cannot be discussed in this paper, it will only be mentioned.* The other minor changes which did occur were the introduction of methods designed to facilitate the quick posting of journal entries to the ledger, and the easier detection of errors and frauds†

While it is quite clear that double-entry bookkeeping was not the only or even the most common system of accounting employed, it is interesting to examine why the system was advocated by teachers and used by some business men. This should throw some light on the problem of which *need(s)* caused the double-entry system to emerge.

We can now tap another source of information, the textbooks which were published after 1494, when the first treatise on bookkeeping, in Pacioli's *Summa*, saw the light of day. It is difficult to tedermine to what extent the textbooks are accurate mirrors of mercantile practice, and how far the observations made by teachers concerning the system were shared by business men. We are warned by Kelly in his *Elements of Bookkeeping* (1801) that most of the writers were "Schoolmasters and Teachers" and that "the works themselves evidently shew that those writers, in general, followed each others plans, and took their documents from printed Books more than from real Business." Considering, however, the striking unanimity revealed by the textbooks, the fact that not a few writers were business men and that in some cases the examples illustrating the text were taken from practice it may be confidently assumed that tf there was any divergence between teaching and practice, it lay more in the form than in the substance.

Double-entry bookkeeping was useful for the same reasons which prompted merchants to keep some sort of accounts in the period before its adoption. Accounting was useful to assist the memory in the regulation of credit dealings, and in the control of property. Accounting records were also useful because they could facilitate the administration of the proprietor's estate after his death. They could also, in certain circumstances, be used as evidence of the existence of debt.‡ But these needs for records could not have stimulated the development of double-entry bookkeeping, because they were satisfied quite adequately by the earlier methods. The existence of these needs cannot explain the introduction of nominal accounts, or the use of money entries in goods accounts, or the unification of the entire framework. We must therefore turn to the special characteristics of double-entry bookkeeping as then practised, and examine their usefulness

The Balance Account as a Statement of Financial Condition

The double-entry bookkeeping system is characterised by the fact that within its structure there is room for a profit and loss account, capital account and balance account (the forerunner of the balance sheet). The advantages, from the modern point of view, of having these three accounts are that they give the reader in a clear and concise manner information about the present position and past progress of the business; or, as the American writers express it, about "status" and "operations."

The first merchants using double-entry, according to Sieveking, did not realise this quality of the new system. The important Iralian firm, Donado Soranzo Brothers (1406-34) could only with the greatest difficulty make an estimate of their capital from their records, and eventually the matter was taken out of their hands and settled by the Court.

But the idea that double-entry bookkeeping could be useful to throw light on status and operations was eventually realised and finds expression in most of the books on bookkeeping. Pacioli says that from the capital account "you may always learn what your fortune is.† Moreover, a definition of bookkeeping as "the Art of arranging the Transactions of Persons in Business, so as to exhibit a State of their Affairs in a concise and satisfactory manner"‡ was very common

If we examine the bookkeeping texts more closely we find that the position is not as straightforward as ot seems. A distinction must be drawn between a balance account drawn up on the basis of the account balances appearing in the ledger, and a balance account incorporating the facts as revealed by an actual inventory where the possessions of the firm are examined and valued. The former may be called a crude or book balance, and the latter an inventory balance. The former does not necessarily or usually show the true condition of the enterprise but only a list of ledger balances; the latter shows the present value of the firm's property. The former may be completed from information contained in the books of double-entry; for the compilation of the latter further information is required. The former statement is the product of the double-entry system; the latter may be used in connection with any system, and if used in conjunction with double entry it is superimpsed on the books of account and must be tied-in with the double-entry records

Many of the balance accounts found in the early mercantile ledgers are of the crude balance type The balance accounts drawn up by Andrea Barbarigo

* See R. S. Edwards: *A Survey of French Contributions to the Study of Cost Accounting during the 19th Century*, 1937, *passim*.

† This tendency is reflected in the English textbooks, e.g. Power: *Bookkeeping no Bugbear*, 1815; Lambert: *The Perpetual Balance*, 1812.

‡ In this connection it should be noted that it is most unlikely that the law, more particularly in this early period, would have initiated any accounting practice. It generally gives formal recognition to existing practice.

* Sieveking, *op. cit.* p. 317.

† Geijsbeek's translation in *Ancient Double-Entry Bookkeeping* 1914, p. 73.

‡ For example, see Morrison's *The Elements of Bookkeeping*, 1810.

(1430-49), whose books are described by Peragallo* as marking " one of the high points in the evolution of double-entry," were of this nature.† And the text writers in the overwhelming majority of cases described the drawing up of crude balances. John Mair, whose two books on *Book-keeping Methodiz'd* and *Book-keeping Moderniz'd* went through many editions in the eighteenth century, describes how to draw up a balance account on the sole basis of the records in the ledger. The cash account will show the merchant the amount of his cash on hand " without the trouble of counting his coin," while the quantitative entries in the goods accounts will reveal the contents of the warehouse " without being put to the trouble of inspecting his warehouse." Mair clearly shows the difference between an inventory balance and a crude balance where he says, concerning the usual practice adopted, that : " When a man begins the world, and first sets up to trade, the inventory is to be gathered from a survey of the particulars that make up his real estate ; but ever after it is to be collected from the balance of his old books, and carried to the new."

It is evident from the treatment of stocks of merchandise on hand that no attempt at valuation in the light of conditions at the balancing date was made. At least nine-tenths of the writers before 1840 advocated the valuation of stocks at cost, or, as it was sometimes called, at " prime cost." Other examples of the absence of valuation may be found in the customary treatment of the following items : in uncompleted consignments no attempt at profit determination was made, but the difference between expenses and proceeds to date carried forward in the balance account ; fixed property accounts showed the cost of repairs as additions to the " value " of the property, and the amount of rent received as a deduction ; in funded debt accounts the excess of the whole purchase price over the proceeds of the portion sold was usually taken as the balance account " value."

Many writers did introduce some elements of the taking of an inventory. Often instructions were given to examine and count the merchandise on hand, and the data in the quantity columns of the goods accounts were adjusted for wastage or leakage revealed by the stock-taking. The " value " of the stock was then calculated by taking the appropriate portion of the original cost as computed by the Rule of Three. Some writers, while advocating a physical stock-taking, did not even allow it to have this limited effect on the valuation. Hager, in his *Buchhalten* (1660), though finding that some of the parcels of goods had diminished in weight, still assigned the total cost as the balance account " value " of these parcels.

Taking into account the evidence afforded by the textbooks one may say with some degree of certainty that in England, and on the Continent, the actual taking of a complete and thorough inventory was the exceptional practice. Isolated examples of the compilation of inventory balances can be found.

* Peragallo *op. cit.* p. 36.

† Sieveking *op. cit.* p. 323

Dr. Penndorf states that the early German writer, Sartorius, desired an inventory. Probably the first English writer to advocate an inventory was Robert Hamilton in his *An Introduction to Merchandise*, first published in 1788. The Germans Magelsen (*Die Ersten Gründe*, 1772) and Wagner (*Neues Vollständiges Lehrbuch*, 1802) also stressed the need for an inventory. But despite these few cases it is doubtful whether the interesting pronouncement of Cory in his *Practical Treatise on Accounts* (1839) is factual : " It is a universal principle among merchants in keeping their books, both at the commencement and at every rest in the progress of business, to affix to all the articles of stock [= capital] their values in money, for without this they would be unable at any time to ascertain their profits and losses. And as estimates and allowances are yearly made for wear and tear, for accidents, for the alteration in value of the leases and patents by the effluxion of time, and of funded property by the fluctuations of the funds, and the like, the whole system depends upon this practice of valuation."

The history of commercial legislation may suggest that French accounting development represents the exception to the general practice concerning inventories. Dr. Simon, referring to the *Ordonnance de Commerce* of 1673 says : " The closing inventory balance must have been evolved in the first half of the seventeenth century ; because, when French legislation embracing accounting was passed, we find this as one of the requirements demanded of it."* However, it is quite clear, as Dr. Simon states, apparently contradicting his earlier statement, that in practice the merchants of France, even after 1673, omitted the compilation of an inventory balance at the closing of their books.† In the works of de la Porte, which were designed expressly to comply with the requirements of the *Ordonnance*, only crude balances are discussed ; and he states : " There can be no doubt, that when the balance account is drawn up as I have taught, then it is . . . the merchant's inventory, which . . . the commercial edict of 1673 directs and compels him to make every two years."‡

Some modern authors§ have deplored the lack of inventory balance accounts in the accounting practice of the sixteenth and later centuries as the greatest deficiency of early accounting. Though this may appear to be a serious shortcoming, the absence of an inventory account in those times was probably no great disadvantage. If the books are those of a proprietor who supervises the drawing up of the balance account and if it is intended solely for his

* Simon : *Die Bilanzen der Aktiengesellschaften*, 1898, p 34. See also Schmalenbach : *Dynamische Bilanz*, 5th Edition, 1931, p. 62, and Sieveking *op. cit.* p. 324. Sombart in *Der Moderne Kapitalismus*, 6th Edition, Vol. II, p. 117, doubts whether the *Ordonnance* applied to firms using double-entry bookkeeping.

† Simon *op. cit.* p. 35.

‡ From the German translation (1764) of de la Porte's *Guide des Negocians* (first published 1716).

§ See Sombart *op. cit.* p. 115 ; Penndorf *op. cit.* p. 44 ; Jäger : *Beiträge*, 1874, p. 95.

use,* then it matters little what value he puts against each item. He can gauge his financial position merely by surveying the enumeration of the assets and the description of each. Valuation is of minor significance.

It would be erroneous to conclude from the above that the crude balance accounts showed values far divorced from reality. When only a small portion of an individual's wealth is tied up in fixed property or long-lived assets, the book values as a rule would be close to current values. Only when production and trade become more capitalistic do book values and current values diverge markedly.

The Closing of the Ledger

It appears that the real reason for the drawing up of the balance account, and the explanation of the valuation technique adopted, is to be found not in the desire to obtain an abstract of the ledger displaying the magnitude and composition of the owner's capital, but in the need for a concise, neat, and orderly method of closing one ledger and transferring all the essential information to its successor.

The fact that until a late date balance accounts were drawn up only when a ledger was filled, and not at regular intervals, supports this view.† The titles given to the balance account by various writers clearly indicate the purpose of the account. Schweicker in his *Zwifach Buchhalten* (1549) heads his balance account: "To close this book, debit . . ." a literal translation of the Italian terminology. The English writer styling himself W. P. in his *Pathway to Knowledge* (1596), a direct translation of Nicolaus Petri's *Practique* (1596), uses the following as the title of the debit side of his balance account: "Ballance of Accompt is Debitor by these Percels following founde by the shutting up of diuers accompts, which to shut up they are made Creditors in this Booke A. and carried Debitors into the Booke B." Finally, the fact that neither Pacioli nor the early writers before Ympyn (1543)‡ incorporated their balance accounts in the account books adds weight to the contention that these balances were not statements desired for their own sake. As Postlethwayt says in his *Universal Dictionary of Trade and Commerce* (1751): "The account of balance is opened in the ledger, only for the closing of the books."

The need for a convenient method of closing an old ledger and opening a new one is evident when one realises that it was both unnecessary and cumbersome to transfer all open accounts to the new ledger. Some process of weeding out the unwanted accounts, the "refuse and dregs" as Mair called them, was required. The process of balancing is the reduction of the mass of accounts to workable proportions preparatory to their transfer to the new ledger. Some account balances had to be included in the new ledger so that it could contain all the information the proprietor would require, and the completed ledger could be stored away.* The information required chiefly concerned the asset and liability accounts, which were useful as controls over their respective assets and liabilities. Therefore, at the closing of the old ledger the balances of these accounts, and of any other account useful for the merchant's purposes, had to be collected and transferred to the new ledger. The balance account proved to be the useful medium for accomplishing this in a clear and systematic manner.

This use of the balance account explains why, when a business was commenced, an inventory had to be compiled to serve as a basis for the first ledger; and why the subsequent making of an inventory was unnecessary. The inventory contained details of those items which formed the basis of the essential ledger accounts. The description of these items was the important part; but as some values had to be used, the most obvious values—current values—were taken. But once the accounting system was in full swing the books of account contained the necessary descriptions of the essential items. Both the descriptions and the book values were transferred; but the latter were retained not because they were significant,† but because they were conveniently available.‡ It was unnecessary to find other values. In this connection it may be suggested that double-entry bookkeeping was used precisely for this reason, that it rendered the taking of subsequent inventories superfluous. However, none of the texts make special mention of this fact.§

The Profit and Loss Account

The function of the profit and loss account was to collect all those account balances which the proprietor did not want or did not need to transfer to the new ledger. Thus in the first published treatise on bookkeeping Pacioli writes: "But as to those accounts which you should not care to transfer to Ledger A. [new], as for instance, your own personal accounts of which you are not obliged to give an account for another, as for instance, small mercantile expenses . . . all these accounts should be closed in the Cross Ledger [old] into the favor and damage account." The accounts which it was desirable to exclude from the balance account and not to transfer to the new ledger were those which did not represent either positive or negative items of wealth. This idea of the nature of profit and loss items is occasionally found in the English texts, an example being Richard Hayes in his *The Gentleman's Complete Book-keeper* (1741).

* There were cases where the balance accounts were intended for owners who knew very little about the state of affairs of their business. Joint stock companies submitting accounts to their shareholders are not unknown in this period. But it appears as if these cases had no influence on accounting practice.

† See Row Fogo in Brown *op. cit.* p. 107.

‡ See de Waal: *De leer van het Boekhouden in de Nederlanden tijdens de Zestiende eeuw*, 1927, p. 118.

* The Flemish writers Savonne (*Instruction*, 1567) and de Renterghem (*Instruction Nouvelle*, 1592) particularly stress the latter point. See de Waal *op. cit.* pp. 151 and 233.

† Except in the case of personal accounts, where the book figures themselves are important.

‡ Some of the early authors, e.g. Mellema (*Boekhouden*, 1590), Petri (1596), Flügel (*Theoretische Abhandlung*, 1781), and Postlethwayt (1751) appear to be indifferent as to which of suggested bases for valuing stocks should be used. The lack of significance of any figure may be the explanation of this.

§ Mair's remarks (p. 10 above) are interesting. It should be noted that any accounting system having property accounts would dispense with the need of making inventories.

|| Geijsbeek *op. cit.* p. 73.

where he says : "And for all such accounts as are of the same nature with Stock [= capital], being such as you can make no Demand upon, nor them upon you; such as House Expences, Pocket Expences, Charges of Merchandize, &c., to make even such accounts, you must Dt. the Account of Profit and Loss."

The technique of closing the ledgers explains the concept of profit which the early writers and business men appear to have adopted. Except in so far as actual revaluation was rarely resorted to, their profit figure reflected the increase or decrease in the value of the firm's possessions between two successive "rests" or balancing dates. The drawings of the proprietor, the expenses of lottery tickets, the winnings, if any, and the receipt of legacies were invariably treated as profit and loss items. The profit figure represented changes in "value" from *all* causes. This concept of profit was not adopted because the resultant figure was more useful than any alternative one, but because it was the only one consistent with the procedure of closing the books. The theoretical implications of the concept were probably never given a thought.

This does not mean that the nature of the profit concept was not understood. Thus Deighan in his *A Complete Treatise on Bookkeeping* (1807) explains the inclusion in the profit and loss account of the private expenses which "is not properly loss" because "as it has the same effect in diminishing the Stock, it is placed in the same manner to the Dr. of Profit and Loss." Ympyn, or more correctly,* the author on whose treatise the *Nieuwe Instructie* (1543) is based, also realises that not all the entries in the profit and loss account are connected with the results of trading. Real profit items contain the words "gained" or "profited"; while the entry for household expenses is: "to expenses of housekeeping brought here to close the book."

The vast majority of business proprietors would not need information from their books to enlighten them whether their business was prospering or on the retrograde. The very fact that the profit and loss account was balanced only when the ledger was full shows that the business man did not rely upon it for vital information. However, all the text writers realised that their profit and loss accounts did to some extent reveal the measure of the enterprise's success. The name of the account tells what it is supposed to show.

The Treatment of Bad Debts

The treatment of bad and doubtful debts is interesting and illuminating in connection with the technique and purpose of balancing the books, and of bookkeeping practice in general.

It was realised that to open separate accounts for each doubtful debt when beginning a new ledger would make the task of transferring the details from the old to the new ledger unnecessarily laborious. Therefore, says Alexander Malcolm in his *A New Treatise of Arithmetick and Book-keeping* (1718): "For what Debts are lost by Bankrupts, when they appear plainly irrecoverable, make Profit, etc. Debtor to the Bankrupt, that your Books may be no longer troubled with his Accompt."

* See Cosmo Gordon *op. cit.* p. 21.

But until the debtor had been declared bankrupt and had paid his final composition there was uncertainty as to how much of the debt would be recovered; and there was always the possibility that at a later date the bankrupt might settle his former debt. Some readily available record of the debt was necessary. So the more popular method of dealing with bad debts was that described by Macghie in his *The Principles of Book-keeping Explain'd* (1718). He says: "I judge it better to enter an Accompt of Desperate Debts, Debitor, rather than Profit and Loss; for by this Way of Entring it, we are still put in Mind that such a Sum was never yet paid, if so be the said Bankrupt should set up to trade again." Here bad debts were not closed into the profit and loss account but retained in an omnibus account, which in the words of Hamilton (1788) "saves the trouble of transferring the particular accompts from ledger to ledger." As Flügel points out in his *Wegweiser* (1741), "if one opens new accounts for each of the doubtful debtors, in many businesses a half a ream of paper will be necessary for them alone."

The omnibus account would not lead to confusion, as would an omnibus account for all debtors with whom the business is still dealing, because as Flügel in his *Theoretische Abhandlung* (1781) and Hustcraft Stephens in his *Italian Book-keeping Reduced into an Art* (1735) explain, it would very rarely be used because few entries would affect it. But if the doubtful debts appeared in the ledger or balance account without any distinguishing mark, the reader might possibly have been misled. The title of the omnibus account, which according to Stephens is "capable of demonstrating the true Nature and Quality of the Debts," would prevent any misunderstanding.

The treatment of bad debts shows that the balance account was the epitome of all the essential information that had to be carried from the old to the new ledger. It also shows that the reader of the accounts relied more on the description of the items than on the valuation figures. It also shows how considerations of the profit figure were ignored or made subsidiary to the need for comprehensive records.*

Partnership Profit and Loss Accounts

While the proprietor of a business may be able to judge the profitability of his business without the use of detailed accounting records, yet if, for some reason, he has to produce an exact profit figure, he will be constrained to use some accounting data. One reason for computing exact profit figures is the division of profits among business partners. Here we

* It is necessary to mention that Magelsen (*Die Ersten Gründe*, 1772) suggests setting up a reserve for doubtful debts, by debiting profit and loss account and crediting an account to appear in the balance account.

must examine the contentions that a complete system of accounting, such as double entry, is indispensable to determine the partners' shares of the total profits,* and that "in this necessity . . . we find the prime motive for creating a system of bookkeeping."†

A distinction must be made between profit and loss accounts made during the existence of the partnership and the final settlement made at the dissolution of the partnership. The first type results in the crediting to the partners' capital accounts of their shares of the profit. Assets are generally not revalued for such purposes. This method is not followed when the final settlement is made, on the basis of which the partners withdraw their shares of th epartnership assets. Either the partners must agree to the valuations of the various assets, that is, an inventory; or else the assets must themselves be distributed or be converted into money and distributed *pro rata* to the partners.

This method of calculating the shares of the partners in the profits can be used without double-entry bookkeeping, as it is based on an inventory at the time of dissolution. Records of the partners' drawings and contributions must be kept, but the incomplete single-entry system will readily provide this information. It is true that an interim profit and loss account (i.e. of the first type) cannot be compiled from single-entry records without making an actual inventory; but it is best to regard these interim balances as the result of closing the ledger and not as statements drawn up on account of their usefulness. It is most unlikely that the withdrawal of funds by the partners are made on the basis of the book profit figure; and if there is any over or under-crediting of the partners' profits owing to the use of the book values of the assets, this will eventually be adjusted (if the partners have funds available) when the final inventory is compiled.

In the early partnerships the profits were divided on the basis of final inventories.‡ The Medici partnerships are interesting examples.§ Normally they were formed for periods of three or five years, and though annual accounts were often prescribed by contract, these were rarely settled. At the termination of the partnership an inventory of the assets was compiled and the assets distributed to the partners according to the terms of the agreement. This procedure preceded the introduction of double entry and was continued after its adoption. In the measurement of total profit single-entry is as efficient as double-entry.

PROFIT CALCULATIONS AND BUSINESS PLANNING

The question whether the profit figures derived from double-entry bookkeeping records were used as a basis for forecasting and the planning of business

* See Murray: *Chapters in the History of Bookkeeping, Accountancy, and Commercial Arithmetic*, 1930, p. 140.

† Row Fogo in Brown *op. cit.* p. 96.

‡ See Littleton *op. cit.* p. 137.

§ See Edler: *Glossary of Medieval Terms of Business*, 1934, Appendix I, *passim*.

policy is of some importance, because not a few economic historians* regard rational economic behaviour as one of the important characteristics of the capitalist system. And adequate records of past activities and results are regarded as useful, if not indispensable, for rational business planning. Some economic historians hold the view that these records must be in the form of double-entry bookkeeping to be useful for this purpose. Alfred Weber defines "a rational capitalistic establishment" as one "which determines its income yielding power by calculation according to the methods of modern [i.e. double-entry] bookkeeping and the striking of a balance."† Mickwitz thinks that double-entry is essential if one wishes to measure the yield against the capital invested, because without double-entry one cannot show the amortisation of fixed assets.‡

These views do not appear to be very accurate. As has been shown earlier, calculations of capital and total profits by means of periodic inventories are at least as effective as double-entry calculations, which, to be at all accurate, must embody the results of an actual inventory. The calculation of depreciation may be accomplished without double-entry bookkeeping by revaluing the particular asset; and in the isolated instances where depreciation appears in early accounts and textbooks such depreciation represents value declines determined in that way.§ If by "amortisation" is meant an, of necessity, arbitrary charge against profit, one may at least question its significance and relevance to rational planning.

Moreover, from the point of view of rational management, the total profit figure is of much less significance than data of the relative profitability of the various activities carried out by the business firm. To-day the provision of this data is regarded as a separate branch of accounting, cost accounting, the development of which cannot be discussed in this paper. But the financial accounting of the fifteenth and subsequent centuries has some resemblance to modern cost accounting in so far as the expenses and receipts connected with particular lots or types of goods, ventures, trading voyages, consignments, and other business activities were entered in the ledger accounts in such a way that the profit or loss on each could be found. This type of accounting, which is possible only where comprehensive records are kept, as in the double-entry system, may imply a significant advance in this respect as compared with earlier bookkeeping methods. Of the earlier period Mick-

* See G. Mickwitz: "Zur Problem der Betriebsführung in der Antiken Wirtschaft" in *Vierteljahrschrift für Sozial- und Wirtschaftsgeschichte*, 32 Band Heft 1., p. 1.

† Weber: *General Economic History*, p. 275.

‡ Mickwitz *op. cit.* p. 15. For the view that double-entry bookkeeping has been of great importance in the development of capitalist society see Mickwitz *op. cit.* p. 24; Sombart *op. cit.* p. 118; Robertson: *Aspects of the Rise of Economic Individualism*, 1933, p. 53. If our conclusions are correct, then the influence of double-entry bookkeeping must have been negligible.

§ See Penndorf: *Luca Pacioli*, 1933, p. 36. It is interesting to note that one of the earliest references to percentage depreciation (in Magelsen, 1772) advocates its application only where actual valuation is difficult or cumbersome.

witz* describes how the accounts were not capable of guiding the agriculturist in the choice of crops, or in the general management of industry and trade.

But it is difficult to assess whether very great use was made or could have been made of the individual profit figures shown by double-entry records. Before specialisation of commercial activities became pronounced, past results were of little use as an aid to future policy, because it was unlikely that the merchant would be engaged in the same line of business in the immediate future. Success depended largely on the ability rapidly to size up the changing market conditions and to take advantage of any opportunity that presented itself.

Nevertheless, text writers occasionally mention that double-entry records show the profit on each separate activity. Flugel (1741) and Wagner (1802), while aware that both double-entry and single-entry bookkeeping can show the total profit figure, point out that only the former method can show the individual profit figures, and is therefore to be preferred. Abraham de Graaf in his *Instructie* (1693) stresses the importance of this information, more particularly to a trader whose transactions consist of separate ventures. Certainly the most striking discussion on the usefulness of the individual profit figures is given by Wardaugh Thompson in his *Accomptant's Oracle* (1777): "Book-keeping by Double Entry, or what is commonly called the Italian method of Book-keeping, is the art of keeping our accompts in such a manner, as will not only exhibit to us our neat gain or loss upon the whole, but our particular gain or loss upon each article we deal in, by which we are instructed what branches to pursue, and which to decline; a piece of knowledge so very essential to every man in business, that without it a person can only be said to deal at random, or at best can be called but guess'd work." Yet despite this clear statement one may conclude that, in view of the scant attention given to the subject in most of the textbooks, it was not until large-scale, specialised business enterprises became common that the use of past records as an aid to business planning became important.

The Trial Balance

Besides serving as a medium for transferring account balances from one ledger to another, the process of balancing and closing the ledger provides a check on the completeness of the entries in the ledger. Unless there is a debit entry for each credit entry the balance would be upset and indicate some error or omission in the ledger. It has been suggested† that double-entry may have been devised to provide such a check.

The need for a check was certainly pressing, for there appears to have been much difficulty in getting the books to balance. Edward Jones in his *An Address to Bankers, Merchants, Tradesmen, etc.* (1795) writes: "To Balance a set of Books at the first trial appears wonderful, and is mentioned with astonishment; and for the same person to do so two or three years following, he is considered to possess a portion of infallability, and is freely allowed to boast of the exploit as long as he lives. But in how few compting-houses hath this been effected." If errors and omissions remain undetected the value of the books would obviously be greatly diminished.

The fact that double-entry bookkeeping provides an easy means of checking the completeness and arithmetic correctness of the postings from the journal to the ledger was realised by the earliest writers.* Peragallo, in his recent book,† holds the contrary view and states: "Manzoni, as well as Paciolo, fell into a grave error when he took off his *summa summarium* [*sic*]: both drew up the trial balance of the old ledger only after it had been completely balanced, closed, and all open accounts transferred to the new ledger. It was thus bound to balance in all cases, even if the ledger were full of errors, because both sides of the accounts were made equal by transferring their balance to the new ledger A trial balance of these closed ledger accounts was not a true trial balance at all: it proved nothing. This is clearly seen in the example. Neither the true function of the trial balance nor its proper construction were known in the early sixteenth century." However, in his fourteenth chapter Pacioli correctly describes the nature and source of the trial balance when he says: "You must never make a credit entry without making the same entry with its respective amount in the debit. Upon this depends the obtaining of the trial balance (bilancio) of the Ledger."‡ From the instructions contained in the summary (chapter 36) there can be no doubt that Pacioli's trial balance was an effective check on the duality of the postings.

In Manzoni's *Quaderno doppia* (1540) the trial balance appears in the worked example and each account is shown as having an equal debit and credit total. As this equality is brought about not by the unsystematic evening-up of the accounts, but by the methodical transfer of the account balances to the capital account, the fact that the capital account ultimately balances is proof that the total credits equal the total debits.

It is more difficult to determine whether the trial balance was used as a check in the early practice of double-entry. A statement of the Venetian Bank of St. George dated 1408 resembling a trial balance was examined by Sieveking,§ who found that it did not balance owing to a small error. De Roover found a correct trial balance in a Flemish account book dated 1369 and states that "the absence of error in com-

* See Mickwitz *op. cit. passim*, and his "Economic Rationalism in Graeco-Roman Agriculture" in *English Historical Review*, V. 52 (1937).

† See Row Fogo in Brown *op. cit.* p. 97; Littleton: *Accounting Review*, Vol. XII (1937), p. 440.

* See de Waal *op cit.* p. 58; Littleton *Accounting Evolution*, p. 81.

† Peragallo *op. cit.* p. 64.

‡ Geijsbeek *op. cit.* p. 47.

§ Sieveking *op. cit.* p. 310.

puting, listing, and totalling the balances allows the inference that the preparation of such a statement was not an unusual task."† These isolated cases alone can prove nothing, and we must turn to other evidence.

Considering the detailed instructions given by most of the authors from Pacioli onwards of how to check the postings by calling-over or "pricking" the journal with the ledger entries, there is much to be said for Row Fogo's opinion‡ that not much reliance was placed on the trial balance as a check. However, there is some evidence that suggests that the trial balance check was advocated by early writers. Ympyn in his twenty-fifth chapter clearly indicates that if the trial balance totals agree "then no errors have been committed in the ledger." He adds that "this seldom happens; because there are many ways of going astray." In such cases, he says, "then there is nothing else to do" but to check the castings and postings. Ympyn's advice about the use of the trial balance is repeated by Coutereels in *Den Stijl van Boeck-houden* (1603), and quite frequently by later writers.

Some writers regarded the duality check as the great virtue of double-entry bookkeeping. Stephen Monteage (1682) claims: "This way of accounting which we Treat of, carries with it its own Proof: And here lies the supreme Excellency and Usefulness of this mystery." Postlethwayt (1751) speaks of the "agreeable satisfaction" of getting a trial balance to balance, and says the trial balance will "shew you, that this, of all methods, is the most excellent."

Interesting, also, is the remark made by Malcolm (1718) that "there are also imaginary [i.e. nominal] Accompts useful in this Method, which beside the keeping that admirable Balance in the Books, serve to shew the various Situation of Affairs." Macghie's (1718) statement is similar: "Fictitious or Nominal Accompts, are such as are contriv'd on Purpose to supply the Defect of a Debitor or Creditor, in all personal or real accompts, seeing that no Accompt can alone consist of a Debitor without a Creditor, or vice versa." They do suggest that the maintenance of the equality of debit and credit was one reason for having nominal accounts.

Conclusion

The fragmentary records of early bookkeeping before double-entry make it impossible to state with certainty whether any given change in bookkeeping method was associated with the emergence of a new business need. However, making use of the available evidence, it has been comparatively easy to reconstruct a probable course of early accounting development as the continual adaptation of bookkeeping technique to meet increasing requirements.

It is much more difficult to explain satisfactorily the appearance of double-entry bookkeeping as the solution of some urgent problem. It has been shown that double-entry was not necessary for the measurement of profit. There is little to suggest that it appeared in response to a need either for the analysis of the total profit figure, or for the arithmetic check it provides. It is more likely that double-entry came about in some other way. Possibly it was the product of some mathematical brain*; possibly it came about by merchants automatically extending the practice of making dual entries for some transactions to all transactions†; possibly the accounts kept by agents for their masters had some influence upon the origin of double-entry.‡ These possibilities cannot be discussed here.

There is still the question why double-entry, after it had made its appearance, was employed by merchants and praised by many text-writers. There is no conclusive evidence that it was widely employed specially on account of its real or alleged advantages. The balance account and the profit and loss account, which to-day are regarded as providing the central benefits of double-entry, were at first mere incidentals, performing purely technical functions.

One probable reason for its employment may have been the completeness and orderliness of double-entry records. Another probable explanation may be that the double-entry system appealed to the scholarly minds of the professional bookkeepers or teachers who kept the books of merchants or instructed them in the "mysteries" of bookkeeping. In this way double-entry became the standard form of "good" bookkeeping, and was used by merchants without necessarily subjecting it to the test of its suitability in every particular set of circumstances. There is much to suggest that even to-day in many cases more importance is attached to the reputation of double-entry bookkeeping and traditional accounting procedures than to their merits in the light of present-day requirements.

[*Note*: My thanks are due to the Institute of Chartered Accountants in England and Wales for granting me access to their excellent collection of historical works.]

† Carman *op. cit.* p. 114.
‡ Row Fogo in Brown *op. cit.* p. 106.

* See Augspurg in *Zeitschrift für Buchhaltung*, 1897, p. 4
† See Littleton *op. cit.* p. 38.
‡ See de Waal *op. cit.* p. 282.

John J. Williams
PENNSYLVANIA STATE UNIVERSITY

A NEW PERSPECTIVE ON THE EVOLUTION OF DOUBLE-ENTRY BOOKKEEPING

Abstract: Inquiry into the origin of double entry accounting has typically focused on form as the causal factor. In the present article the arguments supporting this view are reviewed and challenged by developing the substantive framework of double entry accounting in equation form and linking it to the evolution of mathematics in the Arab-Hindu cultures. The article concludes with specific suggestions for obtaining empirical evidence which might support the "substantive hypothesis" as the causal factor of double entry accounting.

One of the great evolutionary advances in the history of accounting was the conceptualization of "double-entry" and its subsequent manifestation in form and substance. Accounting historians agree that Paciolo's famous treatise of 1494 represents the first complete synthesis of double-entry bookkeeping in *published* form.[1] Substantially less agreement exists in the literature on the underlying stimuli responsible for the "state of the art" prevailing at the end of the fifteenth century.

The methodology employed by accounting researchers in addressing the latter issue is largely inductive and is akin to that of historians in general. By the same token, general observations on the "form" of double-entry bookkeeping as *evidence of origin* requires a deductive approach which is extremely fragile within an historical context. This paper examines, in a brief manner, the major hypotheses debated in the literature as to the causal factors giving rise to double-entry bookkeeping and offers an alternative explanation in view of the amassed empirical evidence.

Writing in 1494, Paciolo explicitly denied any responsibility for the origin of double-entry accounting and asserted that he was merely "writing down the system" which had been in existence for roughly two hundred years in Venice.[2] However, Paciolo apparently did express his acknowledgment to one renown mathematician of this era namely Leonardo da Pisa.[3] The possible contribution of this medieval scholar and the genesis of his knowledge appear to have been extremely understated and perhaps omitted entirely as a source of *first order* importance to the development of double-entry bookkeeping. This will become more evident after we define the fundamental elements underlying the framework of "double-entry" accounting and review some of the major arguments.

If Paciolo simply unified the existing practice of his time, what were the developments contributing to the accounting systems which he borrowed from in writing his *Summa de Arithmetica, Geometria, Proportioni et Proportionalita*. The empirical evidence usually relied upon in attempting to answer this question are the historical accounts of various bankers, family enterprises, and merchant ventures which dominated the expansionary growth experienced throughout Italy during the Renaissance era. One eminent accounting historian exhaustively studied several such sources. In presenting his evidence, de Roover claims that "Double entry does not depend in the least upon the form in which accounts are presented."[4] From his viewpoint, the fundamental criterion is revealed by the following test: "At the end do we have a real balance showing the assets on one side and the liabilities and the owners' equity on the other? Only if this question can be answered affirmatively, is one justified in speaking without hesitation of books kept in double entry."[5]

This question is so critical to the present purpose that it deserves elaboration before we confront any arguments from the literature. Littleton divided the problem into one of form versus substance.[6] The former explicitly encompasses the condition of duality and equilibrium in the various phases of recordkeeping. According to Littleton, we could have three forms of duality: (1) duality of books; (2) duality of account form; and (3) duality of entry.[7] Littleton probed further and suggested that equilibrium of results may be the cornerstone of double entry.[8] However, he argued convincingly that these two conditions (i.e. form and equilibrium) were not sufficient for a complete, coordinated system of double entry bookkeeping. The substantive element of "proprietorship", with its primary emphasis on the calculation of gains and losses, was absent.[9]

Unfortunately, Littleton did not elaborate on precisely *how* his definition of "substance" was manifested in a complete system. Schrader, on the other hand, offers a provocative insight into this matter.[10] Employing an inductive approach, he demonstrates that debits are in fact "consideration received" while credits are "consideration given" in an exchange transaction (i.e. for goods and/or services) which is the "essence of business activity."[11] Moreover, Schrader indicates that at the whole life level of analysis, net income results *naturally* from the recording process with no further manipulations of data.

Schrader's analysis illustrates unequivocally that the accounting equation is an *equivalence* of values between *two* fundamentally different attributes (i.e. variables) expressed as debits and credits. Classification in the usual accounting sense of the word does not change the nature of these attributes.

Introducing periodicity into the exchange activities of an entity does not disturb the standard (i.e. transaction) for admission of the data into the system. However, to generate the real balances cited by de Roover, or Littleton's complete system, a concept of net income is mandatory. Again, under the historical cost model, accountants have agreed in principle that criteria be established for "revenue recognition" (the independent variable) and matching of related expenses (the dependent variable). Net income is merely the balancing residual in the system.[12]

Clearly, all three writers have in mind a bi-variate equation system (i.e. the historical cost model) based on an entity, exchange transactions, and a common monetary unit. To avoid any misunderstanding later, it should be observed that the historical cost model *does not compete* with a "current value" model since the phenomena under observation are entirely different. The latter model focuses on "things" or "elements of wealth" as the fundamental attribute. Price coefficients are attached to these things and summed: equilibrium is attained by setting the aggregate total (i.e. assets) equal to liabilities and equities. Obviously, the equation is an identity and represents a uni-variate model since only one kind of attribute (i.e. "asset" or "thing") is involved. Net income emerges as the difference between the net assets at two points in time assuming no capital adjustments. It should be apparent that an understanding or conceptualization of the bi-variate model (i.e. historical cost) requires a more profound knowledge of the relationship between variables than the identity equation of the current value model which is nothing but an equilibrium feature of any uni-variate model.

Returning to the arguments on the origin of double-entry accounting, de Roover notes that in Tuscany, approximately midway through the fourteenth century, double-entry was achieved before the general adoption of the bilateral or tabular form.[13] Prior to 1350, the northern part of Italy had been exposed to the bilateral form—as early as 1327 in Genoa for example. Despite this movement away from the narrative form of accounts and balances, Roman numerals remained the accepted mode of presentation. De Roover further asserts that:

> . . . improvement was achieved by placing the amounts in extension columns instead of inserting them in the narrative. Summations were thereby greatly facilitated, but the use of Roman numerals continued to impose the aid of the abacus.[14]

It is difficult to comprehend how the vertical arrayment of Roman numerals and their characteristic absence of place value would be comfortable to summation. If one wants to add, say, 1,012 and 1,308, writing down MXII and MCCCVIII in columnar format contributes nothing to the process of summation. Another authority, de Ste. Croix, specifically suggests that this limitation in the Roman numeral system prevented the concepts of debit and credit from emerging and therefore inhibited any notion of double-entry bookkeeping.[15]

A somewhat different viewpoint on the emanation of double-entry form centers on our conventional Arabic numeral system. De Ste. Croix is of the opinion that the arrangement of figures in columns in our notation is not an intrinsic virtue but an incidental defect due to a combination of its two greatest virtues: place-value and the small number of symbols it uses. Furthermore, this defect, paradoxically, provided the stimulus toward the advanced concepts of debits and credits.[16]

Both of the above positions imply that form, augmented by some type of number system, was instrumental in yielding the substantive element in double-entry accounting. Why should form alone necessarily lead to the complete concept of double-entry; is it not equally plausible that the idea was first conceptualized and that the element of form merely reflected a lag effect in the application or modification of existing accounts? De Roover's own testimony on the state of accounting in Tuscany tends to lend credence to the latter possibility. But even if form is accepted as a causal factor, what underlying event or set of phenomena can explain the motive behind the emergence of the bilateral form, in a total framework of duality (i.e., journal entries, trial balance, and final ledger balances) regardless of the number system (i.e., Roman vs. Arabic).

Unfortunately, an inductive approach can not provide solutions to this question and some resort to deductive reasoning is essential. At issue here is *not* the appearance of double-entry *form*, which at one time, was generally understood to be in Genoa around 1340. In fact, de Roover claims that this hypothesis has virtually been shattered and the focal point is now the simultaneous emergence in several Italian trading centers around the beginning of the thirteenth century.[17] Instead, the question of interest lies in discovering the compelling force that provided the substantive element of double-entry bookkeeping. Several alternatives are couched in the literature but they appear to be incomplete upon further emphasis.

De Roover, for example suggests that three factors, namely partnership, credit, and agency were of paramount importance. The notion of partnership, with extant documents dating from 1157, is singled out as the most important because it generated the concept of entity. Borrowing from Kats,[18] both Littleton[19] and Gilman[20] have argued though, that the charge-discharge record of the Roman master-slave relationship is sufficient for conceptualizing a separate entity from proprietorship. Credit, enhanced substantially by the Crusade movement, is offered as a second factor. But trade and credit have co-existed since antiquity and the rise of money economies merely added varying degrees of intensity to the complementarity of these two factors. Keister, for instance, rigorously documents the existence of columnar form, summations and a relatively sophisticated level of trade as far back as ancient Mesopotamia.[21] The third factor, agency, is plainly evident generations prior to the advent of Italian merchants. In short, these three factors have paralleled one another for centuries.

As a prelude to discussing these three factors, de Roover emphasizes the duality of exchange transactions embedded in the nature of business and then asks the interesting question "Is it then surprising that the merchants would *eventually* hit upon a system founded on an *equation* between debits and credits?"[22] (emphasis added). In the absence of any additional stimulus, the answer seems to be affirmative. Partnership, credit, and agency, in any proportion would not necessarily yield a complete bi-variate system of equations (i.e. in the Littleton or Schrader framework). Nor is it at all clear that the thinking of merchants or businessmen of any description would envelop and comprehend the relationship of independent and dependent variables from an evolutionary process of partnership, credit, and agency. The analogy of gunpowder and ancient weaponry is an interesting paradigm. No amount of improvement in the technology of making spears, swords, knives, etc. would match (or transform them into) the explosive power of a chemical mixture.

A competing hypothesis is advanced by de Ste. Croix who revives the idea that the rise of the substantive element of double-entry accounting can be closely linked with the introduction of the Hindu-Arabic system of numeration.[23] However, he is careful to point out that this idea has been totally rejected, by the accounting historians Melis and Besta, on two grounds.[24]

First, there is the argument that even though double-entry bookkeeping appeared not later than the first half of the fourteenth century, literally all of the extant accounts were maintained in Roman numerals until about 1500. But Struik, a mathematics historian, writes that the statutes of the *Arte del Cambio* of 1299 prohibited the bankers of Florence from using Arabic numerals; yet they are found on documents dating back to 976 and 1275.[25] Undoubtedly, our contemporary number system was both known and in use prior to the fourteenth century. It should be carefully noted though, that this evidence does not adequately defend the polemic that double-entry bookkeeping requires the Hindu-Arabic number system. Moreover, the legal interference (i.e., the statutes) may explain why de Roover discovered substantive double-entry in the Tuscany accounts but lacking in form.

The second argument repudiating the connection between the Hindu-Arabic number system and double-entry bookkeeping is that the abacus, which was in general use throughout the Middle Ages, precluded the need for a place-value system complete with a zero characteristic. While the observation on the use of the abacus cannot be refuted, it contributes little or no basis whatsoever for rejecting the substantive appearance of double-entry bookkeeping.

Cognizant of these objections, de Ste. Croix nonetheless suspects that the maturation of double-entry bookkeeping can be traced to the seminal work *Liber Abbaci* written in 1202 by Leonardo da Pisa, himself a merchant as well as a mathematician. In translating directly from the original Latin script, de Ste. Croix observes that da Pisa traveled extensively throughout the Mediterranean as a merchant prior to 1200. Not only did he encourage adoption of the Hindu-Arabic numerals for commercial accounting, but he actually set out an account contrasting completely the Roman figures versus the Arabic numerals.[26]

Unfortunately, de Ste. Croix is biased in the same manner as other historians by suggesting that account *form* was the causal factor leading to a complete double-entry system. He states that:

> Once figures began to be disposed in a *single* column, instead of being scattered all over the page and reduced to order only outside the account-book, on the abacus or in the mind, the advantages of having *two* clearly separated columns, simply to facilitate computation, would very quickly become apparent; and this would of itself result

> in the emergence of the bilateral form of account, with debits and credits visibly distinguished. The final step, the further advance to double entry, could then equally well be made by those (no doubt still the large majority) who continued to employ Roman numerals.[27]

This conclusion leads us full circle from the arguments raised earlier and still leaves undetermined the order of form and substance in the emergence of a unified, complete system of double-entry bookkeeping.

It is evident from the above analysis that various social factors—trade, partnerships, and so forth—in combination with technical factors such as accounts and a numeral system, are necessary for double-entry bookkeeping. It is the view of this writer however, that taken together, they are not sufficient for explaining the appearance of a complete double-entry system. Perhaps some process of serendipity did take place at some point but the transition in "accounting" from the middle of the twelfth century to approximately the end of the thirteenth century seems to have required a *radical change of thinking*.

One possibility lies not merely in the introduction of the Hindu-Arabic number system but in the fundamental system of equations which accompanied its introduction into Spain by the Moors. The former event is obviously well-known in the accounting literature; the crux of the hypothesis of mathematics which did not necessarily emanate *from* the *Liber Abbaci* but rather, *pre-dated* it. The reasons for adopting this avenue of inquiry are several. Prior to the Arabs, Europe was virtually ignorant of mathematics. However, the Arabs, having obtained, preserved, and translated the great works of Greek geometry and, also having acquired the Hindu numerical notation complete with the algebra of linear and quadratic equations, made this body of knowledge accessible to Europeans in the colleges at Granada, Cordova, and Seville around the beginning of the twelfth century.[28] Not only did Leonardo da Pisa become exposed to this knowledge, but he also traveled extensively throughout Egypt, Syria, Greece, and Sicily, eventually returning to Italy where his famous *Liber Abbaci* was published in Latin during the year 1202. There is some likelihood that da Pisa was influenced by the commercial activities of these other cultures but no definitive evidence has thus far been uncovered.

Also, there was a contemporary mathematician at the time of Leonardo da Pisa by the name of Jordanus Nemorarius who introduced the use of letters for magnitudes in his algebra. Apparently this was a significant step forward in the evolution of algebraic symbolism.[29] The dispersion of this knowledge was quite slow since all of the Arab script was translated into Latin first and then retranslated into various vernaculars. Nonetheless, this particular development may have been linked to the conceptualization of debits and credits because symbolic representation of these two concepts would permit a surrogate generalization at the "system" level in addition to the apposed physical numbers at the "transaction" level.

But why should mathematics, especially the notion of equations, serve such a paramount role? In the first place, equations require an equality of variables, both independent and dependent. It then becomes a logical step to delineate the equivalence of two variables in an exchange transaction which is the basis of Littleton's concept of duality. Finally, there emerges a rationale for the substantive element in the Littleton-Schrader framework—the calculation of entity income which requires a precise understanding of an independent variable (usually revenue) and a dependent variable (usually expense). Naturally, a condition of equilibrium is maintained at any balance sheet date if the equivalence of exchange transactions is preserved.

Although higher level mathematics found its way into the Arab culture, why did it traverse the boundaries of north Africa *vis-à-vis* the Moors and culminate in the Spanish universities before spreading to Italy as opposed to a movement across land through Syria and northward, or via Syria by sea-trade. The reason for eliminating the land route through Syria is answered in most medieval history books. Apparently, the empires that lay between Syria and Italy were not in the least culturally interactive.[30] This is certainly a tenable proposition since history is replete with examples of colonization (conquest even) where isolated communities for trading were established while, paradoxically, there was a failure (intentional or othrwise) to abstract even a modicum of the indigenous culture. Preserving the ideology and customs of the homeland was the rule rather than the exception. Intriguing as it may be, this phenomenon did not exist among the cultures dominating trade in the western Mediterranean, including Sicily, Corsica, Pisa, Spain, southern France, and the north African coast.[31] Historically then, cultural transmission from the eastern Mediterranean lagged substantially behind economic trade with the western Mediterranean.

The same rationale would appear to nullify sea-trade with Syria as a possible source of mathematical knowledge from the Arabs. Byrne offers some supporting evidence for this position:

> By 1154 Genoese merchants are found trading freely, through most of the year, with Sardinia, Sicily, southern France, Spain, northern Africa; but trade with the Orient, and especially with Syria, was undertaken only at regular intervals.[32]

Moreover, Byrne indicates that:

> Between 1154 and 1164, it can be said with assurance that only five commercial ventures to Syria were made; between 1177 and 1206, only fifteen years can be cited in which voyages were certainly undertaken.[33]

It would be astonishing indeed if such a small number of trading missions dominated by mostly sailors, one or two merchants, and a scribe for inventory control, could have imbibed an understanding of mathematics and carried it back to Italy.

In summary, the relationship of the evolution of mathematics to accounting development seems remarkably direct. Almost all accounting historians speak of the *concepts* of debit and credit which requires a plurality of variables. But even more important, the idea of the fundamental balance sheet equation, alluded to by de Roover, could possibly have emanated from this source of knowledge. Having grasped the equilibrium nature of the final double-entry product, it would then be a matter of decomposing the whole framework into a series of logical component parts, i.e. the journal entries, a trial balance, and a ledger account complete with calculations of profit. This would imply that substance preceded form and not vice-versa as suggested by the spurious reasons documented in the literature. If this is a tenable hypothesis, it need not matter what particular numerical format is superimposed on the basic equation, for a complete double-entry system will manifest itself in the final analysis. Of course efficiency and understanding would eventually dominate the accepted form and numerical base as witnessed by history.

Providing direct evidence for the "substantive" hypothesis is beyond the immediate purpose of this paper. However, future research by accountants with the requisite skills might focus on several areas which are currently absent in the accounting literature. One approach could center on the historical teachings, artifacts, and other documents located in the various universities and museums throughout Spain with emphasis on the Moorish influence. Alternatively, a rigorous search of the lifetime works of special individuals such as Leonardo da Pisa and others who were in contact with the influx of the Hindu-Arabic number system into Spain may prove rewarding. Finally, a thorough search of the Arabic and Hindu cultures themselves may reveal a knowledge of the substantive element in double entry accounting. Not only did they experience trade, credit, various forms of business, account formats, and a number system, but they also created and commanded the higher power of mathematics—an essential ingredient for a complete system of double-entry bookkeeping.

FOOTNOTES

[1]Some accounting historians maintain that Paciolo plagiarized the work of Giorgio Chiarini which pre-dated Paciolo's synthesis but was published later. Taylor, "Luca Pacioli", in Littleton and Yamey, "Studies in the History of Accounting", p. 180, challenges this accusation: "Pacioli in this and other writings has been wrongly accused of plagiarism."

[2]Taylor, p 180.

[3]Taylor, p. 180.

[4]de Roover, p. 115

[5]de Roover, p. 119.

[6]Littleton, pp. 24-27.

[7]Littleton, p. 24.

[8]Littleton, p. 25.

[9]Littleton, pp. 26-27.

[10]Schrader, pp. 645-649.

[11]Schrader, p. 646.

[12]Schrader, pp. 45-54.

[13]de Roover, p. 115

[14]de Roover, p. 119.

[15]de Ste. Croix, p. 60.

[16]de Ste. Croix, p. 55

[17]de Roover, p. 115.

[18]Kats pp. 203-210.

[19]Littleton, p 32.

[20]Gilman, pp. 40-41.

[21]Keister, pp 371-376.

[22]de Roover, p 115

[23]de Ste Croix p 64.

[24]de Ste. Croix, p 64.

[25]Struik, "A Concise History of Mathematics," p. 87. He further specified that the 976 manuscript, *Codex Vigilanus*, written in Spain is the oldest dated European document containing Hindu-Arabic numerals The earliest French document dates from 1275

[26]de Ste. Croix p. 65

[27]de Ste. Croix, p 66

[28]Sullivan, pp. 18-19.

[29]Sullivan, p. 24.

[30]Braudel, Vol I, Part One, Chapter II, pp. 103-162.

[31]Braudel, Vol. II, Part Two, Chapter VI, pp. 757-835.
[32]Byrne, p. 136.
[33]Byrne, p. 132.

BIBLIOGRAPHY

Braudel, Fernand. *The Mediterranean and the Mediterranean World in the Age of Philip II.* Volume I and II. New York: Harper & Row, Publishers, 1972.

Byrne, E. H. "Commercial Contracts of the Genoese in the Syrian Trade of the Twelfth Century." *Quarterly Journal of Economics,* 1916, pp. 128-70.

de Roover, Raymond. "The Development of Accounting Prior to Luca Pacioli According to the Account-Books of Medieval Merchants," in A. C. Littleton and B. S. Yamey. *Studies in the History of Accounting.* Homewood, Illinois: Richard D. Irwin, Inc., 1956.

de Ste. Croix, G. E. M. "Greek and Roman Accounting", in A. C. Littleton and B. S. Yamey. *Studies in the History of Accounting.* Homewood: Illinois: Richard D. Irwin, Inc., 1956.

Gilman, Stephen. *Accounting Concepts of Profit.* New York: The Ronald Press Company, 1939.

Kats, P. "Early History of Bookkeeping by Double Entry." *Journal of Accountancy,* April, 1929, pp. 203-210.

Keister, Orville R. "Commercial Recoıd-Keeping in Ancient Mesopotamia", *The Accounting Review,* April, 1963, pp. 371-376.

Littleton, A. C. *Accounting Evolution to 1900* New York: American Institute Publishing Co., Inc., 1933.

Schrader, William J. "An Inductive Approach to Accounting Theory," *The Accounting Review,* October, 1962, pp. 645-649.

———. "A Critical Evaluation of Income Measurement by 'Products' and 'Periods'." *Industrial Research Bulletin No. 6,* Bureau of Business Research, The Pennsylvania State University, 1962. pp. 1-169.

Struik, Dirk J. *A Concise History of Mathematics.* New York: Dover Publications, Inc., 1967.

Sullivan, J. W. N. *The History of Mathematics in Europe.* London: Oxford University Press, 1925.

Taylor, R. Emmett. "Luca Pacioli", in A. C. Littleton and B. S. Yamey. *Studies in the History of Accounting.* Homewood, Illinois: Richard D Irwin, Inc , 1956